BORDERS®
CLASSICS

VYASA

The Bhagavad Gita

and

Two Upanishads

BORDERS.
CLASSICS

Please direct sales or editorial inquiries to:
BordersTradeBookInventoryQuestions@bordersgroupinc.com

This edition is published by
Borders Classics, an imprint of Borders Group, Inc.,
by special arrangement with
Ann Arbor Media Group, LLC
2500 South State Street, Ann Arbor, MI 48104

Printed and bound in the United States of America
by Edwards Brothers, Inc.

Quality Paperback ISBN 13: 978-1-58726-487-0
ISBN 10: 1-58726-487-0

11   10   09   08   07   10 9 8 7 6 5 4 3 2 1

CONTENTS

THE BHAGAVAD GITA

Translated by
William Q. Judge

1

OM!

DHRITARASHTRA

Tell me, O Sanjaya, what the people of my own party and those of Pandu, who are assembled at Kurukshetra resolved upon war, have been doing.

SANJAYA

King Duryodhana, having just beheld the army of the Pandus drawn up in battle array, went to his preceptor and spoke these words:

"Behold! O Master, the mighty army of the sons of Pandu drawn up by thy pupil, the clever son of Drupada. In it are warriors with great bows, equal to Bhima and Arjuna in battle, namely, Yuyudhana, and Virata, and Drupada on his great car; Dhrishtaketu, Chekitana, and the valiant king of Kashi, and Purujit, and Kuntibhoja, with Shaivya, chief of men; Yudhamanyu the strong, and Uttamauja the brave; the son of Subhadra, and all the sons of Draupadi, too, in their huge chariots. Be acquainted also with the names of those of our party who are the most distinguished. I will mention a few of those who are amongst my generals, by way of example. There is thyself, my Preceptor, and Bhishma, Karna and Kripa, the conqueror in battle, and Aswatthama, and Vikarna, and the son of Soma-datta, with others in vast numbers, who for my service risk their life. They are all of them practiced in the use of arms, armed with divers weapons, and experienced in every mode of fight. This army of ours, which is commanded by Bhishma, is not sufficient, while their forces, led by Bhima, are sufficient. Let all the generals, according to their respective divisions, stand at their posts, and one and all resolve Bhishma to support."

The ancient chief, brother of the grandsire of the Kurus, then, to raise the spirits of the Kuru chief, blew his shell, sounding like the lion's roar; and instantly innumerable shells and other warlike instruments were sounded on all sides, so that the clangor was excessive. At this time Krishna and Arjuna, standing in a splendid chariot drawn by white horses, also sounded their shells, which were of celestial form: the name of the one which Krishna blew was Panchajanya, and that of Arjuna was called Deva-datta—"the gift of the Gods." Bhima, of terrific power, blew his capacious shell, Paundra; and Yudhishthira, the royal son of Kunti, sounded Ananta-Vijaya; Nakula and Sahadeva blew their shells also, the one called Sughosha, the other Manipushpaka. The prince of Kashi, of the mighty bow; Sikhandi, Dhrishtadyumna, Virata, Satyaki, of invincible arm; Drupada and the sons of his royal daughter; Krishna, with the son, Subhadra, and all the other chiefs and nobles, blew also their respective shells, so that their shrill-sounding voices pierced the hearts of the Kurus and reechoed with a dreadful noise from heaven to earth.

Then Arjuna, whose crest was Hanuman, perceiving that the sons of Dhritarashtra stood ready to begin the fight, and that the flying of arrows had commenced, having raised his bow, addressed these words to Krishna.

ARJUNA

"I pray thee, Krishna, cause my chariot to be placed between the two armies, that I may behold who are the men that stand ready, anxious to commence the battle; with whom it is I am to fight in this ready field; and who they are that are here assembled to support the evil-minded son of Dhritarashtra in the battle."

SANJAYA

Krishna being thus addressed by Arjuna, drove the chariot, and, having caused it to halt in the space between the two armies, bade Arjuna cast his eyes towards the ranks of the Kurus, and behold where stood the aged Bhishma, and Drona, with all the chief nobles of their party. Standing there Arjuna surveyed both the armies, and beheld, on either side, grandsires, uncles, cousins, tutors, sons, and brothers, near relations, or bosom friends; and when he had gazed for awhile and beheld all his kith and kin drawn up in battle array, he was moved by extreme pity, and, filled with despondency, he thus in sadness spoke:

ARJUNA

"Now, O Krishna, that I have beheld my kindred thus standing anxious for the fight, my members fail me, my countenance withereth, the hair standeth on end upon my body, and all my frame trembleth with horror! Even Gandiva, my bow, slips from my hand, and my skin is parched and dried up. I am not able to stand; for my mind, as it were, whirleth round, and I behold on all sides adverse omens. When I shall have destroyed my kindred, shall I longer look for happiness? I wish not for victory, Krishna; I want not pleasure; for what are dominion and the enjoyments of life, or even life itself, when those for whom dominion, pleasure, and enjoyment were to be coveted have abandoned life and fortune, and stand here in the field ready for the battle? Tutors, sons and fathers, grandsires and grandsons, uncles and nephews, cousins, kindred, and friends! Although they would kill me, I wish not to fight them: no, not even for the dominion of the three regions of the universe, much less for this little earth! Having killed the sons of Dhritarashtra, what pleasure, O thou who art prayed to by mortals, can we enjoy? Should we destroy them, tyrants though they are, sin would take refuge with us. It therefore behooveth us not to kill such near relations as these. How, O Krishna, can we be happy hereafter, when we have been the murderers of our race? What if they, whose minds are depraved by the lust of power, see no sin in the extirpation of their race, no crime in the murder of their friends, is that a reason why we should not resolve to turn away from such a crime—we who abhor the sin of extirpating our own kindred? On the destruction of a tribe the ancient virtue of the tribe and family is lost; with the loss of virtue, vice and impiety overwhelm the whole of a race. From the influence of impiety the females of a family grow vicious; and from women that are become vicious are born the spurious caste called Varna Sankar. Corruption of caste is a gate of hell, both for these destroyers of a tribe and for those who survive; and their forefathers, being deprived of the ceremonies of cakes and water offered to their manes, sink into the infernal regions. By the crimes of the destroyers of a tribe and by those who cause confusion of caste, the family virtue and the virtue of a whole tribe are forever done away with; and we have read in sacred writ, O Krishna, that a sojourn in hell awaits those mortals whose generation hath lost its virtue. Woe is me! What a great crime are we prepared to commit! Alas! that from the desire for sovereignty and pleasure we stand here ready to slay our own kin! I would rather patiently suffer that the sons of Dhritarashtra, with their weapons in their hands, should come upon me, and, unopposed, kill me unresisting in the field."

SANJAYA

When Arjuna had ceased to speak, he sat down in the chariot between the two armies; and, having put away his bow and arrows, his heart was overwhelmed with despondency.

2

Krishna, beholding him thus influenced by compunction, his eyes overflowing with a flood of tears, and his heart oppressed with deep affliction, addressed him in the following words:

KRISHNA

"Whence, O Arjuna, cometh upon thee this dejection in matters of difficulty, so unworthy of the honorable, and leading neither to heaven nor to glory? It is disgraceful, contrary to duty, and the foundation of dishonor. Yield not thus to unmanliness, for it ill-becometh one like thee. Abandon, O tormentor of thy foes, this despicable weakness of thy heart, and stand up."

ARJUNA

"How, O slayer of Madhu, shall I with my shafts contend in battle against such as Bhishma and Drona, who of all men are most worthy of my respect? For it were better to beg my bread about the world than be the murderer of my preceptors, to whom such awful reverence is due. Were I to destroy such friends as these, I should partake of possessions, wealth, and pleasures polluted with their blood. Nor can we tell whether it would be better that we should defeat them, or they us. For those drawn up, angrily confronting us—and after whose death, should they perish by my hand, I would not wish to live—are the sons and people of Dhritarashtra. As I am of a disposition which is affected by compassion and the fear of doing wrong, I ask thee which is it better to do? Tell me that distinctly! I am thy disciple; wherefore instruct in my duty me who am under thy tuition; for my understanding is confounded by the dictates of my duty, and I see nothing that may assuage the grief which drieth up my faculties, although I were to obtain a kingdom without a rival upon earth, or dominion over the hosts of heaven."

Arjuna having thus spoken to Krishna, became silent, saying: "I shall not fight, O Govinda." Krishna, tenderly smiling, addressed these words to the prince thus standing downcast between the two armies:

"Thou grievest for those that may not be lamented, whilst thy sentiments are those of the expounders of the letter of the law. Those who are wise in spiritual things grieve neither for the dead nor for the living. I myself never was not, nor thou, nor all the princes of the earth; nor shall we ever hereafter cease to be. As the lord of this mortal frame experienceth therein infancy, youth, and old age, so in future incarnations will it meet the same. One who is confirmed in this belief is not disturbed by anything that may come to pass. The senses, moving toward their appropriate objects, are producers of heat and cold, pleasure and pain, which come and go and are brief and changeable; these do thou endure, O son of Bharata! For the wise man, whom these disturb not and to whom pain and pleasure are the same, is fitted for immortality. There is no existence for that which does not exist, nor is there any non-existence for what exists. By those who see the truth and look into the principles of things, the ultimate characteristic of these both is seen. Learn that He by whom all things were formed is incorruptible, and that no one is able to effect the destruction of IT which is inexhaustible. These finite bodies, which envelope the souls inhabiting them, are said to belong to Him, the eternal, the indestructible, unprovable Spirit, who is in the body: wherefore, O Arjuna, resolve to fight. The man who believeth that it is this Spirit which killeth, and he who thinketh that it may be destroyed, are both alike deceived; for it neither killeth nor is it killed. It is not a thing of which a man may say, 'It hath been, it is about to be, or is to be hereafter;' for it is without birth and meeteth not death; it is ancient, constant, and eternal, and is not slain when this its mortal frame is destroyed. How can the man who believeth that it is incorruptible, eternal, inexhaustible, and without birth, think that it can either kill or cause to be killed? As a man throweth away old garments and putteth on new, even so the dweller in the body, having quitted its old mortal frames, entereth into others which are new. The weapon divideth it not, the fire burneth it not, the water corrupteth it not, the wind drieth it not away; for it is indivisible, inconsumable, incorruptible, and is not to be dried away; it is eternal, universal, permanent, immovable; it is invisible, inconceivable, and unalterable; therefore, knowing it to be thus, thou shouldst not grieve. But whether thou believest it to be of eternal birth and duration, or that it dieth with the body, still thou hast no cause to lament it. Death is certain to all things which are born, and rebirth to all mortals; wherefore it doth not behoove thee to grieve about the inevitable. The antenatal state of beings is unknown; the middle state is evident; and their state after death is not to be discovered. What in this is there to lament? Some regard the indwelling spirit as a wonder, whilst some speak and others hear of it with astonishment; but no one realizes it, although he may have heard it described. This spirit can never be destroyed in the mortal frame which it inhabiteth, hence it is unworthy for thee to be troubled for all these mortals. Cast but thine eyes towards the duties of thy particular tribe, and it will ill become thee to tremble. A soldier of the Kshatriya tribe hath no duty superior to lawful war, and just to thy wish the door of heaven is found open before thee, through this glorious unsought fight which only fortune's favored soldiers may obtain. But if thou wilt not perform the duty of thy calling and fight out the field, thou wilt abandon thy natural duty and thy honor, and be guilty of a crime. Mankind will speak of thy ill fame as infinite, and for one who hath been respected in the world ill fame is worse than death. The generals of the armies will think that thy retirement from the field arose from fear, and even amongst those by whom thou wert wont to be thought great of soul thou shalt become despicable. Thine enemies will speak of thee in words which are unworthy to be spoken, depreciating thy courage and abilities; what can be more dreadful than this! If thou art slain thou shalt attain heaven; if victorious, the world shall be thy reward; wherefore, son of Kunti, arise with determination fixed for the battle. Make pleasure and pain, gain and loss, victory and defeat, the same to thee, and then prepare for battle, for thus and thus alone shalt thou in action still be free from sin.

"Thus before thee has been set the opinion in accordance with the Sankhya doctrine, speculatively; now hear what it is in the practical, devotional one, by means of which, if fully imbued therewith, thou shalt forever burst the bonds of Karma and rise above them. In this system of Yoga no effort is wasted, nor are there any evil consequences, and even a little of this practice delivereth a man from great risk. In this path there is only one single object, and this of a steady, constant nature; but widely-branched is the faith and infinite are the objects of those who follow not this system.

"The unwise, delighting in the controversies of the Vedas, tainted with worldly lusts, and preferring a transient enjoyment of heaven to eternal absorption, whilst they declare there is no other reward, pronounce, for the attainment of worldly riches and enjoyments, flowery sentences which promise rewards in future births for present action, ordaining also many special ceremonies the fruit of which is merit leading to power and objects of enjoyment. But those who thus desire riches and enjoyment have no certainty of soul and least hold on meditation. The subject of the Vedas is the assemblage of the three qualities. Be thou free from these qualities, O Arjuna! Be free from the 'pairs of opposites' and constant in the quality of Sattwa, free from worldly anxiety and the desire to preserve present possessions, self-centred and uncontrolled by objects of mind or sense. As many benefits as there are in a tank stretching free on all sides, so many are there for a truth-realizing Brahman in all the Vedic rites.

"Let, then, the motive for action be in the action itself, and not in the event. Do not be incited to actions by the hope of their reward, nor let thy life be spent in inaction. Firmly persisting in Yoga, perform thy duty, O Dhananjaya, and laying aside all desire for any benefit to thyself from action, make the event equal to thee, whether it be success or failure. Equal-mindedness is called Yoga.

"Yet the performance of works is by far inferior to mental devotion, O despiser of wealth. Seek an asylum, then, in this mental devotion, which is knowledge; for the miserable and unhappy are those whose impulse to action is found in its reward. But he who by means of Yoga is mentally devoted dismisses alike successful and unsuccessful results, being beyond them; Yoga is skill in the performance of actions: therefore do thou aspire to this devotion. For those who are thus united to knowledge and devoted, who have renounced all reward for their actions, meet no rebirth in this life, and go to that eternal blissful abode which is free from all disease and untouched by troubles.

"When thy heart shall have worked through the snares of delusion, then thou wilt attain to high indifference as to those doctrines which are already taught or which are yet to be taught. When thy mind once liberated from the Vedas shall be fixed immovably in contemplation, then shalt thou attain to devotion."

ARJUNA

"What, O Keshava, is the description of that wise and devoted man who is fixed in contemplation and confirmed in spiritual knowledge? What may such a sage declare? Where may he dwell? Does he move and act like other men?"

KRISHNA

"A man is said to be confirmed in spiritual knowledge when he forsaketh every desire which entereth into his heart, and of himself is happy and content in the Self through the Self. His mind is undisturbed in adversity; he is happy and contented in prosperity, and he is a stranger to anxiety, fear, and anger. Such a man is called a Muni. When in every condition he receives each event, whether favorable or unfavorable, with an equal mind which neither likes nor dislikes, his wisdom is established, and, having met good or evil, neither rejoiceth at the one nor is cast down by the other. He is confirmed in spiritual knowledge, when, like the tortoise, he can draw in all his senses and restrain them from their wonted purposes. The hungry man loseth sight of every other object but the gratification of his appetite, and when he is become acquainted with the Supreme, he loseth all taste for objects of whatever kind. The tumultuous senses and organs hurry away by force the heart even of the wise man who striveth after perfection. Let a man, restraining all these, remain in devotion at rest in me, his true self; for he who hath his senses and organs in control possesses spiritual knowledge.

"He who attendeth to the inclinations of the senses, in them hath a concern; from this concern is created passion, from passion anger, from anger is produced delusion, from delusion a loss of the memory, from the loss of memory loss of discrimination, and from loss of discrimination loss of all! But he who, free from attachment or repulsion for objects, experienceth them through the senses and organs, with his heart obedient to his will, attains to tranquility of thought. And this tranquil state attained, therefrom shall soon result a separation from all troubles; and his mind being thus at ease, fixed upon one object, it embraceth wisdom from all sides. The man whose heart and mind are not at rest is without wisdom or the power of contemplation; who doth not practice reflection, hath no calm; and how can a man without calm obtain happiness? The uncontrolled heart, following the dictates of the moving passions, snatcheth away his spiritual knowledge, as the storm the bark upon the raging ocean. Therefore, O great armed one, he is possessed of spiritual knowledge whose senses are withheld from objects of sense. What is night to those who are unenlightened is as day to his gaze; what seems as day is known to him as night, the night of ignorance. Such is the self-governed Sage!

"The man whose desires enter his heart, as waters run into the unswelling passive ocean, which, though ever full, yet does not quit its bed, obtaineth happiness; not he who lusteth in his lusts.

"The man who, having abandoned all desires, acts without covetousness, selfishness, or pride, deeming himself neither actor nor possessor, attains to rest. This, O son of Pritha, is dependence upon the Supreme Spirit, and he who possesseth it goeth no more astray; having obtained it, if therein established at the hour of death, he passeth on to Nirvana in the Supreme."

3

ARJUNA

"If according to thy opinion, O giver of all that men ask, knowledge is superior to the practice of deeds, why then dost thou urge me to engage in an undertaking so dreadful as this? Thou, as it were with doubtful speech, confusest my reason; wherefore choose one method amongst them by which I may obtain happiness and explain it unto me."

KRISHNA

"It hath before been declared by me, O sinless one, that in this world there are two modes of devotion: that of those who follow the Sankhya, or speculative science, which is the exercise of reason in contemplation; and that of the followers of the Yoga school, which is devotion in the performance of action.

"A man enjoyeth not freedom from action from the non-commencement of that which he hath to do; nor doth he obtain happiness from a total abandonment of action. No one ever resteth a moment inactive. Every man is involuntarily urged to act by the qualities which spring from nature. He who remains inert, restraining the senses and organs, yet pondering with his heart upon objects of sense, is called a false pietist of bewildered soul. But he who having subdued all his passions performeth with his active faculties all the duties of life, unconcerned as to their result, is to be esteemed. Do thou perform the proper actions: action is superior to inaction. The journey of thy mortal frame cannot be accomplished by inaction. All actions performed other than as sacrifice unto God make the actor bound by action. Abandon, then, O son of Kunti, all selfish motives, and in action perform thy duty for him alone. When in ancient times the lord of creatures had formed mankind, and at the same time appointed his worship, he spoke and said: 'With this worship, pray for increase, and let it be for you Kamaduk, the cow of plenty, on which ye shall depend for the accomplishment of all your wishes. With this nourish the Gods, that the Gods may nourish you; thus mutually nourishing ye shall obtain the highest felicity. The Gods being nourished by worship with sacrifice, will grant you the enjoyment of your wishes. He who enjoyeth what hath been given unto him by them, and offereth not a portion unto them, is even as a thief.' But those who eat not but what is left of the offerings shall be purified of all their transgressions. Those who dress their meat but for themselves eat the bread of sin, being themselves sin incarnate. Beings are nourished by food, food is produced by rain, rain comes from sacrifice, and sacrifice is performed by action. Know that action comes from the Supreme Spirit who is one; wherefore the all-pervading Spirit is at all times present in the sacrifice.

"He who, sinfully delighting in the gratification of his passions, doth not cause this wheel thus already set in motion to continue revolving, liveth in vain, O son of Pritha.

"But the man who only taketh delight in the Self within, is satisfied with that and content with that alone, hath no selfish interest in action. He hath no interest either in that which is done or that which is not done; and there is not, in all things which have been created, any object on which he may place dependence. Therefore perform thou that which thou hast to do, at all times unmindful of the event; for the man who doeth that which he hath to do, without attachment to the result, obtaineth the Supreme. Even by action Janaka and others attained perfection. Even if the good of mankind only is considered by thee, the performance of thy duty will be plain; for whatever is practised by the most excellent men, that is also practiced by others. The world follows whatever example they set. There is nothing, O son of Pritha, in the three regions of the universe which it is necessary for me to perform, nor anything possible to obtain which I have not obtained; and yet I am constantly in action. If I were not indefatigable in action, all men would presently follow my example, O son of Pritha. If I did not perform actions these creatures would perish; I should be the cause of confusion of castes, and should have slain all these creatures. O son of Bharata, as the ignorant perform the duties of life from the hope of reward, so the wise man, from the wish to bring the world to duty and benefit mankind, should perform his actions without motives of interest. He should not create confusion in the understandings of the ignorant, who are inclined to outward works, but by being himself engaged in action should cause them to act also. All actions are effected by the qualities of nature. The man deluded by ignorance thinks, 'I am the actor.' But he, O strong-armed one! who is acquainted with the nature of the two distinctions of cause and effect, knowing that the qualities act only in the qualities, and that the Self is distinct from them, is not attached in action.

"Those who have not this knowledge are interested in the actions thus brought about by the qualities; and he who is perfectly enlightened should not unsettle those whose discrimination is weak and knowledge incomplete, nor cause them to relax from their duty.

"Throwing every deed on me, and with thy meditation fixed upon the Higher Self, resolve to fight, without expectation, devoid of egotism and free from anguish.

"Those men who constantly follow this my doctrine without reviling it, and with a firm faith, shall be emancipated even by actions; but they who revile it and do not follow it are bewildered in regard to all knowledge, and perish, being devoid of discrimination.

"But the wise man also seeketh for that which is homogeneous with his own nature. All creatures act according to their natures; what, then, will restraint effect? In every purpose of the senses are fixed affection and dislike. A wise man should not fall in the power of these two passions, for they are the enemies of man. It is better to do one's own duty, even though it be devoid of excellence, than to perform another's duty well. It is better to perish in the performance of one's own duty; the duty of another is full of danger."

ARJUNA

"By what, O descendant of Vrishni, is man propelled to commit offences; seemingly against his will and as if constrained by some secret force?"

KRISHNA

"It is lust which instigates him. It is passion, sprung from the quality of *rajas*; insatiable, and full of sin. Know this to be the enemy of man on earth. As the flame is surrounded by smoke, and a mirror by rust, and as the womb envelopes the foetus, so is the universe surrounded by this passion. By this—the constant enemy of the wise man, formed from desire which rageth like fire and is never to be appeased—is discriminative knowledge surrounded. Its empire is over the senses and organs, the thinking principle and the discriminating faculty also; by means of these it cloudeth discrimination and deludeth the Lord of the body. Therefore, O best of the descendants of Bharata, at the very outset restraining thy senses, thou shouldst conquer this sin which is the destroyer of knowledge and of spiritual discernment.

"The senses and organs are esteemed great, but the thinking self is greater than they. The discriminating principle is greater than the thinking self, and that which is greater than the discriminating principle is He. Thus knowing what is greater than the discriminating principle and strengthening the lower by the Higher Self, do thou of mighty arms slay this foe which is formed from desire and is difficult to seize."

4

KRISHNA

"This exhaustless doctrine of Yoga I formerly taught unto Vivaswat; Vivaswat communicated it to Manu and Manu made it known unto Ikshwaku; and being thus transmitted from one unto another it was studied by the Rajarshees, until at length in the course of time the mighty art was lost, O harasser of thy foes! It is even the same exhaustless, secret, eternal doctrine I have this day communicated unto thee because thou art my devotee and my friend."

ARJUNA

"Seeing that thy birth is posterior to the life of Ikshwaku, how am I to understand that thou wert in the beginning the teacher of this doctrine?"

KRISHNA

"Both I and thou have passed through many births, O harasser of thy foes! Mine are known unto me, but thou knowest not of thine.

"Even though myself unborn, of changeless essence, and the lord of all existence, yet in presiding over nature—which is mine—I am born but through my own *maya*, the mystic power of self-ideation, the eternal thought in the eternal mind. I produce myself among creatures, O son of Bharata, whenever there is a decline of virtue and an insurrection of vice and injustice in the world; and thus I incarnate from age to age for the preservation of the just, the destruction of the wicked, and the establishment of righteousness. Whoever, O Arjuna, knoweth my divine birth and actions to be even so doth not upon quitting his mortal frame enter into another, for he entereth into me. Many who were free from craving, fear, and anger, filled with my spirit, and who depended upon me, having been purified by the ascetic fire of knowledge, have entered into my being. In whatever way men approach me, in that way do I assist them; but whatever the path taken by mankind, that path is mine, O son of Pritha. Those who wish for success to their works in this life sacrifice to the gods; and in this world success from their actions soon cometh to pass.

"Mankind was created by me of four castes distinct in their principles and in their duties according to the natural distribution of the actions and qualities. Know me, then, although changeless and not acting, to be the author of this. Actions affect me not, nor have I any expectations from the fruits of actions. He who comprehendeth me to be thus is not held by the bonds of action to rebirth. The ancients who longed for eternal salvation, having discovered this, still performed works. Wherefore perform thou works even as they were performed by the ancients in former times.

"Even sages have been deluded as to what is action and what inaction; therefore I shall explain to thee what is action by a knowledge of which thou shalt be liberated from evil. One must learn well what is action to be performed, what is not to be, and what is inaction. The path of action is obscure. That man who sees inaction in action and action in inaction is wise among men; he is a true devotee and a perfect performer of all action.

"Those who have spiritual discrimination call him wise whose undertakings are all free from desire, for his actions are consumed in the fire of knowledge. He abandoneth the desire to see a reward for his actions, is free, contented, and upon nothing dependeth, and although engaged in action he really doeth nothing; he is not solicitous of results, with mind and body subdued and being above enjoyment from objects, doing with the body alone the acts of the body, he does not subject himself to rebirth. He is contented with whatever he receives fortuitously, is free from the influence of 'the pairs of opposites' and from envy, the same in success and failure; even though he act he is not bound by the bonds of action. All the actions of such a man who is free from self-interest, who is devoted, with heart set upon spiritual knowledge, and whose acts are sacrifices for the sake of the Supreme, are dissolved and left without effect on him. The Supreme Spirit is the act of offering, the Supreme Spirit is the sacrificial butter offered in the fire which is the Supreme Spirit, and unto the Supreme

Spirit goeth he who maketh the Supreme Spirit the object of his meditation in performing his actions.

"Some devotees give sacrifice to the Gods, while others, lighting
the subtler fire of the Supreme Spirit offer up themselves; still others
make sacrifice with the senses, beginning with hearing, in the fire of
self-restraint, and some give up all sense-delighting sounds, and others
again, illuminated by spiritual knowledge, sacrifice all the functions of
the senses and vitality in the fire of devotion through self-constraint.
There are also those who perform sacrifice by wealth given in alms,
by mortification, by devotion, and by silent study. Some sacrifice the
up-breathing in the down-breathing and the down-breathing in the
up-breathing by blocking up the channels of inspiration and expiration; and others by stopping the movements of both the life breaths;
still others by abstaining from food sacrifice life in their life.

"All these different kinds of worshippers are by their sacrifices
purified from their sins; but they who partake of the perfection of
spiritual knowledge arising from such sacrifices pass into the eternal
Supreme Spirit. But for him who maketh no sacrifices there is no part
nor lot in this world; how then shall he share in the other, O best of
the Kurus?

"All these sacrifices of so many kinds are displayed in the sight
of God; know that they all spring from action, and, comprehend-
ing this, thou shalt obtain an eternal release. O harasser of thy foes,
the sacrifice through spiritual knowledge is superior to sacrifice made
with material things; every action without exception is comprehended
in spiritual knowledge, O son of Pritha. Seek this wisdom by doing
service, by strong search, by questions, and by humility; the wise who
see the truth will communicate it unto thee, and knowing which thou
shalt never again fall into error, O son of Bharata. By this knowledge
thou shalt see all things and creatures whatsoever in thyself and then
in me. Even if thou wert the greatest of all sinners, thou shalt be able
to cross over all sins in the bark of spiritual knowledge. As the natural
fire, O Arjuna, reduceth fuel to ashes, so does the fire of knowledge
reduce all actions to ashes. There is no purifier in this world to be
compared to spiritual knowledge; and he who is perfected in devotion
findeth spiritual knowledge springing up spontaneously in himself in
the progress of time. The man who restraineth the senses and organs
and hath faith obtaineth spiritual knowledge, and having obtained
it he soon reacheth supreme tranquility; but the ignorant, those full

of doubt and without faith, are lost. The man of doubtful mind hath no happiness either in this world or in the next or in any other. No actions bind that man who through spiritual discrimination hath renounced action and cut asunder all doubt by knowledge, O despiser of wealth. Wherefore, O son of Bharata, having cut asunder with the sword of spiritual knowledge this doubt which existeth in thy heart, engage in the performance of action. Arise!"

5

ARJUNA

"At one time, O Krishna, thou praisest the renunciation of action, and yet again its right performance. Tell me with certainty which of the two is better."

KRISHNA

"Renunciation of action and devotion through action are both means of final emancipation, but of these two devotion through action is better than renunciation. He is considered to be an ascetic who seeks nothing and nothing rejects, being free from the influence of the 'pairs of opposites,' O thou of mighty arms; without trouble he is released from the bonds forged by action. Children only and not the wise speak of renunciation of action and of right performance of action as being different. He who perfectly practices the one receives the fruits of both, and the place which is gained by the renouncer of action is also attained by him who is devoted in action. That man seeth with clear sight who seeth that the Sankhya and the Yoga doctrines are identical. But to attain to true renunciation of action without devotion through action is difficult, O thou of mighty arms; while the devotee who is engaged in the right practice of his duties approacheth the Supreme Spirit in no long time. The man of purified heart, having his body fully controlled, his senses restrained, and for whom the only self is the Self of all creatures, is not tainted although performing actions. The devotee who knows the divine truth thinketh 'I am doing nothing' in seeing, hearing, touching, smelling, eating, moving, sleeping, breathing; even when speaking, letting go or taking, opening or closing his eyes, he sayeth, 'the senses and organs move by natural impulse to their appropriate objects.' Whoever in acting dedicates his actions to the Supreme Spirit and puts aside all selfish interest in their result is untouched by sin, even as the leaf of the lotus is unaffected by the waters. The truly devoted, for the purification of the heart, perform actions with their bodies, their minds, their understanding, and their senses, putting away all self-interest. The man who is devoted and not attached to the fruit of his actions obtains tranquility; whilst he who through desire has attachment for the fruit of action is bound down thereby. The self-restrained sage having with his heart renounced all actions, dwells at rest in the 'nine gate city of his abode,' neither acting nor causing to act.

"The Lord of the world creates neither the faculty of acting, nor actions, nor the connection between action and its fruits; but nature prevaileth in these. The Lord receives no man's deeds, be they sinful or full of merit. The truth is obscured by that which is not true, and therefore all creatures are led astray. But in those for whom knowledge of the true Self has dispersed ignorance, the Supreme, as if lighted by the sun, is revealed. Those whose souls are in the Spirit, whose asylum is in it, who are intent on it and purified by knowledge from all sins, go to that place from which there is no return.

"The illuminated sage regards with equal mind an illuminated, selfless Brahmin, a cow, an elephant, a dog, and even an outcast who eats the flesh of dogs. Those who thus preserve an equal mind gain heaven even in this life, for the Supreme is free from sin and equal minded; therefore they rest in the Supreme Spirit. The man who knoweth the Supreme Spirit, who is not deluded, and who is fixed on him, doth not rejoice at obtaining what is pleasant, nor grieve when meeting what is unpleasant. He whose heart is not attached to objects of sense finds pleasure within himself, and, through devotion, united with the Supreme, enjoys imperishable bliss. For those enjoyments which arise through the contact of the senses with external objects are wombs of pain, since they have a beginning and an end; O son of Kunti, the wise man delighteth not in these. He who, while living in this world and before the liberation of the soul from the body, can resist the impulse arising from desire and anger is a devotee and blessed. The man who is happy within himself, who is illuminated within, is a devotee, and partaking of the nature of the Supreme Spirit, he is merged in it. Such illuminated sages whose sins are exhausted, who are free from delusion, who have their senses and organs under control, and devoted to the good of all creatures, obtain assimilation with the Supreme Spirit. Assimilation with the Supreme Spirit is on both sides of death for those who are free from desire and anger, temperate, of thoughts restrained; and who are acquainted with the true Self.

"The anchorite who shutteth his placid soul away from all sense of touch, with gaze fixed between his brows; who maketh the breath to pass through both his nostrils with evenness alike in inspiration and expiration, whose senses and organs together with his heart and understanding are under control, and who hath set his heart upon liberation and is ever free from desire and anger, is emancipated from birth and death even in this life. Knowing that I, the great Lord of all worlds, am the enjoyer of all sacrifices and penances and the friend of all creatures, he shall obtain me and be blessed."

6

"He who, unattached to the fruit of his actions, performeth such actions as should be done is both a renouncer of action and a devotee of right action; not he who liveth without kindling the sacrificial fire and without ceremonies. Know, O son of Pandu, that what they call *Sannyas* or a forsaking of action is the same as *Yoga* or the practice of devotion. No one without having previously renounced all intentions can be devoted. Action is said to be the means by which the wise man who is desirous of mounting to meditation may reach thereto; so cessation from action is said to be the means for him who hath reached to meditation. When he hath renounced all intentions and is devoid of attachment to action in regard to objects of sense, then he is called one who hath ascended to meditation. He should raise the self by the Self; let him not suffer the Self to be lowered; for Self is the friend of self, and, in like manner, self is its own enemy. Self is the friend of the man who is self-conquered; so self like a foe hath enmity to him who is not self-conquered. The Self of the man who is self-subdued and free from desire and anger is intent on the Supreme Self in heat and cold, in pain and pleasure, in honor and ignominy. The man who hath spiritual knowledge and discernment, who standeth upon the pinnacle, and hath subdued the senses, to whom gold and stone are the same, is said to be devoted. And he is esteemed among all who, whether amongst his friends and companions, in the midst of enemies or those who stand aloof or remain neutral, with those who love and those who hate, and in the company of sinners or the righteous, is of equal mind.

"He who has attained to meditation should constantly strive to stay at rest in the Supreme, remaining in solitude and seclusion, having his body and his thoughts under control, without possessions and free from hope. He should in an undefiled spot place his seat, firm, neither too high nor too low, and made of kusa grass which is covered with a skin and a cloth. There, for the self's purification he should practice meditation with his mind fixed on one point, the modifications of the thinking principle controlled and the action of the senses and organs restrained. Keeping his body, head, and neck firm and erect, with mind determined, and gaze directed to the tip of his nose without looking in any direction, with heart at peace and free from fear, the Yogee should remain, settled in the vow of a Brahmacharya, his thoughts controlled, and heart fixed on me. The devotee of controlled mind who thus always bringeth his heart to rest in the Supreme reacheth that tranquility, the supreme assimilation with me.

"This divine discipline, Arjuna, is not to be attained by the man who eateth more than enough or too little, nor by him who hath a habit of sleeping much, nor by him who is given to overwatching. The meditation which destroyeth pain is produced in him who is moderate in eating and in recreation, of moderate exertion in his actions, and regulated in sleeping and waking. When the man, so living, centers his heart in the true Self and is exempt from attachment to all desires, he is said to have attained to Yoga. Of the sage of self-centred heart, at rest and free from attachment to desires, the simile is recorded, 'as a lamp which is sheltered from the wind flickereth not.' When regulated by the practice of yoga and at rest, seeing the self by the self, he is contented; when he becometh acquainted with that boundless bliss which is not connected with objects of the senses, and being where he is not moved from the reality; having gained which he considereth no other superior to it, and in which, being fixed, he is not moved even by the greatest grief; know that this disconnection from union with pain is distinguished as yoga, spiritual union or devotion, which is to be striven after by a man with faith and steadfastly.

"When he hath abandoned every desire that ariseth from the imagination and subdued with the mind the senses and organs which impel to action in every direction, being possessed of patience, he by degrees finds rest; and, having fixed his mind at rest in the true Self, he should think of nothing else. To whatsoever object the inconstant mind goeth out he should subdue it, bring it back, and place it upon the Spirit. Supreme bliss surely cometh to the sage whose mind is thus at peace; whose passions and desires are thus subdued; who is thus in the true Self and free from sin. He who is thus devoted and free from sin obtaineth without hindrance the highest bliss—union with the Supreme Spirit. The man who is endued with this devotion and who seeth the unity of all things perceiveth the Supreme Soul in all things and all things in the Supreme Soul. He who seeth me in all things and all things in me looseneth not his hold on me and I forsake him not. And whosoever, believing in spiritual unity, worshippeth me who am in all things, dwelleth with me in whatsoever condition he may be. He, O Arjuna, who by the similitude found in himself seeth but one essence in all things, whether they be evil or good, is considered to be the most excellent devotee."

ARJUNA

"O slayer of Madhu, on account of the restlessness of the mind, I do not perceive any possibility of steady continuance in this yoga of equanimity which thou hast declared. For indeed, O Krishna, the mind is full of agitation, turbulent, strong, and obstinate. I believe the restraint of it to be as difficult as that of the wind."

KRISHNA

"Without doubt, O thou of mighty arms, the mind is restless and hard to restrain; but it may be restrained, O son of Kunti, by practice and absence of desire. Yet in my opinion this divine discipline called yoga is very difficult for one who hath not his soul in his own control; yet it may be acquired through proper means and by one who is assiduous and controlleth his heart."

ARJUNA

"What end, O Krishna, doth that man attain who, although having faith, hath not attained to perfection in his devotion because his unsubdued mind wandered from the discipline? Doth he, fallen from both, like a broken cloud without any support, become destroyed. O strong-armed one, being deluded in the path of the Supreme Spirit? Thou, Krishna, shouldst completely dispel this doubt for me, for there is none other to be found able to remove it."

KRISHNA

"Such a man, O son of Pritha, doth not perish here or hereafter. For never to an evil place goeth one who doeth good. The man whose devotion has been broken off by death goeth to the regions of the righteous, where he dwells for an immensity of years and is then born again on earth in a pure and fortunate family; or even in a family of those who are spiritually illuminated. But such a rebirth into this life as this last is more difficult to obtain. Being thus born again he comes in contact with the knowledge which belonged to him in his former body, and from that time he struggles more diligently towards perfection, O son of Kuru. For even unwittingly, by reason of that past practice, he is led and works on. Even if only a mere enquirer, he reaches beyond the word of the Vedas. But the devotee who, striving with all his might, obtaineth perfection because of efforts continued through many births, goeth to the supreme goal. The man of meditation as thus described is superior to the man of penance and to the man of learning and also to the man of action; wherefore, O Arjuna, resolve thou to become a man of meditation. But of all devotees he is considered by me as the most devoted who, with heart fixed on me, full of faith, worships me."

7

"Hear, O son of Pritha, how with heart fixed on me, practicing meditation and taking me as thy refuge, thou shalt know me completely. I will instruct thee fully in this knowledge and in its realization, which, having learned, there remains nothing else to be known.

"Among thousands of mortals a single one perhaps strives for perfection, and among those so striving perhaps a single one knows me as I am. Earth, water, fire, air, and akasa, Manas, Buddhi, and Ahankara is the eightfold division of my nature. It is inferior; know that my superior nature is different and is the knower; by it the universe is sustained; learn that the whole of creation springs from this too as from a womb; I am the cause, I am the production and the dissolution of the whole universe. There is none superior to me, O conqueror of wealth, and all things hang on me as precious gems upon a string. I am the taste in water, O son of Kunti, the light in the sun and moon, the mystic syllable OM in all the Vedas, sound in space, the masculine essence in men, the sweet smell in the earth, and the brightness in the fire. In all creatures I am the life, and the power of concentration in those whose minds are on the spirit. Know me, O son of Pritha, as the eternal seed of all creatures. I am the wisdom of the wise and the strength of the strong. And I am the power of the strong who in action are free from desire and longing; in all creatures I am desire regulated by moral fitness. Know also that the dispositions arising from the three qualities, *sattva, rajas,* and *tamas,* are from me; they are in me, but I am not in them. The whole world, being deluded by these dispositions which are born of the three qualities, knoweth not me distinct from them, supreme, imperishable. For this my divine illusive power, acting through the natural qualities, is difficult to surmount, and those only can surmount it who have recourse to me alone. The wicked among men, the deluded and the low-minded, deprived of spiritual perception by this illusion, and inclining toward demoniacal dispositions, do not have recourse to me.

"Four classes of men who work righteousness worship me, O Arjuna; those who are afflicted, the searchers for truth, those who desire possessions, and the wise, O son of Bharata. Of these the best is the one possessed of spiritual knowledge, who is always devoted to me. I am extremely dear to the wise man, and he is dear unto me. Excellent indeed are all these, but the spiritually wise is verily myself, because with heart at peace he is upon the road that leadeth to the highest path, which is even myself. After many births the spiritually wise findeth me as the Vasudeva who is all this, for such an one of great soul is difficult to meet. Those who through diversity of desires are deprived of spiritual wisdom adopt particular rites subordinated to their own natures, and worship other Gods. In whatever form a devotee desires with faith to worship, it is I alone who inspire him with constancy therein, and depending on that faith he seeks the propitiation of that God, obtaining the object of his wishes as is ordained by me alone. But the reward of such short-sighted men is temporary. Those who worship the Gods go to the Gods, and those who worship me come unto me. The ignorant, being unacquainted with my supreme condition which is superior to all things and exempt from decay, believe me who am unmanifested to exist in a visible form. Enveloped by my magic illusion I am not visible to the world; therefore the world doth not recognize me the unborn and exhaustless. I know, O Arjuna, all creatures that have been, that are present, as well as all that shall hereafter be, but no one knows me. At the time of birth, O son of Bharata, all beings fall into error by reason of the delusion of the opposites which springs from liking and disliking, O harasser of thy foes. But those men of righteous lives whose sins have ceased, being free from this delusion of the 'pairs of opposites,' firmly settled in faith, worship me. They who depend on me, and labor for deliverance from birth and death know Brahma, the whole Adhyatma, and all Karma. Those who rest in me, knowing me to be the Adhibhuta, the Adhidaivata, and the Adhiyajna, know me also at the time of death."

8

ARJUNA

"What is that Brahman, what is Adhyatma, and what, O best of men! is Karma? What also is Adhibhuta, and what Adhidaivata? Who too is Adhiyajna here, in this body, and how therein, O slayer of Madhu? Tell me also how men who are fixed in meditation are to know thee at the hour of death?"

KRISHNA

"Brahman the Supreme is the exhaustless. Adhyatma is the name of my being manifesting as the Individual Self. Karma is the emanation which causes the existence and reproduction of creatures. Adhibhuta is the Supreme Spirit dwelling in all elemental nature through the mysterious power of nature's illusion. Adhidaivata is the Purusha, the Spiritual Person, and Adhiyajna is myself in this body, O best of embodied men. Whoever at the hour of death abandoneth the body, fixed in meditation upon me, without doubt goeth to me. Whoso in consequence of constant meditation on any particular form thinketh upon it when quitting his mortal shape, even to that doth he go, O son of Kunti. Therefore at all times meditate only on me and fight. Thy mind and Buddhi being placed on me alone, thou shalt without doubt come to me. The man whose heart abides in me alone, wandering to no other object, shall also by meditation on the Supreme Spirit go to it, O son of Pritha. Whosoever shall meditate upon the All-Wise which is without beginning, the Supreme Ruler, the smallest of the small, the Supporter of all, whose form is incomprehensible, bright as the sun beyond the darkness; with mind undeviating, united to devotion, and by the power of meditation concentrated at the hour of death, with his vital powers placed between the eyebrows, attains to that Supreme Divine Spirit.

"I will now make known to thee that path which the learned in the Vedas call indestructible, into which enter those who are free from attachments, and is followed by those desirous of leading the life of a Brahmacharya laboring for salvation. He who closeth all the doors of his senses, imprisoneth his mind in his heart, fixeth his vital powers in his head, standing firm in meditation, repeating the mono-syllable OM, and thus continues when he is quitting the body, goeth to the supreme goal. He who, with heart undiverted to any other object, meditates constantly and through the whole of life on me shall surely attain to me, O son of Pritha. Those great-souled ones who have attained to supreme perfection come unto me and no more incur rebirths rapidly revolving, which are mansions of pain and sorrow.

"All worlds up to that of Brahman are subject to rebirth again and again, but they, O son of Kunti, who reach to me have no rebirth. Those who are acquainted with day and night know that the day of Brahma is a thousand revolutions of the yugas and that his night extendeth for a thousand more. At the coming on of that day all things issue forth from the unmanifested into manifestation, so on the approach of that night they merge again into the unmanifested. This collection of existing things having thus come forth, is dissolved at the approach of the night, O son of Pritha; and now again on the coming of the day it emanates spontaneously. But there is that which upon the dissolution of all things else is not destroyed; it is indi-visible, indestructible, and of another nature from the visible. That called the unmanifested and exhaustless is called the supreme goal, which having once attained they never more return—it is my supreme abode. This Supreme, O son of Pritha, within whom all creatures are included and by whom all this is pervaded, may be attained by a devo-tion which is intent on him alone.

"I will now declare to thee, O best of the Bharatas, at what time yogis dying obtain freedom from or subjection to rebirth. Fire, light, day, the fortnight of the waxing moon, six months of the sun's north-ern course—going then and knowing the Supreme Spirit, men go to the Supreme. But those who depart in smoke, at night, during the fortnight of the waning moon, and while the sun is in the path of his southern journey, proceed for a while to the regions of the moon and again return to mortal birth. These two, *light* and *darkness*, are the world's eternal ways; by one a man goes not to return, by the other he cometh back again upon earth. No devotee, O son of Pritha, who knoweth these two paths is ever deluded; wherefore, O Arjuna, at all times be thou fixed in devotion. The man of meditation who knoweth all this reaches beyond whatever rewards are promised in the Vedas or that result from sacrifices or austerities or from gifts of charity, and goeth to the supreme, the highest place."

9

"Unto thee who findeth no fault I will now make known this most mysterious knowledge, coupled with a realization of it, which having known thou shalt be delivered from evil. This is the royal knowledge, the royal mystery, the most excellent purifier, clearly comprehensible, not opposed to sacred law, easy to perform, and inexhaustible. These who are unbelievers in this truth, O harasser of thy foes, find me not, but revolving in rebirth return to this world, the mansion of death.

"All this universe is pervaded by me in my invisible form; all things exist in me, but I do not exist in them. Nor are all things in me; behold this my divine mystery: myself causing things to exist and supporting them all but dwelling not in them. Understand that all things are in me even as the mighty air which passes everywhere is in space. O son of Kunti, at the end of a kalpa all things return into my nature, and then again at the beginning of another kalpa I cause them to evolve again. Taking control of my own nature I emanate again and again this whole assemblage of beings, without their will, by the power of the material essence. These acts do not bind me, O conqueror of wealth, because I am as one who sitteth indifferent, uninterested in those works. By reason of my supervision nature produceth the animate and inanimate universe; it is through this cause, O son of Kunti, that the universe revolveth.

"The deluded despise me in human form, being unacquainted with my real nature as Lord of all things. They are of vain hopes, deluded in action, in reason and in knowledge, inclining to demoniac and deceitful principles. But those great of soul, partaking of the godlike nature, knowing me to be the imperishable principle of all things, worship me, diverted to nothing else. Fixed in unbroken vows they worship, everywhere proclaiming me and bowing down to me. Others with the sacrifice of knowledge in other ways worship me as indivisible, as separable, as the Spirit of the universe. I am the sacrifice and sacrificial rite; I am the libation offered to ancestors, and the spices; I am the sacred formula and the fire; I am the food and the sacrificial butter; I am the father and the mother of this universe, the grandsire and the preserver; I am the Holy One, the object of knowledge, the mystic purifying syllable OM, the *Rik*, the *Saman*, the *Yajur*, and all the Vedas. I am the goal, the Comforter, the Lord, the Witness, the resting-place, the asylum and the Friend; I am the origin and the dissolution, the receptacle, the storehouse, and the eternal seed. I cause light and heat and rain; I now draw in and now let forth; I am death and immortality; I am the cause unseen and the visible effect. Those enlightened in the three Vedas, offering sacrifices to me and obtaining sanctification from drinking the soma juice, petition me for heaven; thus they attain the region of Indra, the prince of celestial beings, and there feast upon celestial food and are gratified with heavenly enjoyments. And they, having enjoyed that spacious heaven for a period in proportion to their merits, sink back into this mortal world where they are born again as soon as their stock of merit is exhausted; thus those who long for the accomplishment of desires, following the Vedas, obtain a happiness which comes and goes. But for those who, thinking of me as identical with all, constantly worship me, I bear the burden of the responsibility of their happiness. And even those also who worship other gods with a firm faith in doing so, involuntarily worship me, too, O son of Kunti, albeit in ignorance. I am he who is the Lord of all sacrifices, and am also their enjoyer, but they do not understand me truly and therefore they fall from heaven. Those who devote themselves to the gods go to the gods; the worshippers of the pitris go to the pitris; those who worship the evil spirits go to them, and my worshippers come to me. I accept and enjoy the offerings of the humble soul who in his worship with a pure heart offereth a leaf, a flower, or fruit, or water unto me. Whatever thou doest, O son of Kunti, whatever thou eatest, whatever thou sacrificest, whatever thou givest, whatever mortification thou performest, commit each unto me. Thus thou shalt be delivered from the good and evil experiences which are the bonds of action; and thy heart being joined to renunciation and to the practice of action, thou shalt come to me. I am the same to all creatures; I know not hatred nor favor; but those who serve me with love dwell in me and I in them. Even if the man of most evil ways worship me with exclusive devotion, he is to be considered as righteous, for he hath judged aright. Such a man soon becometh of a righteous soul and obtaineth perpetual happiness. I swear, O son of Kunti, that he who worships me never perisheth. Those even who may be of the womb of sin, women, vaisyas, and sudras, shall tread the highest path if they take sanctuary with me. How much more, then, holy brahmans and devotees of kingly race! Having obtained this finite, joyless world, worship me. Serve me, fix heart and mind on me, be my servant, my adorer, prostrate thyself before me, and thus, united unto me, at rest, thou shalt go unto me."

10

"Hear again, O thou of mighty arms, my supreme words, which unto thee who art well pleased I will declare because I am anxious for thy welfare.

"Neither the assemblage of the Gods nor the Adept Kings know my origin, because I am the origin of all the Gods and of the Adepts. Whosoever knoweth me to be the mighty Ruler of the universe and without birth or beginning, he among men, undeluded, shall be liberated from all his sins. Subtle perception, spiritual knowledge, right judgment, patience, truth, self-mastery; pleasure and pain, prosperity and adversity; birth and death, danger and security, fear and equanimity, satisfaction, restraint of body and mind, alms-giving, inoffensiveness, zeal and glory and ignominy, all these the various dispositions of creatures come from me. So in former days the seven great Sages and the four Manus who are of my nature were born of my mind, and from them sprang this world. He who knoweth perfectly this permanence and mystic faculty of mine becometh without doubt possessed of unshaken faith. I am the origin of all; all things proceed from me; believing me to be thus, the wise gifted with spiritual wisdom worship me; their very hearts and minds are in me; enlightening one another and constantly speaking of me, they are full of enjoyment and satisfaction. To them thus always devoted to me, who worship me with love, I give that mental devotion by which they come to me. For them do I out of my compassion, standing within their hearts, destroy the darkness which springs from ignorance by the brilliant lamp of spiritual discernment."

"Thou art Parabrahm! the supreme abode, the great Purification; thou art the Eternal Presence, the Divine Being, before all other

Gods, holy, primeval, all-pervading, without beginning! Thus thou art declared by all the Sages—by Narada, Asita, Devala, Vyasa, and thou thyself now doth say the same. I firmly believe all that thou, O Keshava, sayest unto me; for neither Gods nor demons comprehend thy manifestations. Thou alone knowest thyself by thy Self, Supreme Spirit, Creator and Master of all that lives, God of Gods, and Lord of all the universe! Thou alone can fully declare thy divine powers by which thou hast pervaded and continueth to pervade these worlds. How shall I, constantly thinking of thee, be able to know thee, O mysterious Lord? In what particular forms shall I meditate on thee? O Janardana—besought by mortals—tell me therefore in full thine own powers and forms of manifestation, for I am never sated of drinking of the life-giving water of thy words."

KRISHNA

"O best of Kurus, blessings be upon thee. I will make thee acquainted with the chief of my divine manifestations, for the extent of my nature is infinite.

"I am the Ego which is seated in the hearts of all beings; I am the beginning, the middle, and the end of all existing things. Among Adityas I am Vishnu, and among luminous bodies I am the sun. I am Mrichi among the Maruts, and among heavenly mansions I am the moon. Among the Vedas I am the *Samaveda*, and Indra among the Gods; among the senses and organs I am the Manas, and of creatures the existence. I am Shankara among the Rudras; and Vittesha, the lord of wealth among the Yakshas and Rakshasas. I am Pavaka among the Vasus, and Meru among high-aspiring mountains. And know, O son of Pritha, that I am Brihaspati, the chief of teachers; among leaders of celestial armies Skanda, and of floods I am the ocean. I am Bhrigu among the Adept Kings; of words I am the monoysllable OM; of forms of worship, the silent repetition of sacred texts, and of immovable things I am the Himalaya. Of all the trees of the forest I am Ashwattha, the Pimpala tree; and of the celestial Sages, Narada; among Gandharbhas I am Chitraratha, and of perfect saints, Kapila. Know that among horses I am Uchchisrava, who arose with the Amrita out of the ocean; among elephants, Airavata, and among men their sovereigns. Of weapons I am the thunderbolt; among cows, Kamaduk, the cow of plenty; of procreators, the God of love, and of serpents, Vasuki, their chief. I am Ananta among the Nagas, Varuna among things of the waters; among the ancestors, Aryana, and of all who judge I am Yama. Among the Daityas I am Prahlada, and among computations I am Time itself; the lion among beasts, and Garuda among the feathered tribe. Among purifiers I am Pavana, the air; Rama among those who carry arms, Makara among the fishes, and the Ganges among rivers. Among that which is evolved, O Arjuna, I am the beginning, the middle, and the end; of all sciences I am the knowledge of the Adhyatma, and of uttered sounds the human speech. Among letters I am the vowel A, and of all compound words I am the Dwandwa; I am endless time itself, and the Preserver whose face is turned on all sides. I am all-grasping death, and the birth of those who are to be; among feminine things I am fame, fortune, speech, memory, intelligence, patience, and forgiveness. Among the hymns of the *Samaveda* I am *Brihat Saman,* and the Gayatri among metres; among months I am the month Margashirsha, and of seasons spring called Kusumakra, the time of flowers. Of those things which deceive I am the dice, and splendor itself among splendid things. I am victory, I am perseverance, and the goodness of the good. Of the race of Vrishni I am Vasudeva; of the Pandava I am Arjuna the conqueror of wealth; of perfect saints I am Vyasa, and of prophet-seers I am the bard Oosana. Among rulers I am the rod of punishment, among those desiring conquest I am policy; and among the wise of secret knowledge I am their silence. I am, O Arjuna, the seed of all existing things, and there is not anything, whether animate or inanimate which is without me. My divine manifestations, O harasser of thy foes, are without end, the many which I have mentioned are by way of example. Whatever creature is permanent, of good fortune or mighty, also know it to be sprung from a portion of my energy. But what, O Arjuna, hast thou to do with so much knowledge as this? I established this whole universe with a single portion of myself, and remain separate."

11

"My delusion has been dispersed by the words which thou for my soul's peace hast spoken concerning the mystery of the Adhyatma—the spirit. For I have heard at full length from thee, O thou whose eyes are like lotus leaves, the origin and dissolution of existing things, and also thy inexhaustible majesty. It is even as thou hast described thyself, O mighty Lord; I now desire to see thy divine form, O sovereign Lord. Wherefore, O Lord, if thou thinkest it may be beheld by me, show me, O Master of devotion, thine inexhaustible Self."

KRISHNA

"Behold, O son of Pritha, my forms by hundreds and by thousands, of diverse kinds divine, of many shapes and fashions. Behold the Adityas, Vasus, Rudras, Aswins, and the Maruts, see things wonderful never seen before, O son of Bharata. Here in my body now behold, O Gudakesha, the whole universe animate and inanimate gathered here in one, and all things else thou hast a wish to see. But as with thy natural eyes thou art not able to see me, I will give thee the divine eye. Behold my sovereign power and might!"

SANJAYA

O king, having thus spoken, Hari, the mighty Lord of mysterious power, showed to the son of Pritha his supreme form; with many mouths and eyes and many wonderful appearances, with many divine ornaments, many celestial weapons upraised; adorned with celestial garlands and robes, anointed with celestial ointments and perfumes, full of every marvelous thing, the eternal God whose face is turned in all directions. The glory and amazing splendor of this mighty

Being may be likened to the radiance shed by a thousand suns rising together into the heavens. The son of Pandu then beheld within the body of the God of gods the whole universe in all its vast variety. Overwhelmed with wonder, Dhananjaya, the possessor of wealth, with hair standing on end, bowed down his head before the Deity, and thus with joined palms addressed him:

ARJUNA

"I behold, O God of gods, within thy frame all beings and things of every kind; the Lord Brahma on his lotus throne, all the Rishees and the heavenly Serpents. I see thee on all sides, of infinite forms, having many arms, stomachs, mouths, and eyes. But I can discover neither thy beginning, thy middle, nor thy end, O universal Lord, form of the universe. I see thee crowned with a diadem and armed with mace and chakkra, a mass of splendor, darting light on all sides; difficult to behold, shining in every direction with light immeasurable, like the burning fire or glowing sun. Thou art the supreme inexhaustible Being, the end of effort, changeless, the Supreme Spirit of this universe, the never-failing guardian of eternal law; I esteem thee Purusha, I see thee without beginning, middle, or end, of infinite power with arms innumerable, the sun and moon thy eyes, thy mouth a flaming fire, overmastering the whole universe with thy majesty. Space and heaven, and earth and every point around the three regions of the universe are filled with thee alone. The triple world is full of fear, O thou mighty Spirit, seeing this thy marvellous form of terror. Of the assemblage of the gods some I see fly to thee for refuge, while some in fear with joined hands sing forth thy praise; the hosts of the Maharshis and Siddhas, great sages and saints, hail thee, saying 'svasti,' and glorify thee with most excellent hymns. The Rudras, Adityas, the Vasus, and all those beings—the Sadhyas, Vishwas, the Ashwins, Maruts, and Ushmapas, the hosts of Gandharbhas, Yakshas, and Siddhas—all stand gazing on thee and are amazed. All the worlds alike with me are terrified to behold thy wondrous form gigantic, O thou of mighty arms, with many mouths and eyes, with many arms, thighs and feet, with many stomachs and projecting tusks. For seeing thee thus touching the heavens, shining with such glory, with widely-opened mouths and bright expanded eyes, my inmost soul is troubled and I lose both firmness and tranquility, O Vishnu. Beholding thy dreadful teeth and thy face like the burning of death, I can see neither heaven nor earth; I find no peace; have mercy, O Lord of gods, thou Spirit of the universe! The sons of Dhritarashtra with all these rulers of men, Bhishma, Drona and also Karna and our principal warriors, seem to be impetuously precipitating themselves into thy mouths terrible with tusks; some are seen caught between thy teeth, their heads ground down. As the rapid streams of full-flowing rivers roll on to meet the ocean, even so these heroes of the human race rush into thy flaming mouths. As troops of insects carried away by strong impulse find death in the fire, even so do these beings with swelling force pour into thy mouths for their own destruction. Thou involvest and swallowest all these creatures from every side, licking them in thy flaming lips; filling the universe with thy splendor, thy sharp beams burn, O Vishnu. Reverence be unto thee, O best of Gods! Be favorable! I seek to know thee, the Primeval One, for I know not thy work."

KRISHNA

"I am Time matured, come hither for the destruction of these creatures; except thyself, not one of all these warriors here drawn up in serried ranks shall live. Wherefore, arise! seize fame! Defeat the foe and enjoy the full-grown kingdom! They have been already slain by me; be thou only the immediate agent, O thou both-armed one. Be not disturbed. Slay Drona, Bhishma, Jayadratha, Karna, and all the other heroes of the war who are really slain by me. Fight, thou wilt conquer all thine enemies."

SANJAYA

When he of the resplendent diadem heard these words from the mouth of Keshava, he saluted Krishna with joined palms and trembling with fear, addressed him in broken accents, and bowed down terrified before him.

ARJUNA

"The universe, O Hrishekesha, is justly delighted with thy glory and is filled with zeal for thy service; the evil spirits are affrighted and flee on all sides, while all the hosts of saints bow down in adoration before thee. And wherefore should they not adore thee, O mighty Being, thou who art greater than Brahma, who art the first Maker? O eternal God of gods! O habitation of the universe! Thou art the one indivisible Being, and non-being, that which is supreme. Thou art the first of Gods, the most ancient Spirit; thou art the final supreme receptacle of this universe; thou art the Knower and that which is to be known, and the supreme mansion; and by thee, O thou of infinite form, is this universe caused to emanate. Thou art Vayu, God of wind, Agni, God of fire, Yama, God of death, Varuna, God of waters; thou art the moon; Prajapati, the progenitor and grandfather, art thou. Hail! hail to thee! Hail to thee a thousand times repeated! Again and again hail to thee! Hail to thee! Hail to thee from before! Hail to thee from behind! Hail to thee on all sides, O thou All! Infinite is thy power and might; thou includest all things, therefore thou art all things!

"Having been ignorant of thy majesty, I took thee for a friend, and have called thee 'O Krishna, O son of Yadu, O friend,' and blinded by my affection and presumption, I have at times treated thee without respect in sport, in recreation, in repose, in thy chair, and at thy meals, in private and in public; all this I beseech thee, O inconceivable Being, to forgive.

"Thou art the father of all things animate and inanimate; thou art to be honored as above the guru himself, and worthy to be adored; there is none equal to thee, and how in the triple worlds could there be thy superior, O thou of unrivalled power? Therefore I bow down and with my body prostrate, I implore thee, O Lord, for mercy. Forgive, O Lord, as the friend forgives the friend, as the father pardons his son, as the lover the beloved. I am well pleased with having beheld what was never before seen, and yet my heart is overwhelmed with awe; have mercy then, O God; show me that other form, O thou who art the dwelling-place of the universe; I desire to see thee as before with thy diadem on thy head, thy hands armed with mace and chakra; assume again, O thou of a thousand arms and universal form, thy four-armed shape!"

KRISHNA

"Out of kindness to thee, O Arjuna, by my divine power I have shown thee my supreme form, the universe, resplendent, infinite, primeval, and which has never been beheld by any other than thee. Neither by studying the Vedas, nor by alms-giving, nor by sacrificial rites, nor by deeds, nor by the severest mortification of the flesh can I be seen in this form by any other than thee, O best of Kurus. Having beheld my form thus awful, be not disturbed nor let thy faculties be confounded, but with fears allayed and happiness of heart look upon this other form of mine again."

SANJAYA

Vasudeva having so spoken reassumed his natural form; and thus in milder shape the Great One presently assuaged the fears of the terrified Arjuna.

ARJUNA

"Now that I see again thy placid human shape, O Janardana, who art prayed to by mortals, my mind is no more disturbed and I and self-possessed."

KRISHNA

"Thou hast seen this form of mine which is difficult to be perceived and which even the gods are always anxious to behold. But I am not to be seen, even as I have shown myself to thee, by study of the Vedas, nor by mortifications, nor alms-giving, nor sacrifices. I am to be approached and seen and known in truth by means of that devotion which has me alone as the object. He whose actions are for me alone, who esteemeth me the supreme goal, who is my servant only, without attachment to the results of action and free from enmity towards any creature, cometh to me, O son of Pandu."

12

"Among those of thy devotees who always thus worship thee, which take the better way, those who worship the indivisible and unmanifested, or those who serve thee as thou now art?"

"Those who worship me with constant zeal, with the highest faith and minds placed on me, are held in high esteem by me. But those who, with minds equal toward everything, with senses and organs restrained, and rejoicing in the good of all creatures, meditate on the inexhaustible, immovable, highest, incorruptible, difficult to contemplate, invisible, omnipresent, unthinkable, the witness, undemonstrable, shall also come unto me. For those whose hearts are fixed on the unmanifested the labor is greater, because the path which is not manifest is with difficulty attained by corporeal beings. But for those who worship me, renouncing in me all their actions, regarding me as the supreme goal and meditating on me alone, if their thoughts are turned to me, O son of Pritha, I presently become the savior from this ocean of incarnations and death. Place, then, thy heart on me, penetrate me with thy understanding, and thou shalt without doubt hereafter dwell in me. But if thou shouldst be unable at once steadfastly to fix thy heart and mind on me, strive then, O Dhananjaya, to find me by constant practice in devotion. If after constant practice, thou art still unable, follow me by actions performed for me; for by doing works for me thou shalt attain perfection. But if thou art unequal even to this, then, being self-restrained, place all thy works, failures and successes alike, on me, abandoning in me the fruit of every action. For knowledge is better than constant practice, meditation is superior to knowledge, renunciation of the fruit of action to meditation; final emancipation immediately results from such renunciation.

"My devotee who is free from enmity, well-disposed towards all creatures, merciful, wholly exempt from pride and selfishness, the same in pain and pleasure, patient of wrongs, contented, constantly devout, self-governed, firm in resolves, and whose mind and heart are fixed on me alone, is dear unto me. He also is my beloved of whom mankind is not afraid and who has no fear of man; who is free from joy, from despondency and the dread of harm. My devotee who is unexpecting, pure, just, impartial, devoid of fear, and who hath forsaken interest in the results of action, is dear unto me. He also is worthy of my love who neither rejoiceth nor findeth fault, who neither lamenteth nor coveteth, and being my servant hath forsaken interest in both good and evil results. He also is my beloved servant who is equal-minded to friend or foe, the same in honor and dishonor, in cold and heat, in pain and pleasure, and is unsolicitous about the event of things; to whom praise and blame are as one; who is of little speech, content with whatever cometh to pass, who hath no fixed habitation, and whose heart, full of devotion, is firmly fixed. But those who seek this sacred ambrosia—the religion of immortality—even as I have explained it, full of faith, intent on me above all others, and united to devotion, are my most beloved."

13

"This perishable body, O son of Kunti, is known as Kshetra; those who are acquainted with the true nature of things call the soul who knows it, the Kshetrajna. Know also that I am the Knower in every mortal body, O son of Bharata; that knowledge which through the soul is a realization of both the known and the knower is alone esteemed by me as wisdom. What the Kshetra or body is, what it resembleth, what it produceth, and what is its origin, and also who he is who, dwelling within, knoweth it, as well as what is his power, learn all in brief from me. It has been manifoldly sung by the Rishees with discrimination and with arguments in the various Vedic hymns which treat of Brahma.

"This body, then, is made up of the great elements, Ahankara—egotism, Buddhi—intellect or judgment, the unmanifest, invisible spirit; the ten centers of action, the mind, and the five objects of sense: desire, aversion, pleasure and pain, persistency of life, and firmness, the power of cohesion. Thus I have made known unto thee what the Kshetra or body is with its component parts.

"True wisdom of a spiritual kind is freedom from self-esteem, hypocrisy, and injury to others; it is patience, sincerity, respect for spiritual instructors, purity, firmness, self-restraint, dispassion for objects of sense, freedom from pride, and a meditation upon birth, death, decay, sickness, and error; it is an exemption from self-identifying attachment for children, wife, and household, and a constant unwavering steadiness of heart upon the arrival of every event whether favorable or unfavorable; it is a never-ceasing love for me alone, the self being effaced, and worship paid in a solitary spot, and a want of pleasure in congregations of men; it is a resolute continuance in the study of Adhyatma, the Superior spirit, and a meditation upon the end of the acquirement of a knowledge of truth;—this is called wisdom or spiritual knowledge; its opposite is ignorance.

"I will now tell thee what is the object of wisdom, from knowing which a man enjoys immortality; it is that which has no beginning, even the supreme Brahma, and of which it cannot be said that it is either Being or Non-Being. It has hands and feet in all directions; eyes, heads, mouths, and ears in every direction; it is immanent in the world, possessing the vast whole. Itself without organs, it is reflected by all the senses and faculties; unattached, yet supporting all; without qualities, yet the witness of them all. It is within and without all creatures animate and inanimate; it is inconceivable because of its subtlety, and although near it is afar off. Although undivided it appeareth as divided among creatures, and while it sustains existing things, it is also to be known as their destroyer and creator. It is the light of all lights, and is declared to be beyond all darkness; and it is wisdom itself, the object of wisdom, and that which is to be obtained by wisdom; in the hearts of all it ever presideth. Thus hath been briefly declared what is the perishable body, and wisdom itself, together with the object of wisdom; he, my devotee, who thus in truth conceiveth me, obtaineth my state.

"Know that *prakriti* or nature, and *purusha* the spirit, are without beginning. And know that the passions and the three qualities are sprung from nature. Nature or *prakriti* is said to be that which operates in producing cause and effect in actions; individual spirit or *purusha* is said to be the cause of experiencing pain and pleasure. For spirit when invested with matter or *prakriti* experienceth the qualities which proceed from *prakriti*; its connection with these qualities is the cause of its rebirth in good and evil wombs. The spirit in the body is called *Maheswara*, the Great Lord, the spectator, the admonisher, the sustainer, the enjoyer, and also the *Paramatma*, the highest soul. He who thus knoweth the spirit and nature, together with the qualities, whatever mode of life he may lead, is not born again on this earth.

"Some men by meditation, using contemplation upon the Self, behold the spirit within, others attain to that end by philosophical study with its realization, and others by means of the religion of works. Others, again, who are not acquainted with it in this manner, but have heard it from others, cleave unto and respect it; and even these, if assiduous only upon tradition and attentive to hearing the scriptures, pass beyond the gulf of death.

"Know, O chief of the Bharatas, that whenever anything, whether animate or inanimate, is produced, it is due to the union of the Kshetra and Kshetrajna—body and the soul. He who seeth the Supreme Being existing alike imperishable in all perishable things, sees indeed. Per-

ceiving the same Lord present in everything and everywhere, he does
not by the lower self destroy his own soul, but goeth to the supreme
end. He who seeth that all his actions are performed by nature only,
and that the self within is not the actor, sees indeed. And when he
realizes perfectly that all things whatsoever in nature are comprehended in the ONE, he attains to the Supreme Spirit. This Supreme
Spirit, O son of Kunti, even when it is in the body, neither acteth nor
is it affected by action, because, being without beginning and devoid
of attributes, it is changeless. As the all-moving Akasa by reason of
its subtlety passeth everywhere unaffected, so the Spirit, though present in every kind of body, is not attached to action nor affected. As a
single sun illuminateth the whole world, even so doth the One Spirit
illumine every body, O son of Bharata. Those who with the eye of wisdom thus perceive what is the difference between the body and Spirit
and the destruction of the illusion of objects, go to the supreme."

14

KRISHNA

"I will explain further the sublime spiritual knowledge superior to all others, by knowing which all the sages have attained to supreme perfection on the dissolution of this body. They take sanctuary in this wisdom, and having attained to my state they are not born again even at the new evolution, nor are they disturbed at the time of general destruction.

"The great Brahma is my womb in which I place the seed; from that, O son of Bharata, is the production of all existing things. This great Brahma is the womb for all those various forms which are produced from any womb, and I am the Father who provideth the seed. The three great qualities called *sattva*, *rajas*, and *tamas*—light or truth, passion or desire, and indifference or darkness—are born from nature, and bind the imperishable soul to the body, O thou of mighty arms. Of these the *sattva* quality by reason of its lucidity and peacefulness entwineth the soul to rebirth through attachment to knowledge and that which is pleasant. Know that *rajas* is of the nature of desire, producing thirst and propensity; it, O son of Kunti, imprisoneth the Ego through the consequences produced from action. The quality of *tamas*, the offspring of the indifference in nature, is the deluder of all creatures, O son of Bharata; it imprisoneth the Ego in a body through heedless folly, sleep, and idleness. The *sattva* quality attaches the soul through happiness and pleasure, the *rajas* through action, and *tamas* quality surrounding the power of judgment with indifference attaches the soul through heedlessness.

"When, O son of Bharata, the qualities of *tamas* and *rajas* are overcome, then that of *sattva* prevaileth; *tamas* is chiefly acting when *sattva* and *rajas* are hidden; and when the *sattva* and *tamas* diminish, then *rajas* prevaileth. When wisdom, the bright light, shall become evident at every gate of the body, then one may know that the *sattva* quality is prevalent within. The love of gain, activity in action, and the initiating of works, restlessness and inordinate desire are produced when the quality of *rajas* is prevalent, whilst the tokens of the predominance of the *tamas* quality are absence of illumination, the presence of idleness, heedlessness, and delusion, O son of Kunti.

"If the body is dissolved when the *sattva* quality prevails, the self within proceeds to the spotless spheres of those who are acquainted with the highest place. When the body is dissolved while the quality of *rajas* is predominant, the soul is born again in a body attached to action; and so also of one who dies while *tamas* quality is prevalent, the soul is born again in the wombs of those who are deluded.

"The fruit of righteous acts is called pure and holy, appertaining to *sattva*; from *rajas* is gathered fruit in pain, and the *tamas* produceth only senselessness, ignorance, and indifference. From *sattva* wisdom is produced, from *rajas* desire, from *tamas* ignorance, delusion and folly. Those in whom the *sattva* quality is established mount on high, those who are full of *rajas* remain in the middle sphere, the world of men, while those who are overborne by the gloomy quality, *tamas*, sink below. But when the wise man perceiveth that the only agents of action are these qualities, and comprehends that which is superior to the qualities, he attains to my state. And when the embodied self surpasseth these three qualities of goodness, action, and indifference—which are coexistent with the body it is released from rebirth and death, old age and pain, and drinketh of the water of immortality."

ARJUNA

"What are the characteristic marks by which the man may be known, O Master, who hath surpassed the three qualities? What is his course of life, and what are the means by which he overcometh the qualities?"

KRISHNA

"He, O son of Pandu, who doth not hate these qualities—illumination, action, and delusion—when they appear, nor longeth for them when they disappear; who, like one who is of no party, sitteth as one unconcerned about the three qualities and undisturbed by them, who being persuaded that the qualities exist, is moved not by them; who is of equal mind in pain and pleasure, self-centred, to whom a lump of earth, a stone, or gold are as one; who is of equal mind with those who love or dislike, constant, the same whether blamed or praised; equally minded in honor and disgrace, and the same toward friendly or unfriendly side, engaging only in necessary actions, such an one hath surmounted the qualities. And he, my servant, who worships me with exclusive devotion, having completely overcome the qualities, is fitted to be absorbed in Brahma the Supreme. I am the embodiment of the Supreme Ruler, and of the incorruptible, of the unmodifying, and of the eternal law, and of endless bliss."

15

"Men say that the *Ashwattha*, the eternal sacred tree, grows with its roots above and its branches below, and the leaves of which are the Vedas; he who knows this knows the Vedas. Its branches growing out of the three qualities with the objects of sense as the lesser shoots, spread forth, some above and some below; and those roots which ramify below in the regions of mankind are the connecting bonds of action. Its form is not thus understood by men; it has no beginning, nor can its present constitution be understood, nor has it any end. When one hath hewn down with the strong axe of dispassion this *Ashwattha* tree with its deeply-imbedded roots, then that place is to be sought after from which those who there take refuge never more return to rebirth, for it is the Primeval Spirit from which floweth the never-ending stream of conditioned existence. Those who are free from pride of self and whose discrimination is perfected, who have prevailed over the fault of attachment to action, who are constantly employed in devotion to meditation upon the Supreme Spirit, who have renounced desire and are free from the influence of the opposites known as pleasure and pain, are undeluded, and proceed to that place which endureth forever. Neither the sun nor the moon nor the fire enlighteneth that place; from it there is no return; it is my supreme abode.

"It is even a portion of myself which, having assumed life in this world of conditioned existence, draweth together the five senses and the mind in order that it may obtain a body and may leave it again. And those are carried by the Sovereign Lord to and from whatever body he enters or quits, even as the breeze bears the fragrance from the flower. Presiding over the eye, the ear, the touch, the taste, and the power of smelling, and also over the mind, he experienceth the objects of sense. The deluded do not see the spirit when it quitteth or remains in the body, nor when, moved by the qualities, it has experience in the world. But those who have the eye of wisdom perceive it, and devotees who industriously strive to do so see it dwelling in their own hearts; whilst those who have not overcome themselves, who are devoid of discrimination, see it not even though they strive thereafter. Know that the brilliance of the sun which illuminateth the whole world, and the light which is in the moon and in the fire, are the splendor of myself. I enter the earth supporting all living things by my power, and I am that property of sap which is taste, nourishing all the herbs and plants of the field. Becoming the internal fire of the living, I associate with the upward and downward breathing, and cause the four kinds of food to digest. I am in the hearts of all men, and from me come memory, knowledge, and also the loss of both. I am to be known by all the Vedas; I am he who is the author of the Vedanta, and I alone am the interpreter of the Vedas.

"There are two kinds of beings in the world, the one divisible, the other indivisible; the divisible is all things and the creatures, the indivisible is called Kutastha, or he who standeth on high unaffected. But there is another spirit designated as the Supreme Spirit—Paramatma—which permeates and sustains the three worlds. As I am above the divisible and also superior to the indivisible, therefore both in the world and in the Vedas am I known as the Supreme Spirit. He who being not deluded knoweth me thus as the Supreme Spirit, knoweth all things and worships me under every form and condition.

"Thus, O sinless one, have I declared unto thee this most sacred science; he who understandeth it, O son of Bharata, will be a wise man and the performer of all that is to be done."

16

"Fearlessness, sincerity, assiduity in devotion, generosity, self-restraint, piety, and alms-givings, study, mortification, and rectitude; harmlessness, veracity, and freedom from anger, resignation, equanimity, and not speaking of the faults of others, universal compassion, modesty, and mildness; patience, power, fortitude, and purity, discretion, dignity, unrevengefulness, and freedom from conceit—these are the marks of him whose virtues are of a godlike character, O son of Bharata. Those, O son of Pritha, who are born with demoniacal dispositions are marked by hypocrisy, pride, anger, presumption, harshness of speech, and ignorance. The destiny of those whose attributes are godlike is final liberation, while those of demoniacal dispositions, born to the Asuras' lot, is continued bondage to mortal birth; grieve not, O son of Pandu, for thou art born with the divine destiny. There are two kinds of natures in beings in this world, that which is godlike, and the other which is demoniacal; the godlike hath been fully declared, hear now from me, O son of Pritha, what the demoniacal is.

"Those who are born with the demoniacal disposition—of the nature of the Asuras—know not the nature of action nor of cessation from action, they know not purity nor right behavior, they possess no truthfulness. They deny that the universe has any truth in it, saying it is not governed by law, declaring that it hath no Spirit; they say creatures are produced alone through the union of the sexes, and that all is for enjoyment only. Maintaining this view, their souls being ruined, their minds contracted, with natures perverted, enemies of the world, they are born to destroy. They indulge insatiable desires, are full of hypocrisy, fast-fixed in false beliefs through their delusions. They indulge in unlimited reflections which end only in annihilation, convinced until death that the enjoyment of the objects of their desires is the supreme good. Fast-bound by the hundred chords of desire, prone to lust and anger, they seek by injustice and the accumulation of wealth for the gratification of their own lusts and appetites.

'This today hath been acquired by me, and that object of my heart I shall obtain; this wealth I have, and that also shall be mine. This foe have I already slain, and others will I forthwith vanquish; I am the lord, I am powerful, and I am happy. I am rich and with precedence among men; where is there another like unto me? I shall make sacrifices, give alms, and enjoy.' In this manner do those speak who are deluded. Confounded by all manner of desires, entangled in the net of delusion, firmly attached to the gratification of their desires, they descend into hell. Esteeming themselves very highly, self-willed, full of pride and ever in pursuit of riches, they perform worship with hypocrisy and not even according to ritual, but only for outward show. Indulging in pride, selfishness, ostentation, power, lust, and anger, they detest me who am in their bodies and in the bodies of others. Wherefore I continually hurl these cruel haters, the lowest of men, into wombs of an infernal nature in this world of rebirth. And they being doomed to those infernal wombs, more and more deluded in each succeeding rebirth, never come to me, O son of Kunti, but go at length to the lowest region.

"The gates of hell are three—desire, anger, covetousness, which destroy the soul; wherefore one should abandon them. Being free from these three gates of hell, O son of Kunti, a man worketh for the salvation of his soul, and thus proceeds to the highest path. He who abandoneth the ordinances of the Scriptures to follow the dictates of his own desires, attaineth neither perfection nor happiness nor the highest path. Therefore, in deciding what is fit and what unfit to be done, thou shouldst perform actions on earth with a knowledge of what is declared in Holy Writ."

17

ARJUNA

"What is the state of those men who, while they neglect the precepts of the Scriptures, yet worship in faith, O Krishna? Is it of the *sattva*, the *rajas*, or the *tamas* quality?"

KRISHNA

"The faith of mortals is of three kinds, and is born from their own disposition; it is of the quality of truth—*sattva*, action—*rajas*, and indifference—*tamas*; hear now what those are.

"The faith of each one, O son of Bharata, proceeds from the *sattva* quality; the embodied soul being gifted with faith, each man is of the same nature as that ideal on which his faith is fixed. Those who are of the disposition which ariseth from the prevalence of the *sattva* or good quality worship the gods; those of the quality of *rajas* worship the celestial powers, the Yakshas and Rakshasas; other men in whom the dark quality of indifference or *tamas* predominates worship elemental powers and the ghosts of dead men. Those who practice severe self-mortification not enjoined in the Scriptures are full of hypocrisy and pride, longing for what is past and desiring more to come. They, full of delusion, torture the powers and faculties which are in the body, and me also, who am in the recesses of the innermost heart; know that they are of an infernal tendency.

"Know that food which is pleasant to each one, as also sacrifices, mortification, and alms-giving, are of three kinds; hear what their divisions are. The food which increases the length of days, vigor and strength, which keeps one free from sickness, of tranquil mind, and contented, and which is savory, nourishing, of permanent benefit and congenial to the body, is that which is attractive to those in whom the *sattva* quality prevaileth. The food which is liked by those of the *rajas* quality is over bitter, too acid, excessively salt, hot, pungent, dry

and burning, and causeth unpleasantness, pain, and disease. Whatever food is such as was dressed the day before, that is tasteless or
rotting, that is impure, is that which is preferred by those in whom
predominates the quality of *tamas* or indifference.

"The sacrifice or worship which is directed by Scripture and is
performed by those who expect no reward but who are convinced
that it is necessary to be done, is of the quality of light, of goodness,
of *sattva*. But know that that worship or sacrifice which is performed
with a view to its results, and also for an ostentation of piety, belongs
to passion, the quality of *rajas*, O best of the Bharatas. But that which
is not according to the precepts of Holy Writ, without distribution of
bread, without sacred hymns, without gifts to brahmans at the conclu-
sion, and without faith, is of the quality of *tamas*.

"Honoring the gods, the brahmans, the teachers, and the wise,
purity, rectitude, chastity, and harmlessness are called mortification
of the body. Gentle speech which causes no anxiety, which is truthful
and friendly, and diligence in the reading of the Scriptures, are said to
be austerities of speech. Serenity of mind, mildness of temper, silence,
self-restraint, absolute straightforwardness of conduct, are called mortification of the mind. This threefold mortification or austerity practiced with supreme faith and by those who long not for a reward is of
the *sattva* quality.

"But that austerity which is practiced with hypocrisy, for the sake
of obtaining respect for oneself or for fame or favor, and which is
uncertain and belonging wholly to this world, is of the quality of *rajas*.
Those austerities which are practiced merely by wounding oneself or
from a false judgment or for the hurting of another are of the quality
of *tamas*. Those gifts which are bestowed at the proper time to the
proper person, and by men who are not desirous of a return, are of
the *sattva* quality, good and of the nature of truth. But that gift which
is given with the expectation of a return from the beneficiary or with
a view to spiritual benefit flowing therefrom or with reluctance, is
of the *rajas* quality, bad and partaketh of untruth. Gifts given out of
place and season and to unworthy persons, without proper attention
and scornfully, are of the *tamas* quality, wholly bad and of the nature
of darkness.

"OM TAT SAT: these are said to be the threefold designation of the
Supreme Being. By these in the beginning were sanctified the knowers of Brahma the Vedas, and sacrifices. Therefore the sacrifices, the
giving of alms, and the practicing of austerities are always, among

those who expound Holy Writ, preceded by the word OM. Among those who long for immortality and who do not consider the reward for their actions, the word TAT precedes their rites of sacrifice, their austerities, and giving of alms. The word SAT is used for qualities that are true and holy, and likewise is applied to laudable actions, O son of Pritha. The state of mental sacrifice when actions are at rest is also called SAT. Whatever is done without faith, whether it be sacrifice, alms-giving, or austerities, is called ASAT, that which is devoid of truth and goodness, O son of Pritha, and is not of any benefit either in this life or after death."

18

"I wish to learn, O great-armed one, the nature of abstaining from action and of the giving up of the results of action, and also the difference between these two, O slayer of Keshin."

KRISHNA

"The bards conceive that the forsaking of actions which have a desired object is renunciation or Sannyasa, the wise call the disregard of the fruit of every action true disinterestedness in action. By some wise men it is said, 'Every action is as much to be avoided as a crime,' while by others it is declared, 'Deeds of sacrifice, of mortification, and of charity should not be forsaken.' Among these divided opinions hear my certain decision, O best of the Bharatas, upon this matter of disinterested forsaking, which is declared to be of three kinds, O chief of men. Deeds of sacrifice, of mortification, and of charity are not to be abandoned, for they are proper to be performed, and are the purifiers of the wise. But even those works are to be performed after having renounced all selfish interest in them and in their fruits; this, O son of Pritha, is my ultimate and supreme decision. The abstention from works which are necessary and obligatory is improper; the not doing of such actions is due to delusion springing from the quality of *tamas*. The refraining from works because they are painful and from the dread of annoyance ariseth from the quality of *rajas* which belongs to passion, and he who thus leaves undone what he ought to do shall not obtain the fruit which comes from right forsaking. The work which is performed, O Arjuna, because it is necessary, obligatory, and proper, with all self-interest therein put aside and attachment to the action absent, is declared to be of the quality of truth and goodness which is known as *sattva*. The true renouncer, full of the quality of goodness, wise and exempt from all doubt, is averse neither to those works which fail nor those which succeed. It is impossible for mortals to utterly abandon actions; but he who gives up the results of action is the true renouncer. The threefold results of action—unwished for, wished for, and mixed—accrue after death to those who do not practice this renunciation, but no results follow those who perfectly renounce.

"Learn, O great-armed one, that for the accomplishment of every work five agents are necessary, as is declared. These are the substratum, the agent, the various sorts of organs, the various and distinct movements and with these, as fifth, the presiding deities. These five agents are included in the performance of every act which a man undertaketh, whether with his body, his speech, or his mind. This being thus, whoever because of the imperfection of his mind beholdeth the real self as the agent thinketh wrongly and seeth not aright. He whose nature is free from egotism and whose power of discrimination is not blinded does not slay though he killeth all these people, and is not bound by the bonds of action. The three causes which incite to action are knowledge, the thing to be known, and the knower, and threefold also is the totality of the action in the act, the instrument, and the agent. Knowledge, the act, and the agent are also distinguished in three ways according to the three qualities; listen to their enumeration after that classification.

"Know that the wisdom which perceives in all nature one single principle, indivisible and incorruptible, not separate in the separate objects seen, is of the *sattva* quality. The knowledge which perceives different and manifold principles as present in the world of created beings pertains to *rajas*, the quality of passion. But that knowledge, wholly without value, which is mean, attached to one object alone as if it were the whole, which does not see the true cause of existence, is of the nature of *tamas*, indifferent and dark.

"The action which is right to be done, performed without attachment to results, free from pride and selfishness, is of the *sattva* quality. That one is of the *rajas* quality which is done with a view to its consequences, or with great exertion, or with egotism. And that which in consequence of delusion is undertaken without regard to its consequences, or the power to carry it out, or the harm it may cause, is of the quality of darkness—*tamas*.

"The doer who performs necessary actions unattached to their consequences and without love or hatred is of the nature of the quality of truth—*sattva*. The doer whose actions are performed with attachment to the result, with great exertion, for the gratification of his lusts and with pride, covetousness, uncleanness, and attended with rejoicing and grieving, is of the quality of *rajas*—passion and desire. The doer who is ignorant, foolish, undertaking actions without ability, without discrimination, with sloth, deceit, obstinacy, mischievousness, and dilatoriness, is of the quality of *tamas*.

"Hear now, O Dhananjaya, conqueror of wealth, the differences which I shall now explain in the discerning power and the steadfast power within, according to the three classes flowing from the divisions of the three qualities. The discerning power that knows how to begin and to renounce, what should and what should not be done, what is to be feared and what not, what holds fast and what sets the soul free, is of the *sattva* quality. That discernment, O son of Pritha, which does not fully know what ought to be done and what not, what should be feared and what not, is of the passion-born *rajas* quality. That discriminating power which is enveloped in obscurity, mistaking wrong for right and all things contrary to their true intent and meaning, is of the dark quality of *tamas*.

"That power of steadfastness holding the man together, which by devotion controls every motion of the mind, the breath, the senses and the organs, partaketh of the *sattva* quality. And that which cherisheth duty, pleasure, and wealth, in him who looketh to the fruits of action is of the quality of *rajas*. But that through which the man of low capacity stays fast in drowsiness, fear, grief, vanity and rashness is from the *tamas* quality, O son of Pritha.

"Now hear what are the three kinds of pleasure wherein happiness comes from habitude and pain is ended. That which in the beginning is as poison and in the end as the water of life, and which arises from a purified understanding, is declared to be of the *sattva* quality. That arising from the connection of the senses with their objects which in the beginning is sweet as the waters of life but at the end like poison, is of the quality of *rajas*. That pleasure is of the dark *tamas* quality which both in the beginning and the end arising from sleep, idleness, and carelessness, tendeth both in the beginning and the end to stupify the soul. There is no creature on earth nor among the hosts in heaven who is free from these three qualities which arise from nature.

"The respective duties of the four castes, of Brahmans, Kshatriyas, Vaisyas, and Sudras, are also determined by the qualities which predominate in the disposition of each, O harasser of thy foes. The natural duty of a Brahman compriseth tranquility, purity, self-mastery, patience, rectitude, learning, spiritual discernment, and belief in the existence of another world. Those of the Kshatriya sprung from his nature, are valor, glory, strength, firmness, not to flee from the field of battle, liberality and a lordly character. The natural duties of the Vaisya are to till the land, tend cattle and to buy and sell; and that of the Sudra is to serve, as is his natural disposition.

"Men being contented and devoted to their own proper duties attain perfection; hear now how that perfection is attained by devotion to natural duty.

"If a man maketh offering to the Supreme Being who is the source of the works of all and by whom this universe was spread abroad, he thus obtaineth perfection. The performance of the duties of a man's own particular calling, although devoid of excellence, is better than doing the duty of another, however well performed; and he who fulfils the duties obligated by nature, does not incur sin. A man's own natural duty, even though stained with faults, ought not to be abandoned. For all human acts are involved in faults, as the fire is wrapped in smoke. The highest perfection of freedom from action is attained through renunciation by him who in all works has an unfettered mind and subdued heart.

"Learn from me, in brief, in what manner the man who has reached perfection attains to the Supreme Spirit, which is the end, the aim, and highest condition of spiritual knowledge.

"Embued with pure discrimination, restraining himself with resolution, having rejected the charms of sound and other objects of the senses, and casting off attachment and dislike; dwelling in secluded places, eating little, with speech, body, and mind controlled, engaging in constant meditation and unwaveringly fixed in dispassion; abandoning egotism, arrogance, violence, vanity, desire, anger, pride, and possession, with calmness ever present, a man is fitted to be the Supreme Being. And having thus attained to the Supreme, he is serene, sorrowing no more, and no more desiring, but alike towards all creatures he attains to supreme devotion to me. By this devotion to me he knoweth fundamentally who and what I am and having thus discovered me he enters into me without any intermediate condition. And even the man who is always engaged in action shall attain by my favor to the eternal and incorruptible imperishable abode, if he puts his trust in me alone. With thy heart place all thy works on me, prefer me to all else, exercise mental devotion continually, and think constantly of me. By so doing thou shalt by my divine favor surmount every difficulty which surroundeth thee; but if from pride thou wilt not listen to my words, thou shalt undoubtedly be lost. And if, indulging self-confidence, thou sayest 'I will not fight,' such a determination will prove itself vain, for the principles of thy nature will impel thee to engage. Being bound by all past karma to thy natural duties, thou, O son of Kunti, wilt involuntarily do from necessity that which in thy folly thou wouldst not do. There dwelleth in the heart of every creature, O Arjuna, the Master—*Ishwara*—who by his magic power causeth all things and creatures to revolve mounted upon the universal wheel of time. Take sanctuary with him alone, O son of Bharata, with all thy soul; by his grace thou shalt obtain supreme happiness, the eternal place.

"Thus have I made known unto thee this knowledge which is a mystery more secret than secrecy itself; ponder it fully in thy mind; act as seemeth best unto thee.

"But further listen to my supreme and most mysterious words which I will now for thy good reveal unto thee because thou art dearly beloved of me. Place thy heart upon me as I have declared myself to be, serve me, offer unto me alone, and bow down before me alone, and thou shalt come to me; I swear it, for thou art dear to me. Forsake every other religion and take refuge alone with me; grieve not, for I shall deliver thee from all transgressions. Thou must never reveal this to one who doth not practice mortification, who is without devotion, who careth not to hear it, nor unto him who despiseth me. He who expoundeth this supreme mystery to my worshippers shall come to me if he perfoms the highest worship of me; and there shall not be among men anyone who will better serve me than he, and he shall be dearest unto me of all on earth. If anyone shall study these sacred dialogues held between us two, I shall consider that I am worshipped by him with the sacrifice of knowledge; this is my resolve. And even the man who shall listen to it with faith and not reviling shall, being freed from evil, attain to the regions of happiness provided for those whose deeds are righteous.

"Hast thou heard all this, O son of Pritha, with mind one-pointed? Has the delusion of thought which arose from ignorance been removed, O Dhananjaya?"

ARJUNA

"By thy divine power, O thou who fallest not, my delusion is destroyed, I am collected once more; I am free from doubt, firm, and will act according to thy bidding."

SANJAYA

Thus have I been an ear-witness of the miraculous astonishing dialogue, never heard before, between Vasudeva and the magnanimous son of Pritha. By the favor of Vyasa I heard this supreme mystery of Yoga—devotion—even as revealed from the mouth of Krishna himself who is the supreme Master of devotion. And as I again and again remember, O mighty king, this wonderful sacred dialogue between Krishna and Arjuna, I am delighted again and again. Also, as I recall to my memory the wonderful form of Hari, the Lord, my astonishment is great, O king, and I rejoice again and again. Wherever Krishna, the supreme Master of devotion, and wherever the son of Pritha, the mighty archer, may be, there with certainty are fortune, victory, wealth, and wise action; this is my belief.

TWO UPANISHADS

Translated by
Robert Ernest Hume

BRIHAD-ARANYAKA
UPANISHAD

1

1

1. Om! Verily, the dawn is the head of the sacrificial horse; the sun, his eye; the wind, his breath; universal fire, his open mouth. The year is the body of the sacrificial horse; the sky, his back; the atmosphere, his belly; the earth, the under part of his belly; the quarters, his flanks; the intermediate quarters, his ribs; the seasons, his limbs; the months and half-months, his joints; days and nights, his feet; the stars, his bones; the clouds, his flesh. Sand is the food in his stomach; rivers are his entrails. His liver and lungs are the mountains; plants and trees, his hair. The orient is his fore part; the occident, his hind part. When he yawns, then it lightens. When he shakes himself, then it thunders. When he urinates, then it rains. Voice, indeed, is his voice.

2. Verily, the day arose for the horse as the sacrificial vessel which stands before. Its place is the eastern sea.

Verily, the night arose for him as the sacrificial vessel which stands behind. Its place is the western sea. Verily, these two arose on both sides of the horse as the two sacrificial vessels.

Becoming a steed, he carried the gods; a stallion, the Gandharvas; a courser, the demons; a horse, men. The sea, indeed, is his relative. The sea is his place.

2

1. In the beginning nothing whatsoever was here. This [world] was covered over with death, with hunger—for hunger is death.

Then he made up his mind: "Would that I had a self!"

So he went on praising. From him, while he was praising, water was produced. "Verily, while I was praising, I had pleasure!" thought he. This, indeed, is the *arka*-nature of what pertains to brightness.

Verily, there is pleasure for him who knows thus that *arka*-nature of what pertains to brightness.

2. The water, verily, was brightness.

That which was the froth of the water became solidified. That became the earth.

On it he [i.e., Death] tortured himself. When he had tortured himself and practised austerity, his heat and essence turned into fire.

3. He divided himself threefold: [fire one third], the sun one third, wind one third. He also is Life divided threefold.

The eastern direction is his head. Yonder one and yonder one are the fore quarters. Likewise the western direction is his tail. Yonder one and yonder one are the hind quarters. South and north are the flanks. The sky is the back. The atmosphere is the belly. This [earth] is the chest. He stands firm in the waters. He who knows this, stands firm wherever he goes.

4. He desired: "Would that a second self of me were produced!" He—death, hunger—by mind copulated with speech. That which was the semen, became the year. Previous to that there was no year. He bore him for a time as long as a year. After that long time he brought him forth. When he was born, Death opened his mouth on him. He cried "*bhan!*" That, indeed, became speech.

5. He bethought himself: "Verily, if I shall intend against him, I shall make the less food for myself." With that speech, with that self he brought forth this whole world, whatsoever exists here: the Hymns [i.e., the Rig-Veda], the Formulas [i.e., the Yajur-Veda], the Chants [i.e., the Sama-Veda], meters, sacrifices, men, cattle.

Whatever he brought forth, that he began to eat. Verily, he eats everything: that is the *aditi*-nature of Aditi (the Infinite). He who knows thus the *aditi*-nature of Aditi, becomes an eater of everything here; everything becomes food for him.

6. He desired: "Let me sacrifice further with a greater sacrifice!" He tortured himself. He practised austerity. When he had tortured himself and practised austerity, glory and vigor went forth. The glory and vigor, verily, are the vital breaths. So when the vital breaths departed, his body began to swell. His mind, indeed, was in his body.

7. He desired: "Would that this [body] of mine were fit for sacrifice! Would that by it I had a self!" Thereupon it became a horse, because it swelled. "It has become fit for sacrifice!" thought he. Therefore the horse-sacrifice is called Asva-medha. He, verily, knows the Asva-medha, who knows it thus.

He kept him [i.e., the horse] in mind without confining him. After a year he sacrificed him for himself. [Other] animals he delivered over to the divinities. Therefore men sacrifice the victim which is consecrated to Prajapati as though offered unto all the gods.

Verily, that [sun] which gives forth heat is the Asva-medha. The year is its embodiment.

This [earthly] fire is the *arka*. The worlds are its embodiments. These are two, the *arka* sacrificial fire and the Asva-medha sacrifice. Yet again they are one divinity, even Death. He [who knows this] wards off death again, death obtains him not, death becomes his body, he becomes one of these deities.

3

1. The gods and the devils were the twofold offspring of Prajapati. Of these the gods were the younger, the devils the older. They were struggling with each other for these worlds.

The gods said: "Come, let us overcome the devils at the sacrifice with the Udgitha."

2. They said to Speech: "Sing for us the Udgitha."

"So be it," said Speech, and sang for them. Whatever pleasure there is in speech, that it sang for the gods; whatever good one speaks, that for itself.

They [i.e., the devils] knew: "Verily, by this singer they will overcome us." They rushed upon it and pierced it with evil. That evil was the improper thing that one speaks. That was the evil.

3. Then they [i.e., the gods] said to the In-breath: "Sing for us the Udgitha."

"So be it," said the In-breath, and sang for them. Whatever pleasure there is in the in-breath, that it sang for the gods; whatever good one breathes in, that for itself.

They [i.e., the devils] knew: "Verily, by this singer they will overcome us." They rushed upon it and pierced it with evil. That evil was the improper thing that one breathes in. This, truly, was that evil.

4. Then they [i.e., the gods] said to the Eye: "Sing for us the Udgitha."

"So be it," said the Eye, and sang for them. Whatever pleasure there is in the eye, that it sang for the gods; whatever good one sees, that for itself.

They [i.e., the devils] knew: "Verily, by this singer they will overcome us." They rushed upon it and pierced it with evil. That evil was the improper thing that one sees. This, truly, was that evil.

5. Then they [i.e., the gods] said to the Ear: "Sing for us the Udgitha."

"So be it," said the Ear, and sang for them. Whatever pleasure there is in the ear, that it sang for the gods; whatever good one hears, that for itself.

They [i.e., the devils] knew: "Verily, by this singer they will overcome us." They rushed upon it and pierced it with evil. That evil was the improper thing that one hears. This, truly, was that evil.

6. Then they [i.e., the gods] said to the Mind: "Sing for us the Udgitha."

"So be it," said the Mind, and sang for them. Whatever pleasure there is in the mind, that it sang for the gods; whatever good one imagines, that for itself.

They [i.e., the devils] knew: "Verily, by this singer they will overcome us." They rushed upon him and pierced him with evil. That evil was the improper thing that one imagines. This, truly, was that evil.

And thus they let out upon these divinities with evil, they pierced them with evil.

7. Then they [i.e., the gods] said to this Breath in the mouth: "Sing for us the Udgitha."

"So be it," said this Breath, and sang for them.

They [i.e., the devils] knew: "Verily, by this singer they will overcome us." They rushed upon him and desired to pierce him with evil. As a clod of earth would be scattered by striking on a stone, even so they were scattered in all directions and perished. Therefore the gods increased, the demons became inferior. He increases with himself, a hateful enemy becomes inferior for him who knows this.

8. Then they said, "What, pray, has become of him who stuck to us thus?" "This one here is within the mouth! " He is called Ayasya Angirasa, for he is the essence of the limbs.

9. Verily, that divinity is Dur by name, for death is far from it. From him who knows this, death is far.

10. Verily, that divinity having struck off the evil of these divinities, even death, made this go to where is the end of the quarters of

heaven. There it set down their evils. Therefore one should not go to [foreign] people, one should not go to the end [of the earth], lest he fall in with evil, with death.

11. Verily, that divinity by striking off the evil, the death, of those divinities carried them beyond death.

12. Verily, it carried Speech over as the first. When that was freed from death, it became fire. This fire, when it has crossed beyond death, shines forth.

13. Likewise it carried Smell across. When that was freed from death, it became wind. This wind, when it has crossed beyond death, purifies.

14. Likewise it carried the Eye across. When that was freed from death, it became the sun. That sun, when it has crossed beyond death, glows.

15. Likewise it carried the Ear across. When that was freed from death, it became the quarters of heaven. These quarters of heaven have crossed beyond death.

16. Likewise it carried the Mind across. When that was freed from death, it became the moon. That moon, when it has crossed beyond death, shines.

Thus, verily, that divinity carries beyond death him who knows this.

17. Then it [i.e., breath] sang out food for itself, for whatever food is eaten is eaten by it. Hereon one is established.

18. Those gods said: "Of such extent, verily, is this universe as food. You have sung it into your own possession. Give us an after-share in this food."

"As such, verily, do ye enter into me."

"So be it." They entered into him from all sides. Therefore whatever food one eats by this breath, these are satisfied by it. Thus, verily, his people come to him, he becomes the supporter of his people, their chief, foremost leader, an eater of food, an overlord—he who knows this. And whoever among his people desires to be the equal of him who has this knowledge suffices not for his dependents. But whoever follows after him and whoever, following after him, desires to support his dependents, he truly suffices for his dependents.

19. He is Ayasya Angirasa, for he is the essence of the limbs. Verily, breath is the essence of the limbs, for verily breath is the essence

of the limbs. Therefore from whatever limb the breath departs, that indeed dries up, for it is verily the essence of the limbs.

20. And also it is Brihaspati. The Brihati is speech. He is her lord, and is therefore Brihaspati.

21. And it is also Brahmanaspati. Prayer, verily, is speech. He is her lord, and is therefore Brahmanaspati.

22. And it is also the Sama-Veda. The Chant, verily, is speech. It is *sa* (she) and *ama* (he). That is the origin of the word *saman*.

Or because it is equal to a gnat, equal to a fly, equal to an elephant, equal to these three worlds, equal to this universe, therefore, indeed, it is the Sama-Veda. He obtains intimate union with the Saman [chant], he wins its world who knows thus that Saman.

23. And it is also the Udgitha. The breath verily is up, for by breath this whole world is upheld. Song, verily, is speech; *ut* and *githa*—that is Udgitha.

24. As also Brahmadatta Caikitaneya, while partaking of King [Soma], said: "Let this king cause this man's head to fall off, if Ayasya Angirasa sang the Udgitha with any other means than that, for," said he, "only with speech and with breath did he sing the Udgitha."

25. He who knows the property of that Saman has that property. Its property, truly, is tone. Therefore let him who is about to perform the duties of an Ritvij priest desire a good tone in his voice. Being possessed of such a voice, let him perform the duties of the Ritvij priest. Therefore people desire to see at the sacrifice one who has a good tone, as being one who has a possession. He has a possession who knows thus the property of the Saman.

26. He who knows the gold of that Saman comes to have gold. The tone, verily, is its gold. He comes to have gold who knows thus that gold of the Saman.

27. He who knows the support of that Saman is indeed supported. Voice, verily, is its support, for when supported on voice the breath sings. But some say it is supported on food.

28. Now next, the praying of the purificatory formulas—

The Prastotri priest (Praiser), verily, begins to praise with the Chant. When he begins to praise, then let [the sacrificer] mutter the following:

> From the unreal lead me to the real!
> From darkness lead me, to light!
> From death lead me to immortality!

When he says "From the unreal lead me to the real," the unreal, verily, is death, the real is immortality. "From death lead me to immortality. Make me immortal"—that is what he says.

"From darkness lead me to light"—the darkness, verily, is death, the light is immortality. "From death lead me to immortality. Make me immortal"—that is what he says.

"From death lead me to immortality"—there is nothing there that seems obscure.

Now whatever other verses there are of a hymn of praise, in them one may win food for himself by singing. And, therefore, in them he should choose a boon, whatever desire he may desire. That Udgatri priest who knows this—whatever desire he desires, either for himself or for the sacrificer, that he obtains by singing. This, indeed, is world-conquering. There is no prospect of his being without a world who knows thus this Saman.

4

1. In the beginning this world was Soul alone in the form of a Person. Looking around, he saw nothing else than himself. He said first: "I am." Thence arose the name "I." Therefore even today, when one is addressed, he says first just "It is I" and then speaks whatever name he has. Since before all this world he burned up all evils, therefore he is a person. He who knows this, verily, burns up him who desires to be ahead of him.

2. He was afraid. Therefore one who is alone is afraid. This one then thought to himself: "Since there is nothing else than myself, of what am I afraid?" Thereupon, verily, his fear departed, for of what should he have been afraid? Assuredly it is from a second that fear arises.

3. Verily, he had no delight. Therefore one alone has no delight. He desired a second. He was, indeed, as large as a woman and a man closely embraced. He caused that self to fall into two pieces. Therefrom arose a husband and a wife. Therefore this [is true]: "Oneself is like a half-fragment," as Yajnavalkya used to say. Therefore this space is filled by a wife. He copulated with her. Therefrom human beings were produced.

4. And she then bethought herself: "How now does he copulate with me after he has produced me just from himself? Come, let me hide myself." She became a cow. He became a bull. With her he did indeed copulate. Then cattle were born. She became a mare, he a stallion. She became a female ass, he a male ass; with her he copulated, of a truth. Thence were born solid-hoofed animals. She became a she-goat, he a he-goat; she a ewe, he a ram. With her he did verily copulate. Therefrom were born goats and sheep. Thus, indeed, he created all, whatever pairs there are, even down to the ants.

5. He knew: "I, indeed, am this creation, for I emitted it all from myself." Thence arose creation. Verily, he who has this knowledge comes to be in that creation of his.

6. Then he rubbed thus. From his mouth as the fire-hole and from his hands he created fire. Both these [i.e., the hands and the mouth] are hairless on the inside, for the fire-hole is hairless on the inside.

This that people say, "Worship this god! Worship that god!"—one god after another—this is his creation indeed! And he himself is all the gods.

Now, whatever is moist, that he created from semen, and that is Soma. This whole world, verily, is just food and the eater of food.

That was Brahma's super-creation: namely, that he created the gods, his superiors; likewise, that, being mortal, he created the immortals. Therefore was it a super-creation. Verily, he who knows this comes to be in that super-creation of his.

7. Verily, at that time the world was undifferentiated. It became differentiated just by name and form, as the saying is: "He has such a name, such a form." Even today this world is differentiated just by name and form, as the saying is: "He has such a name, such a form."

He entered in here, even to the fingernail-tips, as a razor would be hidden in a razor-case, or fire in a fire-holder. Him they see not, for [as seen] he is incomplete. When breathing, he becomes breath by name; when speaking, voice; when seeing, the eye; when hearing, the ear; when thinking, the mind: these are merely the names of his acts. Whoever worships one or another of these—he knows not; for he is incomplete with one or another of these. One should worship with the thought that he is just one's self, for therein all these become one. That same thing, namely, this self, is the trace of this All, for by it one. knows this All. just as, verily, one might find by a footprint, thus—. He finds fame and praise who knows this.

8. That self is dearer than a son, is dearer than wealth, is dearer than all else, since this self is nearer.

If of one who speaks of anything else than the self as dear, one should say, "He will lose what he holds dear," he would indeed be likely to do so. One should reverence the self alone as dear. He who reverences the self alone as dear—what he holds dear, verily, is not perishable.

9. Here people say: "Since men think that by the knowledge of Brahma they become the All, what, pray, was it that Brahma knew whereby he became the All?"

10. Verily, in the beginning this world was Brahma.

It knew only itself: "I am Brahma!" Therefore it became the All. Whoever of the gods became awakened to this, he indeed became it; likewise in the case of seers, likewise in the case of men. Seeing this, indeed, the seer Vamadeva began:

I was Manu and the Sun!

This is so now also. Whoever thus knows "I am Brahma!" becomes this All; even the gods have not power to prevent his becoming thus, for he becomes their self.

So whoever worships another divinity [than his Self], thinking "He is one and I another," he knows not. He is like a sacrificial animal for the gods. Verily, indeed, as many animals would be of service to a man, even so each single person is of service to the gods. If even one animal is taken away, it is not pleasant. What, then, if many? Therefore it is not pleasing to those [gods] that men should know this.

11. Verily, in the beginning this world was Brahma, one only. Being one, he was not developed. He created still further a superior form, the Kshatrahood, even those who are Kshatras (rulers) among the gods: Indra, Varuna, Soma, Rudra, Parjanya, Yama, Mrityu, Isana. Therefore there is nothing higher than Kshatra. Therefore at the Raja-suya ceremony the Brahman sits below the Kshatriya. Upon Kshatrahood alone does he confer this honor. This same thing, namely Brahmanhood, is the source of Kshatrahood. Therefore, even if the king attains supremacy, he rests finally upon Brahmanhood as his own source. So whoever injures him [i.e., a Brahman] attacks his own source. He fares worse in proportion as he injures one who is better.

12. He was not yet developed. He created the Vis, those kinds of gods that are mentioned in numbers: the Vasus, the Rudras, the Adityas, the Visvadevas, the Maruts.

13. He was not yet developed. He created the Sudra caste, Pushan. Verily, this [earth] is Pushan, for she nourishes everything that is.

14. He was not yet developed. He created still further a better form, Law. This is the power of the Kshatriya class, viz Law. Therefore there is nothing higher than Law. So a weak man controls a strong man by Law, just as if by a king. Verily, that which is Law is truth. Therefore they say of a man who speaks the truth, "He speaks the Law," or of a man who speaks the Law, "He speaks the truth." Verily, both these are the same thing.

15. So that Brahma [appeared as] Kshatra, Vis, and Sudra. So among the gods Brahma appeared by means of Agni, among men a Brahman, as a Kshatriya by means of the [divine] Kshatriya, as a Vaisya by means of the [divine] Vaisya, as a Sudra by means of the [divine] Sudra. Therefore people desire a place among the gods in Agni, among men in a Brahman, for by these two forms [pre-eminently] Brahma appeared.

Now whoever departs from this world [i.e., the world of the Atman] without having recognized it as his own, to him it is of no service, because it is unknown, as the unrecited Vedas or any other undone deed [do not help a man].

Verily, even if one performs a great and holy work, but without knowing this, that work of his merely perishes in the end. One should worship the Self alone as his [true] world. The work of him who worships the Self alone as his world does not perish, for out of that very Self he creates whatsoever he desires.

16. Now this Self, verily, is a world of all created things. In so far as a man makes offerings and sacrifices, he becomes the world of the gods. In so far as he learns [the Vedas], he becomes the world of the seers. In so far as he offers libations to the fathers and desires offspring, he becomes the world of the fathers. In so far as he gives lodging and food to men, he becomes the world of men. In so far as he finds grass and water for animals, he becomes the world of animals. In so far as beasts and birds, even to the ants, find a living in his houses, he becomes their world. Verily, as one would desire security for his own world, so all creatures wish security for him who has this knowledge. This fact, verily, is known when it is thought out.

17. In the beginning this world was just the Self, one only. He wished: "Would that I had a wife; then I would procreate. Would that I had wealth; then I would offer sacrifice." So great, indeed, is desire.

Not even if one desired, would he get more than that. Therefore even today when one is lonely one wishes: "Would that I had a wife, then I would procreate. Would that I had wealth, then I would offer sacrifice." So far as he does not obtain any one of these, he thinks that he is, assuredly, incomplete. Now his completeness is as follows: his mind truly is his self; his voice is his wife; his breath is his offspring; his eye is his worldly wealth, for with his eye he finds; his ear is his heavenly [wealth], for with his ear he hears it; his body, indeed, is his work, for with his body he performs work.

The sacrifice is fivefold. The, sacrificial animal is fivefold. A person is fivefold. This whole world, whatever there is, is fivefold. He obtains this whole world who knows this.

5

1. When the Father produced by intellect
   And austerity seven kinds of food,
   One of his [foods] was common to all,
   Of two he let the gods partake,
   Three he made for himself,
   One he bestowed upon the animals
   On this [food] everything depends,
   Both what breathes and what does not.
   How is it that these do not perish
   When they are being eaten all the time
   He who knows this imperishableness—
   He eats food with his mouth,
   He goes to the gods,
   He lives on strength.

Thus the verses.

2. "When the Father produced by intellect and austerity seven kinds of food"—truly by intellect and austerity the Father did produce them.

"One of his [foods] was common to all." That of his which is common to all is the food that is eaten here. He who worships that, is not turned from evil, for it is mixed [i.e., common, not selected].

"Of two he let the gods partake." They are the *huta* and the *pra-huta*. For this reason one sacrifices and offers to the gods. People also say that these two are the new-moon and the full-moon sacrifices. Therefore one should not offer sacrifice [merely] to secure a wish.

"One he bestowed upon the animals"—that is milk, for at first both men and animals live upon milk. Therefore they either make a new-born babe lick butter or put it to the breast. Likewise they call a new-born calf "one that does not eat grass."

"On this [food] everything depends, both what breathes and what does not"—for upon milk everything depends, both what breathes and what does not. This that people say, "By offering with milk for a year one escapes the second death"—one should know that this is not so, since on the very day that he makes the offering he who knows escapes the second death, for he offers all his food to the gods.

"How is it that these do not perish when they are being eaten all the time?" Verily, the Person is imperishableness, for he produces this food again and again.

"He who knows this imperishableness"—verily, a person is imperishableness, for by continuous meditation he produces this food as his work. Should he not do this, all the food would perish.

"He eats food with his mouth." The *pratika* is the mouth. So he eats food with his mouth.

"He goes to the gods, he lives on strength"—this is praise.

3. "Three he made for himself." Mind, speech, breath—these he made for himself.

People say: "My mind was elsewhere; I did not see. My mind was elsewhere; I did not hear. It is with the mind, truly, that one sees. It is with the mind that one hears. Desire, imagination, doubt, faith, lack of faith, steadfastness, lack of steadfastness, shame, meditation, fear—all this is truly mind. Therefore even if one is touched on his back, he discerns it with the mind.

Whatever sound there is, it is just speech. Verily, it comes to an end [as human speech]; verily, it does not [as the heavenly voice].

The in-breath, the out-breath, the diffused breath, the up-breath, the middle-breath—all this is just breath.

Verily, the self consists of speech, mind, and breath.

4. These same are the three worlds. This [terrestrial] world is Speech. The middle [atmospheric] world is Mind. That [celestial] world is Breath.

5. These same are the three Vedas. The Rig-Veda is Speech. The Yajur-Veda is Mind. The Sama-Veda is Breath.

6. The same are the gods, Manes, and men. The gods are Speech. The Manes are Mind. Men are Breath.

7. These same are father, mother, and offspring. The father is Mind. The mother is Speech. The offspring is Breath.

8. These same are what is known, what is to be known, and what is unknown.

Whatever is known is a form of Speech, for Speech is known. Speech, having become this, helps him [i.e., man].

9. Whatever is to be known is a form of Mind, for mind is to be known. Mind, having become this, helps him.

10. Whatever is unknown is a form of Breath, for Breath is unknown. Breath, having become this, helps him.

11. Of this Speech the earth is the body. Its light-form is this [terrestrial] fire. As far as Speech extends, so far extends the earth, so far this fire.

12. Likewise of that Mind the sky is the body. Its light-form is yon sun. As far as Mind extends, so far extends the sky, so far yon sun.

These two [the fire and the sun] entered sexual union. Therefrom was born Breath. He is Indra. He is without a rival. Verily, a second person is a rival. He who knows this has no rival.

13. Likewise of that Breath, water is the body. Its light-form is yon moon. As far as Breath extends, so far extends water, so far yon moon.

These are all alike, all infinite. Verily he who worships them as finite wins a finite world. Likewise he who worships them as infinite wins an infinite world.

14. That Prajapati is the year. He is composed of sixteen parts. His nights, truly, are fifteen parts. His sixteenth part is steadfast. He is increased and diminished by his nights alone. Having, on the new-moon night, entered with that sixteenth part into everything here that has breath, he is born thence on the following morning [as the new moon]. Therefore on that night one should not cut off the breath of any breathing thing, not even of a lizard, in honor of that divinity.

15. Verily, the person here who knows this, is himself that Prajapati with the sixteen parts who is the year. The fifteen parts are his wealth. The sixteenth part is his self. In wealth alone [not in self] is one increased and diminished.

That which is the self is a hub; wealth, a felly. Therefore even if one is overcome by the loss of everything, provided he himself lives, people say merely: "He has come off with the loss of a felly!"

16. Now, there are of a truth three worlds—the world of men, the world of the fathers, and the world of the gods. This world of men is to be obtained by a son only, by no other means; the world of the fathers, by sacrifice; the world of the gods, by knowledge. The world of the gods is verily the best of worlds. Therefore they praise knowledge.

17. Now next, the Transmission—

When a man thinks he is about to depart, he says to his son: "Thou art holy knowledge. Thou art sacrifice. Thou art the world." The son replies: "I am holy knowledge. I am sacrifice. I am the world." Verily, whatever has been learned [from the Vedas], the sum of all this is expressed by the word "knowledge." Verily, whatever sacrifices have been made, the sum of them all is expressed by the word "sacrifice." Whatever worlds there are, they are all comprehended under the word "world." So great, verily, is this all.

"Being thus the all, let him assist me from this world," thus [the father considers]. Therefore they call "world-procuring" a son who has been instructed. Therefore they instruct him.

When one who has this knowledge departs from this world, he enters into his son with these vital breaths [i.e., faculties: Speech, Mind, and Breath]. Whatever wrong has been done by him, his son frees him from it all. Therefore he is called a son. By his son a father stands firm in this world. Then into him [who has made over to his son his mortal breaths] enter those divine immortal breaths.

18. From the earth and from the fire the divine Speech enters him. Verily, that is the divine Speech whereby whatever one says comes to be.

19. Out of the sky and out of the sun the divine Mind enters him. Verily, that is the divine Mind whereby one becomes blissful and sorrows not.

20. Out of the water and out of the moon the divine Breath enters him. Verily, that is the divine Breath which, whether moving or not moving, is not perturbed, nor injured.

He who knows this becomes the Self of all beings. As is that divinity [i.e., Prajapati], so is he. As all beings favor that divinity, so to him who knows this all beings show favor. Whatever sufferings creatures endure, these remain with them. Only good goes to him. Evil, verily, does not go to the gods.

21. Now next, a Consideration of the Activities—

Prajapati created the active functions. They, when they had been created, strove with one another. "I am going to speak," the voice began. "I am going to see," said the eye. "I am going to hear," said the ear. So spake the other functions, each according to his function. Death, appearing as weariness, laid hold and took possession of them; and, taking possession of them, Death checked them. Therefore the voice becomes weary, the eye becomes weary, the ear becomes weary. But Death did not take possession of him who was the middle breath. They sought to know him. They said: "Verily, he is the best of us, since whether moving or not moving, he is not perturbed, nor perishes. Come, let us all become a form of him." Of him, indeed, they became a form. Therefore they are named "vital breaths" after him. In whatever family there is a man who has this knowledge, they call that family after him. Whoever strives with one who knows this, dries up and finally dies—. So much with reference to the self.

22. Now with reference to the divinities—

"Verily, I am going to blaze," began the Fire. "I am going to give forth heat," said the Sun. "I am going to shine," said the Moon. So said the other divinities, each according to his divine nature. As Breath holds the central position among the vital breaths [or functions], so Wind among these divinities; for the other divinities have their decline, but not Wind. The Wind is that divinity which never goes to rest.

23. There is this verse on the subject:

From whom the sun rises
And in whom it sets—

in truth, from Breath it rises, and in Breath it sets—

Him the gods made law;
He only today and tomorrow will be.

Verily, what those [functions] undertook of old, even that they accomplish today. Therefore one should practise but one activity. He should breathe in and breathe out, wishing, "May not the evil one, Death, get me." And the observance which he practises he should desire to fulfil to the end. Thereby he wins complete union with that divinity [i.e., Breath] and residence in the same world.

6

1. Verily, this world is a triad—name, form, and work.

Of these, as regards names, that which is called Speech is their hymn of praise, for from it arise all names. It is their Saman [chant], for it is the same as all names. It is their prayer, for it supports all names.

2. Now of forms—

That which is called the Eye is their hymn of praise, for from it arise all forms. It is their Saman, for it is the same as all forms. It is their prayer, for it supports all forms.

3. Now of works—

That which is called the Body is their hymn of praise, for from it arise all actions. It is their Saman, for it is the same as all works. It is their prayer, for it supports all works.

Although it is that triad, this Soul is one. Although it is one, it is that triad. That is the Immortal veiled by the real. Life [a designation of the Atman], verily, is the Immortal. Name and form are the real. By them this Life is veiled.

2

1

1. Driptabalaki was a learned Gargya. He said to Ajatasatru, [king] of Benares: "I will tell you about Brahma." Ajatasatru said: "We will give a thousand [cows] for such a speech. Verily, people will run hither, crying, 'A Janaka! a Janaka!'"

2. Gargya said: "The Person who is yonder in the sun—him, indeed, I worship as Brahma!"

Ajatasatru said: "Talk not to me about him! I worship him as the pre-eminent, the head and king of all beings. He who worships him as such becomes pre-eminent, the head and king of all beings."

3. Gargya said: "The Person who is yonder in the moon—him, indeed, I worship as Brahma!"

Ajatasatru said: "Talk not to me about him! I worship him as the great, white-robed king Soma. He who worships him as such, for him soma is pressed out and continually pressed out day by day. His food does not fail."

4. Gargya said: "The Person who is yonder in lightning—him, indeed, I worship as Brahma!"

Ajatasatru said: "Talk not to me about him! I worship him, verily, as the Brilliant. He who worships him as such becomes brilliant indeed. His offspring becomes brilliant."

5. Gargya said: "The Person who is here in space—him, indeed, I worship as Brahma!"

Ajatasatru said: "Talk not to me about him! I worship him, verily, as the Full, the non-active. He who worships him as such is filled with offspring and cattle. His offspring goes not forth from this earth."

6. Gargya said: "The Person who is here in wind—him, indeed, I worship as Brahma!"

Ajatasatru said: "Talk not to me about him! Verily, I worship him as Indra, the terrible, and the unconquered army. He who worships him as such becomes indeed triumphant, unconquerable, and a conqueror of adversaries."

7. Gargya said: "The Person who is here in fire—him, indeed, I worship as Brahma!"

Ajatasatru said: "Talk not to me about him! I worship him, verily, as the Vanquisher. He who worships him as such becomes a vanquisher indeed. His offspring become vanquishers."

8. Gargya said: "The Person who is here in water—him, indeed, I worship as Brahma!"

Ajatasatru said: "Talk not to me about him! I worship him, verily, as the Counterpart [of phenomenal objects]. His counterpart comes to him [in his children], not that which is not his counterpart. His counterpart is born from him."

9. Gargya said: "The Person who is here in a mirror—him, indeed, I worship as Brahma!"

Ajatasatru said: "Talk not to me about him! I worship him, verily, as the Shining One. He who worships him as such becomes shining indeed. His offspring shine. He out-shines all those with whom he goes."

10. Gargya said: "The sound here which follows after one as he goes—him, indeed, I worship as Brahma!"

Ajatasatru said: "Talk not to me about him! I worship him, verily, as Life. To him who worships him as such there comes a full length of life in this world. Breath leaves him not before the time."

11. Gargya said: "The Person who is here in the quarters of heaven—him, indeed, I worship as Brahma!"

Ajatasatru said: "Talk not to me about him! I worship him, verily, as the Inseparable Companion. He who worships him as such has a companion. His company is not separated from him."

12. Gargya said: "The Person here who consists of shadow—him, indeed, I worship as Brahma!"

Ajatasatru said: "Talk not to me about him! I worship him, verily, as Death. To him who worships him as such there comes a full length of life in this world. Death does not come to him before the time."

13. Gargya said: "The Person here who is in the body—him, indeed, I worship as Brahma!"

Ajatasatru said: "Talk not to me about him! I worship him, verily, as the Embodied One. He who worships him as such becomes embodied indeed. His offspring becomes embodied."

Gargya became silent.

14. Ajatasatru said: "Is that all?"

Gargya said: "That is all."

Ajatasatru said: "With that much [only] it is not known."

Gargya said: "Let me come to you as a pupil."

15. Ajatasatru said: "Verily, it is contrary to the course of things that a Brahman should come to a Kshatriya, thinking 'He will tell me Brahma.' However, I shall cause you to know him clearly."

He took him by the hand and rose. The two went up to a man who was asleep. They addressed him with these words: "Thou great, white-robed king Soma!" He did not rise. He [i.e., Ajatasatru] woke him by rubbing him with his hand. That one arose.

16. Ajatasatru said: "When this man fell asleep thus, where then was the person who consists of intelligence? Whence did he thus come back?"

And this also Gargya did not know.

17. Ajatasatru said: "When this man has fallen asleep thus, then the person who consists of intelligence, having by his intelligence taken to himself the intelligence of these senses, rests in that place which is the space within the heart. When that person restrains the senses, that person is said to be asleep. Then the breath is restrained. The voice is restrained. The eye is restrained. The ear is restrained. The mind is restrained.

18. When he goes to sleep, these worlds are his. Then he becomes a great king, as it were. Then he becomes a great Brahman, as it were. He enters the high and the low, as it were. As a great king, taking with him his people, moves around in his own country as he pleases, even so here this one, taking with him his senses, moves around in his own body as he pleases.

19. Now when one falls sound asleep, when one knows nothing whatsoever, having crept out through the seventy-two thousand veins, called *hita*, which lead from the heart to the pericardium, one rests in the pericardium. Verily, as a youth or a great king or a great Brahman might rest when he has reached the summit of bliss, so this one now rests.

20. As a spider might come out with his thread, as small sparks come forth from the fire, even so from this Soul come forth all vital energies, all worlds, all gods, all beings. The mystic meaning thereof is 'the Real of the real.' Breathing creatures, verily, are the real. He is their Real."

2

1. Verily, he who knows the new-born infant with his housing, his covering, his post, and his rope, keeps off seven hostile relatives.

Verily, this infant is Breath in the middle. Its housing is this [body]. Its covering is this [head]. Its post is breath. Its rope is food.

2. Seven imperishable beings stand near to serve him. Thus there are these red streaks in the eye. By them Rudra is united with him. Then there is the water in the eye. By it Parjanya is united with him. There is the pupil of the eye. By it the sun is united with him. By the black of the eye, Agni; by the white of the eye, Indra; by the lower eyelash, Earth is united with him; by the upper eyelash, Heaven. He who knows this—his food does not fail.

3. In connection herewith there is this verse:
There is a cup with its mouth below and its bottom up.
In it is placed every form of glory.
On its rim sit seven seers.
Voice as an eighth is united with prayer.

"There is a cup having its mouth below and its bottom up"—this is the head, for that is a cup having its mouth below and its bottom up. "In it is placed every form of glory"—breaths, verily, are the "every form of glory" placed in it; thus he says breaths. "On its rim sit seven seers"—verily, the breaths are the seers. Thus he says breaths. "Voice as an eighth is united with prayer"—for voice as an eighth is united with prayer.

4. These two [sense-organs] here [i.e., the ears] are Gotama and Bharadvaja. This is Gotama and this is Bharadvaja. These two here [i.e., the eyes] are Visvamitra and Jamadagni. This is Visvamitra. This is Jamadagni. These two here [i.e., the nostrils] are Vasishtha and Kasyapa. This is Vasishtha. This is Kasyapa. The voice is Atri, for by the voice food is eaten. Verily, eating is the same as the name Atri. He who knows this becomes the eater of everything; everything becomes his food.

3

1. There are, assuredly, two forms of Brahma: the formed and the formless, the mortal and the immortal, the stationary and the moving, the actual and the yon.

2. This is the formed [Brahma]—whatever is different from the wind and the atmosphere. This is mortal; this is stationary; this is actual. The essence of this formed, mortal, stationary, actual [Brahma] is yonder [sun] which gives forth heat, for that is the essence of the actual.

3. Now the formless [Brahma] is the wind and the atmosphere. This is immortal, this is moving, this is the yon. The essence of this unformed, immortal, moving, yonder [Brahma] is the Person in that sun-disk, for he is the essence of the yon—Thus with reference to the divinities.

4. Now, with reference to the self—
Just that is the formed [Brahma] which is different from breath and from the space which is within the self. This is mortal, this is stationary, this is actual. The essence of this formed, mortal, stationary, actual [Brahma] is the eye, for it is the essence of the actual.

5. Now the formless [Brahma] is the breath and the space which is within the self. This is immortal, this is moving, this is the yon. The essence of this unformed, immortal, moving, yonder [Brahma] is this Person who is in the right eye, for he is the essence of the yonder.

6. The form of this Person is like a saffron-colored robe, like white wool, like the [purple] Indragopa beetle, like a flame of fire, like the [white] lotus-flower, like a sudden flash of lightning. Verily, like a sudden lightning-flash is the glory of him who knows this.

Hence, now, there is the teaching "Not thus! not so!," for there is nothing higher than this, that he is thus. Now the designation for him is "the Real of the real." Verily, breathing creatures are the real. He is their Real.

4

1. "Maitreyi!" said Yajnavalkya, "lo, verily, I am about to go forth from this state. Behold! let me make a final settlement for you and that Katyayani."

2. Then said Maitreyi: "If now, Sir, this whole earth filled with wealth were mine, would I be immortal thereby?"

"No," said Yajnavalkya. "As the life of the rich, even so would your life be. Of immortality, however, there is no hope through wealth."

3. Then said Maitreyi: "What should I do with that through which I may not be immortal? What you know, Sir—that, indeed, tell me!"

4. Then said Yajnavalkya: "Ah! Lo, dear as you are to us, dear is what you say! Come, sit down. I will explain to you. But while I am expounding, do you seek to ponder thereon."

5. Then said he: "Lo, verily, not for love of the husband is a husband dear, but for love of the Soul a husband is dear.

Lo, verily, not for love of the wife is a wife dear, but for love of the Soul a wife is dear.

Lo, verily, not for love of the sons are sons dear, but for love of the Soul sons are dear.

Lo, verily, not for love of the wealth is wealth dear, but for love of the Soul wealth is dear.

Lo, verily, not for love of Brahmanhood is Brahmanhood dear, but for love of the Soul Brahmanhood is dear.

Lo, verily, not for love of Kshatrahood is Kshatrahood dear, but for love of the Soul Kshatrahood is dear.

Lo, verily, not for love of the worlds are the worlds dear, but for love of the Soul the worlds are dear.

Lo, verily, not for love of the gods are the gods dear, but for love of the Soul the gods are dear.

Lo, verily, not for love of the beings are beings dear, but for love of the Soul beings are dear.

Lo, verily, not for love of all is all dear, but for love of the Soul all is dear.

Lo, verily, it is the Soul that should be seen, that should be hearkened to, that should be thought on, that should be pondered on, O Maitreyi. Lo, verily, with the seeing of, with the hearkening to, with the thinking of, and with the understanding of the Soul, this world-all is known.

6. Brahmanhood has deserted him who knows Brahman-hood in aught else than the Soul.

Kshatrahood has deserted him who knows Kshatrahood in aught else than the Soul.

The worlds have deserted him who knows the worlds in aught else than the Soul.

The gods have deserted him who knows the gods in aught else than the Soul.

Beings have deserted him who knows beings in aught else than the Soul.

Everything has deserted him who knows everything in aught else than the Soul.

This Brahmanhood, this Kshatrahood, these worlds, these gods, these beings, everything here is what this Soul is.

7. It is—as, when a drum is being beaten, one would not be able to grasp the external sounds, but by grasping the drum or the beater of the drum the sound is grasped.

8. It is—as, when a conch-shell is being blown, one would not be able to grasp the external sounds, but by grasping the conch-shell or the blower of the conch-shell the sound is grasped.

9. It is—as, when a lute is being played, one would not be able to grasp the external sounds, but by grasping the lute or the player of the lute the sound is grasped.

10. It is—as, from a fire laid with damp fuel, clouds of smoke separately issue forth, so, lo, verily, from this great Being has been breathed forth that which is Rig-Veda, Yajur-Veda, Sama-Veda, [Hymns] of the Atharvans and Angirases, Legend, Ancient Lore, Sciences, Mystic Doctrines, Verses, Aphorisms, Explanations, and Commentaries. From it, indeed, are all these breathed forth.

11. It is—as of all waters the uniting-point is the sea, so of all touches the uniting-point is the skin, so of all tastes the uniting-point is the tongue, so of all smells the uniting-point is the nostrils, so of all forms the uniting-point is the eye, so of all sounds the uniting-point is the ear, so of all intentions the uniting-point is the mind, so of all knowledges the uniting-point is the heart, so of all acts the uniting-point is the hands, so of all pleasures the uniting-point is the generative organ, so of all evacuations the uniting-point is the anus,

so of all journeys the uniting-point is the feet, so of all the Vedas the uniting-point is speech.

12. It is—as a lump of salt cast in water would dissolve right into the water; there would not be [any] of it to seize forth, as it were, but wherever one may take, it is salty indeed—so, lo, verily, this great Being, infinite, limitless, is just a mass of knowledge.

Arising out of these elements, into them also one vanishes away. After death there is no consciousness. Thus, lo, say I." Thus spake Yajnavalkya.

13. Then spake Maitreyi: "Herein, indeed, you have bewildered me, Sir—in saying: 'After death there is no consciousness!'"

Then spake Yajnavalkya: "Lo, verily, I speak not bewilderment. Sufficient, lo, verily, is this for understanding.

14. For where there is a duality, as it were, there one sees another; there one smells another; there one hears another; there one speaks to another; there one thinks of another; there one understands another. Where, verily, everything has become just one's own self, then whereby and whom would one smell? then whereby and whom would one see? then whereby and whom would one hear? then whereby and to whom would one speak? then whereby and on whom would one think? then whereby and whom would one understand? Whereby would one understand him by whom one understands this All? Lo, whereby would one understand the understander?"

5

1. This earth is honey for all creatures, and all creatures are honey for this earth. This shining, immortal Person who is in this earth, and, with reference to oneself, this shining, immortal Person who is in the body—he, indeed, is just this Soul, this Immortal, this Brahma, this All.

2. These waters are honey for all things, and all things are honey for these waters. This shining, immortal Person who is in these waters, and, with reference to oneself, this shining, immortal Person who is made of semen—he is just this Soul, this Immortal, this Brahma, this All.

3. This fire is honey for all things, and all things are honey for

this fire. This shining, immortal Person who is in this fire, and, with reference to oneself, this shining, immortal Person who is made of speech—he is just this Soul, this Immortal, this Brahma, this All.

4. This wind is honey for all things, and all things are honey for this wind. This shining, immortal Person who is in this wind, and, with reference to oneself, this shining, immortal Person who is breath—he is just this Soul, this Immortal, this Brahma, this All.

5. This sun is honey for all things, and all things are honey for this sun. This shining, immortal Person who is in this sun, and, with reference to oneself, this shining, immortal Person who is in the eye—he is just this Soul, this Immortal, this Brahma, this All.

6. These quarters of heaven are honey for all things, and all things are honey for these quarters of heaven. This shining, immortal Person who is in these quarters of heaven, and, with reference to oneself, this shining, immortal Person who is in the ear and in the echo—he is just this Soul, this Immortal, this Brahma, this All.

7. This moon is honey for all things, and all things are honey for this moon. This shining, immortal Person who is in this moon, and, with reference to oneself, this shining, immortal Person consisting of mind—he is just this Soul, this Immortal, this Brahma, this All.

8. This lightning is honey for all things, and all things are honey for this lightning. This shining, immortal Person who is in this lightning, and, with reference to oneself, this shining, immortal Person who exists as heat—he is just this Soul, this Immortal, this Brahma, this All.

9. This thunder is honey for all things, and all things are honey for this thunder. This shining, immortal Person who is in thunder, and, with reference to oneself, this shining, immortal Person who is in sound and in tone—he is just this Soul, this Immortal, this Brahma, this All.

10. This space is honey for all things, and all things are honey for this space. This shining, immortal Person who is in this space, and, with reference to oneself, this shining, immortal Person who is in the space in the heart—he is just this Soul, this Immortal, this Brahma, this All.

11. This Law is honey for all things, and all things are honey for this Law. This shining, immortal Person who is in this Law, and, with reference to oneself, this shining, immortal Person who exists as virtuousness—he is just this Soul, this Immortal, this Brahma, this All.

12. This Truth is honey for all things, and all things are honey for this Truth. This shining, immortal Person who is in this Truth, and, with reference to oneself, this shining, immortal Person who exists as truthfulness—he is just this Soul, this Immortal, this Brahma, this All.

13. This mankind is honey for all things, and all things are honey for this mankind. This shining, immortal Person who is in this mankind, and, with reference to oneself, this shining, immortal Person who exists as a human being—he is just this Soul, this Immortal, this Brahma, this All.

14. This Soul is honey for all things, and all things are honey for this Soul. This shining, immortal Person who is in this Soul, and, with reference to oneself, this shining immortal Person who exists as Soul—he is just this Soul, this Immortal, this Brahma, this All.

15. Verily, this Soul is the overlord of all things, the king of all things. As all the spokes are held together in the hub and felly of a wheel, just so in this Soul all things, all gods, all worlds, all breathing things, all selves are held together.

16. This, verily, is the honey which Dadhyanc Atharvana declared unto the two Asvins. Seeing this, the seer spake:

"That mighty deed of yours,
O ye two heroes, [which ye did] for gain,
I make known, as thunder [makes known the coming] rain,
Even the honey which Dadhyanc Atharvana to you
Did declare by the head of a horse."

17. This, verily, is the honey which Dadhyanc Atharvana declared unto the two Asvins. Seeing this, the seer spake:

"Upon Dadhyanc Atharvana ye Asvins
Did substitute a horse's head.
He, keeping true, declared to you the honey
Of Tvashtri, which is your secret, O ye mighty ones."

18. This, verily, is the honey which Dadhyanc Atharvana declared unto the two Asvins. Seeing this, the seer spake:

"Citadels with two feet he did make.
Citadels with four feet he did make.
Into the citadels he, having become a bird—
Into the citadels the Person entered."

This, verily, is the person dwelling in all cities. There is nothing by which he is not covered, nothing by which he is not hid.

19. This, verily, is the honey which Dadhyanc Atharvana declared unto the two Asvins. Seeing this, the seer spake:
"He became corresponding in form to every form
This is to be looked upon as a form of him.
Indra by his magic powers goes about in many forms;
Yoked are his ten-hundred steeds."

He [i.e., the Soul, Atman], verily, is the steeds. He, verily, is tens and thousands, many and endless. This Brahma is without an earlier and without a later, without an inside and without an outside. This Soul is Brahma, the all-perceiving—Such is the instruction.

6

1. Now the Line of Tradition—
Pautimashya [received this teaching] from Gaupavana,
Gaupavana from Pautimashya,
Pautimashya from Gaupavana,
Gaupavana from Kausika,
Kausika from Kaundinya,
Kaundinya from Sandilya,
Sandilya from Kausika and Gautama,
Gautama [2] from Agnivesya,
Agnivesya from Sandilya and Anabhimlata,
Anabhimlata from Anabhimlata,
Anabhimlata from Anabhimlata,
Anabhimlata from Gautama,
Gautama from Saitava and Pracinayogya,
Saitava and Pracinayogya from Parasarya,
Parasarya from Bharadvaja,
Bharadvaja from Bharadvaja and Gautama,
Gautama from Bharadvaja,
Bharadvaja from Parasarya,
Parasarya from Vaijavapayana,
Vaijavapayana from Kausikayani,
Kausikayani [3] from Ghritakausika,
Ghritakausika from Parasaryayana,
Parasaryayana from Parasarya,

Parasarya from Jatukarnya,
Jatukarnya from Asurayana and Yaska,
Asurayana from Traivani,
Traivani from Aupajandhani,
Aupajandhani from Asuri,
Asuri from Bharadvaja,
Bharadvaja from Atreya,
Atreya from Manti,
Manti from Gautama
Gautama from Gautama,
Gautama from Vatsya,
Vatsya from Sandilya,
Sandilya from Kaisorya Kapya,
Kaisorya Kapya from Kumaraharita,
Kumaraharita from Galava,
Galava from Vidarbhikaundinya,
Vidarbhikaundinya from Vatsanapad Babhrava,
Vatsanapad Babhrava from Panthah Saubhara,
Panthah Saubhara from Ayasya Angirasa,
Ayasya Angirasa from Abhuti Tvashtra,
Abhuti Tvashtra from Visvarupa Tvashtra,
Visvarupa Tvashtra from the two Asvins,
the two Asvins from Dadhyanc Atharvana,
Dadhyanc Atharvana from Atharvan Daiva,
Atharvan Daiva from Mrityu Pradhvamsana,
Mrityu Pradhvamsana from Pradhvamsana,
Pradhvamsana from Eka Rishi,
Eka Rishi from Vipracitti,
Vipracitti from Vyashti,
Vyashti from Sanaru,
Sanaru from Sanatana,
Sanatana from Sanaga,
Sanaga from Parameshtin,
Parameshtin from Brahma.
Brahma is the Self-existent. Adoration to Brahma!

3

1

1. Janaka, [king] of Videha, sacrificed with a sacrifice at which many presents were distributed. Brahmans of the Kurupancalas were gathered together there. In this Janaka of Videha there arose a desire to know which of these Brahmans was the most learned in scripture. He enclosed a thousand cows. To the horns of each ten *padas* [of gold] were bound.

2. He said to them: "Venerable Brahmans, let him of you who is the best Brahman drive away these cows."

Those Brahmans durst not.

Then Yajnavalkya said to his pupil: "Samasravas, my dear, drive them away."

He drove them away.

The Brahmans were angry. "How can he declare himself to be the best Brahman among us?"

Now there was Asvala, the Hotri-priest of Janaka, [king] of Videha. He asked him: "Yajnavalkya, are you now the best Brahman among us?"

He replied, "We give honor to the best Brahman. But we are really desirous of having those cows."

Thereupon Asvala, the Hotri-priest, began to question him.

3. "Yajnavalkya," said he, "since everything here is overtaken by death, since everything is overcome by death, whereby is a sacrificer liberated beyond the reach of death?"

"By the Hotri-priest, by fire, by speech. Verily, speech is the Hotri of sacrifice. That which is this speech is this fire, is the Hotri. This is release, this is complete release."

4. "Yajnavalkya," said he, "since everything here is overtaken by day and night, since everything is overcome by day and night, whereby is a sacrificer liberated beyond day and night?

"By the Adhvaryu-priest, by the eye, by the sun. Verily, the eye is the Adhvaryu of sacrifice. That which is this eye is yonder sun, is the Adhvaryu. This is release, this is complete release."

5. "Yajnavalkya," said he, "since everything here is overtaken by the waxing and waning moon, by what means does a sacrificer obtain release from the waxing and waning moon?"

"By the Udgatri-priest, by the wind, by breath. Verily breath is the Udgatri of the sacrifice. That which is this breath is wind, is the Udgatri. This is release, this is complete release."

6. "Yajnavalkya," said he, "since this atmosphere does not afford a [foot]hold, as it were, by what means of ascent does a sacrificer ascend to the heavenly world?"

"By the Brahman-priest, by the mind, by the moon. Verily, the mind is the Brahman of the sacrifice. That which is this mind is yonder moon, is the Brahman. This is release, this is complete release." Thus [concerning] liberation.

Now the acquirements—

7. "Yajnavalkya," said he, "how many Rig verses will the Hotri make use of today in this sacrifice?"

"Three."

"Which are those three?"

"The introductory verse, the accompanying verse, and the benediction as the third."

"What does one win by these?"

"Whatever there is here that has breath."

8. "Yajnavalkya," said he, "how many oblations will the Adhvaryu pour out today in this sacrifice?"

"Three."

"Which are those three?"

"Those which when offered flame up, those which when offered flow over, those which when offered sink down."

"What does one win by these?"

"By those which when offered flame up, one wins the world of the gods, for the world of the gods gleams, as it were. By those which when offered flow over, one wins the world of the fathers, for the world of the fathers is over, as it were. By those which when offered sink down, one wins the world of men, for the world of men is below as it were."

9. "Yajnavalkya," said he, "with how many divinities does the Brahman protect the sacrifice on the right today?"

"With one."

"Which is that one?"

"The mind. Verily, endless is the mind. Endless are the All-gods. An endless world he wins thereby."

10. "Yajnavalkya," said he, "how many hymns of praise will the Udgatri chant today in this sacrifice?"

"Three."

"Which are those three?"

"The introductory hymn, the accompanying hymn, and the benediction hymn as the third."

"Which are those three with reference to the self?"

"The introductory hymn is the in-breath. The accompanying hymn is the out-breath. The benediction hymn is the diffused breath."

"What does one win by these?"

"One wins the earth-world by the introductory hymn, the atmosphere-world by the accompanying hymn, the sky-world by the benediction hymn."

Thereupon the Hotri-priest Asvala held his peace.

2

1. Then Jaratkarava Artabhaga questioned him. "Yajnavalkya," said he, "how many apprehenders are there? How many over-apprehenders?"

"Eight apprehenders. Eight over-apprehenders."

"Those eight apprehenders and eight over-apprehenders—which are they?"

2. "Breath, verily, is an apprehender. It is seized by the out-breath as an over-apprehender, for by the out-breath one smells an odor.

3. Speech, verily, is an apprehender. It is seized by name as an over-apprehender, for by speech one speaks names.

4. The tongue, verily, is an apprehender. It is seized by taste as an over-apprehender, for by the tongue one knows tastes.

5. The eye, verily, is an apprehender. It is seized by appearance as an over-apprehender, for by the eye one sees appearances.

6. The ear, verily, is an apprehender. It is seized by sound as an over-apprehender, for by the ear one hears sounds.

7. The mind, verily, is an apprehender. It is seized by desire as an over-apprehender, for by the mind one desires desires.

8. The hands, verily, are an apprehender. It is seized by action as an over-apprehender, for by the hands one performs action.

9. The skin, verily, is an apprehender. It is seized by touch as an over-apprehender, for by the skin one is made to know touches."

10. "Yajnavalkya," said he, "since everything here is food for death, who, pray, is that divinity for whom death is food?"

"Death, verily, is a fire. It is the food of water. He overcomes a second death [who knows this]."

11. "Yajnavalkya," said he, "when a man dies, do the breaths go out of him, or no?"

"No," said Yajnavalkya. "They are gathered together right there. He swells up. He is inflated. The dead man lies inflated."

12. "Yajnavalkya," said he, "when a man dies, what does not leave him?"

"The name. Endless, verily, is the name. Endless are the All-gods. An endless world he wins thereby."

13. "Yajnavalkya," said he, "when the voice of a dead man goes into fire, his breath into wind, his eye into the sun, his mind into the moon, his hearing into the quarters of heaven, his body into the earth, his soul into space, the hairs of his head into plants, the hairs of his body into trees, and his blood and semen are placed in water, what then becomes of this person?"

"Artabhaga, my dear, take my hand. We two only will know of this. This is not for us two [to speak of] in public."

The two went away and deliberated. What they said was *karma* (action). What they praised was *karma*. Verily, one becomes good by good action, bad by bad action.

Thereupon Jaratkarava Artabhaga held his peace.

3

1. Then Bhujyu Lahyayani questioned him. "Yajnavalkya," said he, "we were traveling around as wanderers among the Madras. As such we came to the house of Patancala Kapya. He had a daughter who was possessed by a Gandharva. We asked him: "Who are you?" He said: "I am Sudhanvan, a descendant of Angiras." When we were asking him about the ends of the earth, we said to him: "What has become

of the Parikshitas? What has become of the Parikshitas?"—I now ask you, Yajnavalkya. What has become of the Parikshitas?"

2. He said: "That one doubtless said, 'They have, in truth, gone whither the offerers of the horse-sacrifice go.'"

"Where, pray, do the offerers of the horse-sacrifice go?"

"This inhabited world, of a truth, is as broad as thirty-two days [i.e., days' journeys] of the sun-god's chariot. The earth, which is twice as wide, surrounds it on all sides. The ocean, which is twice as wide, surrounds the earth on all sides. Then there is an interspace as broad as the edge of a razor or the wing of a mosquito. Indra, taking the form of a bird, delivered them [i.e., the Parikshitas] to Wind. Wind, placing them in himself, led them where the offerers of the horse-sacrifice were. Somewhat thus he [i.e., Sudhanvan] praised Wind. Therefore Wind alone is individuality. Wind is totality. He who knows this overcomes a second death."

Thereupon Bhujyu Lahyayani held his peace.

4

1. Then Ushasta Cakrayana questioned him. "Yajnavalkya," said he, "explain to me him who is the Brahma present and not beyond our ken, him who is the Soul in all things."

"He is your soul, which is in all things."

"Which one, O Yajnavalkya, is in all things?"

"He who breathes in with your breathing in is the Soul of yours, which is in all things. He who breathes out with your breathing out is the Soul of yours, which is in all things. He who breathes about with your breathing about is the Soul of yours, which is in all things. He who breathes up with your breathing up is the Soul of yours, which is in all things. He is your soul, which is in all things."

2. Ushasta Cakrayana said: "This has been explained to me just as one might say, 'This is a cow. This is a horse.' Explain to me him who is just the Brahma present and not beyond our ken, him who is the Soul in all things."

"He is your soul, which is in all things."

"Which one, O Yajnavalkya, is in all things?"

"You could not see the seer of seeing. You could not hear the hearer of hearing. You could not think the thinker of thinking. You could not understand the understander of understanding. He is your soul, which is in all things. Aught else than Him [or, than this] is wretched."

Thereupon Ushasta Cakrayana held his peace.

5

1. Now Kahola Kaushitakeya questioned him. "Yajnavalkya," said he, "explain to me him who is just the Brahma present and not beyond our ken, him who is the Soul in all things."

"He is your soul, which is in all things."

"Which one, O Yajnavalkya, is in all things?"

"He who passes beyond hunger and thirst, beyond sorrow and delusion, beyond old age and death—Brahmans who know such a Soul overcome desire for sons, desire for wealth, desire for worlds, and live the life of mendicants. For desire for sons is desire for wealth, and desire for wealth is desire for worlds, for both these are merely desires. Therefore let a Brahman become disgusted with learning and desire to live as a child. When he has become disgusted both with the state of childhood and with learning, then he becomes an ascetic. When he has become disgusted both with the non-ascetic state and with the ascetic state, then he becomes a Brahman."

"By what means would he become a Brahman?"

"By that means by which he does become such a one. Aught else than this Soul is wretched."

Thereupon Kahola Kaushitakeya held his peace.

6

Then Gargi Vacaknavi questioned him. "Yajnavalkya," said she, "since all this world is woven, warp and woof, on water, on what, pray, is the water woven, warp and woof?"

"On wind, O Gargi."

"On what then, pray, is the wind woven, warp and woof?"

"On the atmosphere-worlds, O Gargi."

"On what then, pray, are the atmosphere-worlds woven, warp and woof?"

"On the worlds of the Gandharvas, O Gargi."

"On what then, pray, are the worlds of the Gandharvas woven, warp and woof?"

"On the worlds of the sun, O Gargi."

"On what then, pray, are the worlds of the sun woven, warp and woof?"

"On the worlds of the moon, O Gargi."

"On what then, pray, are the worlds of the moon woven, warp and woof?"

"On the worlds of the stars, O Gargi."

"On what then, pray, are the worlds of the stars woven warp and woof?"

"On the worlds of the gods, O Gargi."

"On what then, pray, are the worlds of the gods woven, warp and woof?"

"On the worlds of Indra, O Gargi."

"On what then, pray, are the worlds of Indra woven, warp and woof?"

"On the worlds of Prajapati, O Gargi."

"On what then, pray, are the worlds of Prajapati woven, warp and woof?"

"On the worlds of Brahma, O Gargi."

"On what then, pray, are the worlds of Brahma woven, warp and woof?"

Yajnavalkya said: "Gargi, do not question too much, lest your head fall off. In truth you are questioning too much about a divinity about which further questions cannot be asked. Gargi, do not over-question."

Thereupon Gargi Vacaknavi held her peace.

7

1. Then Uddalaka Aruni questioned him. "Yajnavalkya," said he, "we were dwelling among the Madras in the house of Patancala Kapya, studying the sacrifice. He had a wife possessed by a spirit. We asked him: 'Who are you?' He said: 'I am Kabandha Atharvana.' He said to

Patancala Kapya and to us students of the sacrifice: 'Do you know, O Kapya, that thread by which this world and the other world and all things are tied together?' Patancala Kapya said: 'I do not know it, Sir.' He said to Patancala Kapya and to us students of the sacrifice: 'Pray do you know, O Kapya, that Inner Controller who from within controls this world and the other world and all things?' Patancala Kapya said: 'I do not know him, Sir.' He said to Patancala Kapya and to us students of the sacrifice: 'Verily, Kapya, he who knows that thread and the so-called Inner Controller knows Brahma, he knows the worlds, he knows the gods, he knows the Vedas, he knows created things, he knows the Soul, he knows everything.' Thus he [i.e., the spirit] explained it to them. And I know it. If you, O Yajnavalkya, drive away the Brahma-cows without knowing that thread and the Inner Controller, your head will fall off."

"Verily, I know that thread and the Inner Controller, O Gautama."

"Any one might say 'I know, I know.' Do you tell what you know."

2. He [i.e., Yajnavalkya] said: "Wind, verily, O Gautama, is that thread. By wind, verily, O Gautama, as by a thread, this world and the other world and all things are tied together.

Therefore, verily, O Gautama, they say of a deceased person, 'His limbs become unstrung,' for by wind, O Gautama, as by a thread, they are strung together."

"Quite so, O Yajnavalkya. Declare the Inner Controller."

3. "He who, dwelling in the earth, yet is other than the earth, whom the earth does not know, whose body the earth is, who controls the earth from within—He is your Soul, the Inner Controller, the Immortal.

4. He who, dwelling in the waters, yet is other than the waters, whom the waters do not know, whose body the waters are, who controls the waters from within—He is your Soul, the Inner Controller, the Immortal.

5. He who, dwelling in the fire, yet is other than the fire, whom the fire does not know, whose body the fire is, who controls the fire from within—He is your Soul, the Inner Controller, the Immortal.

6. He who, dwelling in the atmosphere, yet is other than the atmosphere, whom the atmosphere does not know, whose body the atmosphere is, who controls the atmosphere from within—He is your Soul, the Inner Controller, the Immortal.

7. He who, dwelling in the wind, yet is other than the wind,

whom the wind does not know, whose body the wind is, who controls the wind from within—He is your Soul, the Inner Controller, the Immortal.

8. He who, dwelling in the sky, yet is other than the sky, whom the sky does not know, whose body the sky is, who controls the sky from within—He is your Soul, the Inner Controller, the Immortal.

9. He who, dwelling in the sun, yet is other than the sun, whom the sun does not know, whose body the sun is, who controls the sun from within—He is your Soul, the Inner Controller, the Immortal.

10. He who, dwelling in the quarters of heaven, yet is other than the quarters of heaven, whom the quarters of heaven do not know, whose body the quarters of heaven are, who controls the quarters of heaven from within—He is your Soul, the Inner Controller, the Immortal.

11. He who, dwelling in the moon and stars, yet is other than the moon and stars, whom the moon and stars do not know, whose body the moon and stars are, who controls the moon and stars from within—He is your Soul, the Inner Controller, the Immortal.

12. He who, dwelling in space, yet is other than space, whom space does not know, whose body space is, who controls space from within—He is your Soul, the Inner Controller, the Immortal.

13. He who, dwelling in the darkness, yet is other than the darkness, whom the darkness does not know, whose body the darkness is, who controls the darkness from within—He is your Soul, the Inner Controller, the Immortal.

14. He who, dwelling in the light, yet is other than the light, whom the light does not know, whose body the light is, who controls the light from within—He is your Soul, the Inner Controller, the Immortal.—

Thus far with reference to the divinities. Now with reference to material existence—

15. He who, dwelling in all things, yet is other than all things, whom all things do not know, whose body all things are, who controls all things from within—He is your Soul, the Inner Controller, the Immortal.

Thus far with reference to material existence. Now with reference to the self.

16. He who, dwelling in breath, yet is other than breath, whom the breath does not know, whose body the breath is, who controls the breath from within—He is your Soul, the Inner Controller, the Immortal.

17. He who, dwelling in speech, yet is other than speech, whom the speech does not know, whose body the speech is, who controls the speech from within—He is your Soul, the Inner Controller, the Immortal.

18. He who, dwelling in the eye, yet is other than the eye, whom the eye does not know, whose body the eye is, who controls the eye from within—He is your Soul, the Inner Controller, the Immortal.

19. He who, dwelling in the ear, yet is other than the ear, whom the ear does not know, whose body the ear is, who controls the ear from within—He is your Soul, the Inner Controller, the Immortal.

20. He who, dwelling in the mind, yet is other than the mind, whom the mind does not know, whose body the mind is, who controls the mind from within—He is your Soul, the Inner Controller, the Immortal.

21. He who, dwelling in the skin, yet is other than the skin, whom the skin does not know, whose body the skin is, who controls the skin from within—He is your Soul, the Inner Controller, the Immortal.

22. He who, dwelling in the understanding, yet is other than the understanding, whom the understanding does not know, whose body the understanding is, who controls the understanding from within— He is your Soul, the Inner Controller, the Immortal.

23. He who, dwelling in the semen, yet is other than the semen, whom the semen does not know, whose body the semen is, who controls the semen from within—He is your Soul, the Inner Controller, the Immortal.

He is the unseen Seer, the unheard Hearer, the unthought Thinker, the ununderstood Understander. Other than He there is no seer. Other than He there is no hearer. Other than He there is no thinker. Other than He there is no understander. He is your Soul, the Inner Controller, the Immortal."

Thereupon Uddalaka Aruni held his peace.

8

1. Then [Gargi] Vacaknavi said: "Venerable Brahmans, lo, I will ask him [i.e., Yajnavalkya] two questions. If he will answer me these, not one of you will surpass him in discussions about Brahma."

"Ask, Gargi."

2. She said: "As a noble youth of the Kasis or of the Videhas might rise up against you, having strung his unstrung bow and taken two foe-piercing arrows in his hand, even so, O Yajnavalkya, have I risen up against you with two questions. Answer me these."

Yajnavalkya said: "Ask Gargi."

3. She said: "That, O Yajnavalkya, which is above the sky, that which is beneath the earth, that which is between these two, sky and earth, that which people call the past and the present and the future—across what is that woven, warp and woof?"

4. He said: "That, O Gargi, which is above the sky, that which is beneath the earth, that which is between these two, sky and earth, that which people call the past and the present and the future—across space is that woven, warp and woof."

5. She said: "Adoration to you, Yajnavalkya, in that you have solved this question for me. Prepare yourself for the other."

"Ask, Gargi."

6. She said: "That, O Yajnavalkya, which is above the sky, that which is beneath the earth, that which is between these two, sky and earth, that which people call the past and the present and the future—across what is that woven, warp and woof?"

7. He said: "That, O Gargi, which is above the sky, that which is beneath the earth, that which is between these two, sky and earth, that which people call the past and the present and the future—across space alone is that woven, warp and woof."

"Across what then, pray, is space woven, warp and woof?"

8. He said: "That, O Gargi, Brahmans call the Imperishable. It is not coarse, not fine, not short, not long, not glowing [like fire], not adhesive [like water], without shadow and without darkness, without air and without space, without stickiness, (intangible), odorless, tasteless, without eye, without ear, without voice, without wind, without energy, without breath, without mouth, (without personal or family name, unaging, undying, without fear, immortal, stainless, not uncovered, not covered), without measure, without inside and without outside.

It consumes nothing soever.

No one soever consumes it.

9. Verily, O Gargi, at the command of that Imperishable the sun and the moon stand apart. Verily, O Gargi, at the command of that

Imperishable the earth and the sky stand apart. Verily, O Gargi, at the command of that Imperishable the moments, the hours, the days, the nights, the fortnights, the months, the seasons, and the years stand apart. Verily, O Gargi, at the command of that Imperishable some rivers flow from the snowy mountains to the east, others to the west, in whatever direction each flows. Verily, O Gargi, at the command of that Imperishable men praise those who give, the gods are desirous of a sacrificer, and the fathers [are desirous] of the Manes-sacrifice.

10. Verily, O Gargi, if one performs sacrifices and worship and undergoes austerity in this world for many thousands of years, but without knowing that Imperishable, limited indeed is that [work] of his. Verily, O Gargi, he who departs from this world without knowing that Imperishable is pitiable. But, O Gargi, he who departs from this world knowing that Imperishable is a Brahman.

11. Verily, O Gargi, that Imperishable is the unseen Seer, the unheard Hearer, the unthought Thinker, the ununderstood Understander. Other than It there is naught that sees. Other than It there is naught that hears. Other than It there is naught that thinks. Other than It there is naught that understands. Across this Imperishable, O Gargi, is space woven, warp and woof."

12. She said: "Venerable Brahmans, you may think it a great thing if you escape from this man with [merely] making a bow. Not one of you will surpass him in discussions about Brahma."

Thereupon [Gargi] Vacaknavi held her peace.

9

1. Then Vidagdha Sakalya questioned him. "How many gods are there, Yajnavalkya?"

He answered in accord with the following *Nivid* (invocationary formula): "As many as are mentioned in the *Nivid* of the Hymn to All the Gods, namely, three hundred and three, and three thousand and three [= 3,306]."

"Yes," said he, "but just how many gods are there, Yajnavalkya?"

"Thirty-three."

"Yes," said he, "but just how many gods are there, Yajnavalkya?"

"Six."

"Yes," said he, "but just how many gods are there, Yajnavalkya?"
"Three."
"Yes," said he, "but just how many gods are there, Yajnavalkya?"
"Two."
"Yes," said he, "but just how many gods are there, Yajnavalkya?"
"One and a half."
"Yes," said he, "but just how many gods are there, Yajnavalkya?"
"One."
"Yes," said he, "which are those three hundred and three, and those three thousand and three?"

2. He [i.e., Yajnavalkya] said: "Those are only their powers. There are just thirty-three gods."
"Which are those thirty-three?"
"Eight Vasus, eleven Rudras, twelve Adityas. Those are thirty-one. Indra and Prajapati make thirty-three."

3. "Which are the Vasus?"
"Fire, earth, wind, atmosphere, sun, sky, moon, and stars. These are Vasus, for upon them this excellent world is set, (for they give a dwelling to the world). Therefore they are called Vasus."

4. "Which are the Rudras?"
"These ten breaths in a person, and the self as the eleventh. When they go out from this mortal body, they make us lament. So, because they make us lament, therefore they are Rudras."

5. "Which are the Adityas?"
"Verily, the twelve months of the year. These are Adityas, for they go carrying along this whole world. Since they go carrying along this whole world, therefore they are called Adityas."

6. "Which is Indra? Which is Prajapati?"
"The thunder, verily, is Indra. The sacrifice is Prajapati."
"Which is the thunder?"
"The thunderbolt."
"Which is the sacrifice?"
"The sacrificial animals."

7. "Which are the six [gods]?"
"Fire, earth, wind, atmosphere, sun, and sky. These are the six, for the whole world is these six."

8. "Which are the three gods?"
"They, verily, are the three worlds, for in them all these gods exist."
"Which are the two gods?"

"Food and breath."

"Which is the one and a half?"

"This one here who purifies [i.e., the wind]."

9. Then they say: "Since he who purifies is just like one, how then is he one and a half?"

"Because in him this whole world did prosper. Therefore he is one and a half."

"Which is the one god?"

"Breath," said he. "They call him Brahma, the Yon."

10. [Sakalya said:] "Verily, he who knows that Person whose abode is the earth, whose world is fire, whose light is mind, who is the last source of every soul—he, verily, would be a knower, O Yajnavalkya."

[Yajnavalkya said:] "Verily, I know that Person, the last source of every soul, of whom you speak. This very person who is in the body is He. Tell me, Sakalya, who is his god?"

"The Immortal," said he.

11. [Sakalya said:] "Verily, he who knows that Person whose abode is desire, whose world is the heart, whose light is mind, who is the last source of every soul—he, verily, would be a knower, O Yajnavalkya."

[Yajnavalkya said:] "Verily, I know that Person, the last source of every soul, of whom you speak. This very person who is made of desire is He. Tell me, Sakalya, who is his god?"

"Women," said he.

12. [Sakalya said:] "Verily, he who knows that Person whose abode is forms, whose world is the eye, whose light is mind, who is the last source of every soul he, verily, would be a knower, O Yajnavalkya."

"Verily, I know that Person, the last source of every soul, of whom you speak. That very person who is in the sun is He. Tell me, Sakalya, who is his god?"

"Truth," said he.

13. [Sakalya said:] "Verily, he who knows that Person whose abode is space, whose world is the ear, whose light is mind, who is the last source of every soul—he, verily, would be a knower, O Yajnavalkya."

"Verily, I know that Person, the last source of every soul, of whom you speak. This very person who is in hearing and who is in echo is He. Tell me, Sakalya, who is his god?"

"The quarters of heaven," said he.

14. [Sakalya said:] "Verily, he who knows that Person whose abode is darkness, whose world is the heart, whose light is mind,

who is the last source of every soul—he, verily, would be a knower, O Yajnavalkya."

"Verily, I know that Person, the last source of every soul, of whom you speak. This very person who is made of shadow is He. Tell me, Sakalya, who is his god?"

"Death," said he.

15. [Sakalya said:] "Verily, he who knows that Person whose abode is forms, whose world is the eye, whose light is mind, who is the last source of every soul—he, verily, would be a knower, O Yajnavalkya."

"Verily, I know that Person, the last source of every soul, of whom you speak. This very person who is in the mirror is He. Tell me, Sakalya, who is his god?"

"Life," said he.

16. [Sakalya said:] "Verily, he who knows that Person whose abode is water, whose world is the heart, whose light is mind, who is the last source of every soul—he, verily, would be a knower, O Yajnavalkya."

"Verily, I know that Person, the last source of every soul, of whom you speak. This very person who is in the waters is He. Tell me, Sakalya, who is his god?"

"Varuna," said he.

17. [Sakalya said:] "Verily, he who knows that Person whose abode is semen, whose world is the heart, whose light is mind, who is the last source of every soul—he, verily, would be a knower, O Yajnavalkya."

"Verily, I know that Person, the last source of every soul, of whom you speak. This very person who is made of a son is He. Tell me, Sakalya, who is his god?"

"Prajapati," said he.

18. "Sakalya," said Yajnavalkya, "have those Brahmans made you their coal-destroyer?"

19. "Yajnavalkya," said Sakalya, "by knowing what Brahma is it that you have talked down the Brahmans of the Kurupancalas?"

"I know the quarters of heaven together with their gods and their bases."

"Since you know the quarters of heaven together with their gods and their bases, [20] what divinity have you in this eastern quarter?"

"The sun."

"That sun—on what is it based?"

"On the eye."

"And on what is the eye based?"

"On appearance, for with the eye one sees appearances."

"And on what are appearances based?"

"On the heart," he said, "for with the heart one knows appearances, for on the heart alone appearances are based."

"Quite so, Yajnavalkya."

21. [Sakalya said:] "What divinity have you in this southern quarter?"

"Yama."

"That Yama—on what is he based?"

"On sacrifice."

"And on what is sacrifice based?"

"On gifts to the priests."

"And on what are the gifts to the priests based?"

"On faith, for when one has faith, then one gives gifts to the priests. Verily, on faith the gifts to the priests are based."

"On what is faith based?"

"On the heart," he said, "for with the heart one knows faith. Verily, on the heart alone faith is based."

"Quite so, Yajnavalkya."

22. [Sakalya said:] "What divinity have you in this western quarter?"

"Varuna."

"That Varuna—on what is he based?"

"On water."

"And on what is water based?"

"On semen."

"And on what is semen based?"

"On the heart. Therefore they say of a son who is just like his father, 'He has slipped out from his heart, as it were. He is built out of his heart.' For on the heart alone semen is based."

"Quite so, Yajnavalkya."

23. [Sakalya said:] "What divinity have you in this northern quarter?"

"Soma."

"That Soma—on what is he based?"

"On the Diksha [initiatory] rite."

"And on what is the Diksha rite based?"

"On truth. Therefore they say to one who is initiated, 'Speak the truth!' For on truth alone the Diksha rite is based."

"And on what is truth based?"

"On the heart," he said, "for with the heart one knows truth. Verily, on the heart alone truth is based."

"Quite so, Yajnavalkya."

24. [Sakalya said:] "What divinity have you in this fixed quarter [i.e., the zenith]?"

"The god Agni."

"That Agni—on what is he based?"

"On speech."

"And on what is speech based?"

"On the heart."

"And on what is the heart based?"

25. "You idiot," said Yajnavalkya, "that you will think that it could be anywhere else than in ourselves! for if it were anywhere else than in ourselves, the dogs might eat it or the birds might tear it to pieces."

26. "On what are you and your soul based?"

"On the in-breath."

"And on what is the in-breath based?"

"On the out-breath."

"And on what is the out-breath based?"

"On the diffused breath."

"And on what is the diffused breath based?"

"On the up-breath."

"And on what is the up-breath based?"

"On the middle [or equalizing] breath."

"That Soul is not this, it is not that. It is unseizable, for it is not seized. It is indestructible, for it is not destroyed. It is unattached, for it does not attach itself. It is unbound. It does not tremble. It is not injured.

"These are the eight abodes, the eight worlds, the eight gods, the eight persons. He who plucks apart and puts together these persons and passes beyond them—that is the Person taught in the Upanishads about whom I ask you.

> If him to me ye will not tell,
> Your head indeed will then fall off."
> But him Sakalya did not know,
> And so indeed his head fell off.

Indeed, robbers carried off his bones, thinking they were something else.

27. Then he [i.e., Yajnavalkya] said: "Venerable Brahmans, let him

of you that desires question me. Or do ye all question me. Or I will question him of you that desires [to be questioned]; or I will question all of you."

Those Brahmans, however, durst not.

28. Then he [i.e., Yajnavalkya] questioned them with these verses:

> As a tree of the forest,
> Just so, surely, is man.
> His hairs are leaves,
> His skin the outer bark.
> From his skin blood,
> Sap from the bark flows forth.
> From him when pierced there comes forth
> A stream, as from the tree when struck.
> His pieces of flesh are under-layers of wood.
> The fibre is muscle-like, strong.
> The bones are the wood within.
> The marrow is made resembling pith.
> A tree, when it is felled, grows up
> From the root, more new again;
> A mortal, when cut down by death—
> From what root does he grow up?
> Say not "from semen,"
> For that is produced from the living,
> As the tree, forsooth, springing from seed,
> Clearly arises without having died.
> If with its roots they should pull up
> The tree, it would not come into being again.
> A mortal, when cut down by death—
> From what root does he grow up?
> When born, indeed, he is not born [again].
> Who would again beget him?
> Brahma is knowledge, is bliss,
> The final goal of the giver of offerings,
> Of him, too, who stands still and knows It.

4

1

1. Janaka, [king] of Videha, was seated. Yajnavalkya came up. To him he said: "Yajnavalkya, for what purpose have you come? Because you desire cattle or subtle disputations?"

"Indeed, for both, your Majesty," he said.

2. "Let us hear what anybody may have told you," [continued Yajnavalkya].

"Jitvan Sailini told me: 'Brahma, verily, is speech,'" [said Janaka].

"As a man might say that he had a mother, that he had a father, that he had a teacher, so did that Sailina say, 'Brahma, verily, is speech.' For he might have thought, 'What can one have who can not speak?' But did he tell you Its seat and support?"

"He did not tell me."

"Forsooth, your Majesty, that is a one-legged [Brahma]."

"Verily, Yajnavalkya, do you here tell us."

"Its seat is just speech; Its support, space. One should worship It as intelligence."

"What is Its quality of intelligence, Yajnavalkya?"

"Just speech, your Majesty," said he. "Verily, by speech, your Majesty, a friend is recognized. By speech alone, your Majesty, the Rig-Veda, the Yajur-Veda, the Sama-Veda, the [Hymns] of the Atharvans and Angirases, Legends, Ancient Lore, Sciences, Mystic Doctrines, Verses, Aphorisms, Explanations, Commentaries, what is offered in sacrifice and as oblation, food and drink, this world and the other, and all beings are known. The highest Brahma, your Majesty, is in truth speech. Speech does not desert him who, knowing this, worships it as such. All things run unto him. He, having become a god, goes even to the gods."

"I will give you a thousand cows with a bull as large as an elephant," said Janaka, [king] of Videha.

Yajnavalkya replied: "My father thought that without having instructed one should not accept."

3. "Let us hear what anybody may have told you," [continued Yaj-navalkya].

"Udanka Saulbayana told me: 'Brahma, verily, is the breath of life.'"

"As a man might say that he had a mother, that he had a father, that he had a teacher, so did that Saulbayana say, 'Brahma is the breath of life.' For he might have thought, 'What can one have who is without the breath of life?' But did he tell you Its seat and support?"

"He did not tell me."

"Forsooth, your Majesty, that is a one-legged [Brahma]."

"Verily, Yajnavalkya, do you here tell us."

"Its seat is just the breath of life; Its support, space. One should worship It as the dear."

"What is Its dearness, Yajnavalkya?"

"The breath of life itself, your Majesty," said he. "Verily, out of love for the breath of life, your Majesty, one has sacrifice offered for him for whom one should not offer sacrifice, one accepts from him from whom one should not accept. Out of love of just the breath of life, your Majesty, there arises fear of being killed wherever one goes. The highest Brahma, your Majesty, is in truth the breath of life. The breath of life leaves not him who, knowing this, worships it as such. All things run unto him. He, having become a god, goes even to the gods."

"I will give you a thousand cows with a bull as large as an elephant," said Janaka, [king] of Videha.

Yajnavalkya replied: "My father thought that without having instructed one should not accept."

4. "Let us hear what anybody may have told you," [continued Yaj-navalkya].

"Barku Varshna told me: 'Brahma, verily, is sight.'"

"As a man might say that he had a mother, that he had a father, that he had a teacher, so did that Varshna say, 'Brahma is sight.' For he might have thought, 'What can one have who can not see?' But did he tell you Its seat and support?"

"He did not tell me."

"Forsooth, your Majesty, that is a one-legged [Brahma]."

"Verily, Yajnavalkya, do you here tell us."

"Its seat is just sight; Its support, space. One should worship It as the true."

"What is Its truthfulness, Yajnavalkya?"

"Sight alone, your Majesty," said he. "Verily, your Majesty, when they say to a man who sees with his eyes, 'Have you seen?' and he says, 'I have seen,' that is the truth. Verily, your Majesty, the highest Brahma is sight. Sight leaves not him who, knowing this, worships it as such. All things run unto him. He, becoming a god, goes to the gods."

"I will give you a thousand cows with a bull as large as an elephant," said Janaka, [king] of Videha.

Yajnavalkya replied: "My father thought that without having instructed one should not accept."

5. "Let us hear what anybody may have told you," [continued Yajnavalkya].

"Gardabhivipita Bharadvaja told me: 'Brahma, verily, is hearing.'"

"As a man might say that he had a mother, that he had a father, that he had a teacher, so did that Bharadvaja say, 'Brahma is hearing.' For he might have thought, 'What can one have who can not hear?' But did he tell you Its seat and support?"

"He did not tell me."

"Forsooth, your Majesty, that is a one-legged [Brahma]."

"Verily, Yajnavalkya, do you here tell us."

"Its seat is just hearing; Its support, space. One should worship It as the endless."

"What is Its endlessness, Yajnavalkya?"

"Just the quarters of heaven, your Majesty," said he. "Therefore, verily, your Majesty, to whatever quarter one goes, he does not come to the end of it, for the quarters of heaven are endless. Verily, your Majesty, the quarters of heaven are hearing. Verily, your Majesty, the highest Brahma is hearing. Hearing does not desert him who, knowing this, worships it as such. All things run unto him. He, becoming a god, goes to the gods."

"I will give you a thousand cows with a bull as large as an elephant," said Janaka, [king] of Videha.

Yajnavalkya replied: "My father thought that without having instructed one should not accept."

6. "Let us hear what anybody may have told you," [continued Yajnavalkya].

"Satyakama Jabala told me: 'Brahma, verily, is mind.'"

"As a man might say that he had a mother, that he had a father, that he had a teacher, so did that Jabala say, 'Brahma is mind.' For he might have thought, 'What can one have who is without a mind?' But did he tell you Its seat and support?"

"He did not tell me."

"Forsooth, your Majesty, that is a one-legged [Brahma]."

"Verily, Yajnavalkya, do you here tell us."

"Its seat is just the mind; Its support, space. One should worship It as the blissful."

"What is Its blissfulness, Yajnavalkya?"

"Just the mind, your Majesty," said he. "Verily, your Majesty, by the mind one betakes himself to a woman. A son like himself is born of her. He is bliss. Verily, your Majesty, the highest Brahma is mind. Mind does not desert him who, knowing this, worships it as such. All things run unto him. He, becoming a god, goes to the gods."

"I will give you a thousand cows with a bull as large as an elephant," said Janaka, [king] of Videha.

Yajnavalkya replied: "My father thought that without having instructed one should not accept."

7. "Let us hear what anybody may have told you," [continued Yajnavalkya].

"Vidagdha Sakalya told me: 'Brahma, verily, is the heart.'"

"As a man might say that he had a mother, that he had a father, that he had a teacher, so did that Sakalya say, 'Brahma is the heart.' For he might have thought, 'What can one have who is without a heart?' But did he not tell you Its seat and support?"

"He did not tell me."

"Forsooth, your Majesty, that is a one-legged [Brahma]."

"Verily, Yajnavalkya, do you here tell us."

"Its seat is just the heart; Its support, space. One should worship It as the steadfast."

"What is Its steadfastness, Yajnavalkya?"

"Just the heart, your Majesty," said he. "Verily, your Majesty, the heart is the seat of all things. Verily, your Majesty, the heart is the support of all things, for on the heart alone, your Majesty, all things are established. Verily, your Majesty, the highest Brahma is the heart. The heart does not leave him, who, knowing this, worships it as such. All things run unto him. He, becoming a god, goes to the gods."

"I will give you a thousand cows with a bull as large as an elephant," said Janaka, [king] of Videha.

Yajnavalkya replied: "My father thought that without having instructed one should not accept."

2

1. Janaka, [king] of Videha, descending from his cushion and approaching, said: "Adoration to you, Yajnavalkya. Do you instruct me."

He [i.e., Yajnavalkya] said: "Verily, as a king about to go on a great journey would prepare a chariot or a ship, even so you have a soul prepared with these mystic doctrines. So, being at the head of a troop, and wealthy, learned in the Vedas, and instructed in mystic doctrines, whither, when released hence, will you go?"

"That I know not, noble Sir—whither I shall go."

"Then truly I will tell you that—whither you will go."

"Tell me, noble Sir."

2. "Indha (i.e., the Kindler) by name is this person here in the right eye. Him, verily, who is that Indha people call 'Indra' cryptically, for the gods are fond of the cryptic, as it were, and dislike the evident.

3. Now that which has the form of a person in the left eye is his wife, Viraj. Their meeting-place [literally, their common praise, or concord] is the space in the heart. Their food is the red lump in the heart. Their covering is the net-like work in the heart. The path that they go is that vein which goes upward from the heart. Like a hair divided a thousandfold, so are the veins called *hita*, which are established within the heart. Through these flows that which flows on [i.e., the food], Therefore that [soul which is composed of Indha and Viraj] is, as it were, an eater of finer food than is this bodily self.

4. The eastern breaths are his eastern quarter. The southern breaths are his southern quarter. The western breaths are his western quarter. The northern breaths are his northern quarter. The upper breaths are his upper quarter [i.e., the zenith]. The lower breaths are his lower quarter [i.e., the nadir]. All the breaths are all his quarters.

But the Soul is not this, it is not that. It is unseizable, for it cannot be seized. It is indestructible, for it cannot be destroyed. It is unattached, for it does not attach itself. It is unbound. It does not tremble. It is not injured.

Verily, Janaka, you have reached fearlessness."—Thus spake Yajnavalkya.

Janaka, [king] of Videha, said: "May fearlessness come unto you, noble Sir, you who make us to know fearlessness. Adoration to you! Here are the Videhas, here am I [as your servants]."

3

1. Yajnavalkya came to Janaka, [king] of Videha. He thought to himself: "I will not talk."

But [once] when Janaka, [king] of Videha, and Yajnavalkya were discussing together at an Agnihotra, Yajnavalkya granted the former a boon. He chose asking whatever question he wished. He granted it to him. So [now] the king, [speaking] first, asked him:

2. "Yajnavalkya, what light does a person here have?"

"He has the light of the sun, O king," he said, "for with the sun, indeed, as his light one sits, moves around, does his work, and returns."

"Quite so, Yajnavalkya.

3. But when the sun has set, Yajnavalkya, what light does a person here have?"

"The moon, indeed, is his light," said he, "for with the moon, indeed, as his light one sits, moves around, does his work, and returns."

"Quite so, Yajnavalkya.

4. But when the sun has set, and the moon has set, what light does a person here have?"

"Fire, indeed, is his light," said he, "for with fire, indeed, as his light one sits, moves around, does his work, and returns."

"Quite so, Yajnavalkya.

5. But when the sun has set, Yajnavalkya, and the moon has set, and the fire has gone out, what light does a person here have?"

"Speech, indeed, is his light," said he, "for with speech, indeed, as his light one sits, moves around, does his work, and returns. Therefore, verily, O king, where one does not discern even his own hands, when a voice is raised, then one goes straight towards it."

"Quite so, Yajnavalkya.

6. But when the sun has set, Yajnavalkya, and the moon has set, and the fire has gone out, and speech is hushed, what light does a person here have?"

"The soul, indeed, is his light," said he, "for with the soul, indeed, as his light one sits, moves around, does his work, and returns."

7. "Which is the soul?"

"The person here who among the senses is made of knowledge, who is the light in the heart. He, remaining the same, goes along both worlds, appearing to think, appearing to move about, for upon becoming asleep he transcends this world and the forms of death.

8. Verily, this person, by being born and obtaining a body, is joined with evils. When he departs, on dying, he leaves evils behind.

9. Verily, there are just two conditions of this person: the condition of being in this world and the condition of being in the other world. There is an intermediate third condition, namely, that of being in sleep. By standing in this intermediate condition one sees both those conditions, namely being in this world and being in the other world. Now whatever the approach is to the condition of being in the other world, by making that approach one sees the evils [of this world] and the joys [of yonder world].

When one goes to sleep, he takes along the material of this all-containing world, himself tears it apart, himself builds it up, and dreams by his own brightness, by his own light. Then this person becomes self-illuminated.

10. There are no chariots there, no spans, no roads. But he projects from himself chariots, spans, roads. There are no blisses there, no pleasures, no delights. But he projects from himself blisses, pleasures, delights. There are no tanks there, no lotus-pools, no streams. But he projects from himself tanks, lotus-pools, streams. For he is a creator.

11. On this point there are the following verses:
Striking down in sleep what is bodily,
Sleepless he looks down upon the sleeping [senses].
Having taken to himself light, there returns to his place
The golden person, the one spirit.

12. Guarding his low nest with the breath,
The Immortal goes forth out of the nest.
He goes where'er he pleases—the immortal,
The golden person, the one spirit.

13. In the state of sleep going aloft and alow,
A god, he makes many forms for himself—
Now, as it were, enjoying pleasure with women,
Now, as it were, laughing, and even beholding fearful sights.

14. People see his pleasure-ground;
Him no one sees at all.

"Therefore one should not wake him suddenly," they say. Hard is the curing for a man to whom He does not return.

Now some people say: "That is just his waking state, for whatever things he sees when awake, those too he sees when asleep." [This is not so, for] there [i.e., in sleep] the person is self-illuminated."

[Janaka said:] "I will give you, noble Sir, a thousand [cows]. Declare what is higher than this, for my release [from transmigration]."

15. "Having had enjoyment in this state of deep sleep, having traveled around and seen good and bad, he hastens again, according to the entrance and place of origin, back to sleep. Whatever he sees there [i.e., in the state of deep sleep], he is not followed by it, for this person is without attachments."

[Janaka said:] "Quite so, Yajnavalkya. I will give you, noble Sir, a thousand [cows]. Declare what is higher than this, for my release."

16. "Having had enjoyment in this state of sleep, having traveled around and seen good and bad, he hastens again, according to the entrance and place of origin, back to the state of waking. Whatever he sees there [i.e., in dreaming sleep], he is not followed by it, for this person is without attachments."

[Janaka said:] "Quite so, Yajnavalkya. I will give you, noble Sir, a thousand [cows]. Declare what is higher than this, for my release."

17. "Having had enjoyment in this state of waking, having traveled around and seen good and evil, he hastens again, according to the entrance and place of origin, back to dreaming sleep.

18. As a great fish goes along both banks of a river, both the hither and the further, just so this person goes along both these conditions, the condition of sleeping and the condition of waking.

19. As a falcon, or an eagle, having flown around here in space, becomes weary, folds its wings, and is borne down to its nest, just so this person hastens to that state where, asleep, he desires no desires and sees no dream.

20. Verily, a person has those arteries called *hita*; as a hair subdivided a thousandfold, so minute are they, full of white, blue, yellow, green, and red. Now when people seem to be killing him, when they seem to be overpowering him, when an elephant seems to be tearing him to pieces, when he seems to be falling into a hole—in these circumstances he is imagining through ignorance the very fear which

he sees when awake. When he imagines that he is a god, as it were, that he is a king, as it were, or "I am this world-all," that is his highest world.

21. This, verily, is that form of his which is beyond desires, free from evil, without fear. As a man, when in the embrace of a beloved wife, knows nothing within or without, so this person, when in the embrace of the intelligent Soul, knows nothing within or without. Verily, that is his [true] form in which his desire is satisfied, in which the Soul is his desire, in which he is without desire and without sorrow.

22. There a father becomes not a father; a mother, not a mother; the worlds, not the worlds; the gods, not the gods; the Vedas, not the Vedas; a thief, not a thief. There the destroyer of an embryo becomes not the destroyer of an embryo; a Candala [the son of a Sudra father and a Brahman mother] is not a Candala; a Paulkasa [the son of a Sudra father and a Kshatriya mother] is not a Paulkasa; a mendicant is not a mendicant; an ascetic is not an ascetic. He is not followed by good, he is not followed by evil, for then he has passed beyond all sorrows of the heart.

23. Verily, while he does not there see [with the eyes], he is verily seeing, though he does not see (what is [usually] to be seen); for there is no cessation of the seeing of a seer, because of his imperishability [as a seer]. It is not, however, a second thing, other than himself and separate, that he may see.

24. Verily, while he does not there smell, he is verily smelling, though he does not smell (what is [usually] to be smelled); for there is no cessation of the smelling of a smeller, because of his imperishability [as a smeller]. It is not, however, a second thing, other than himself and separate, that he may smell.

25. Verily, while he does not there taste, he is verily tasting, though he does not taste (what is [usually] to be tasted); for there is no cessation of the tasting of a taster, because of his imperishability [as a taster]. It is not, however, a second thing, other than himself and separate, that he may taste.

26. Verily, while he does not there speak, he is verily speaking, though he does not speak (what is [usually] to be spoken); for there is no cessation of the speaking of a speaker, because of his imperishability [as a speaker]. It is not, however, a second thing, other than himself and separate, to which he may speak.

27. Verily, while he does not there hear, he is verily hearing, though he does not hear (what is [usually] to be heard); for there is no cessation of the hearing of a hearer, because of his imperishability [as a hearer]. It is not, however, a second thing, other than himself and separate, which he may hear.

28. Verily, while he does not there think, he is verily thinking, though he does not think (what is [usually] to be thought); for there is no cessation of the thinking of a thinker, because of his imperishability [as a thinker]. It is not, however, a second thing, other than himself and separate, of which he may think.

29. Verily, while he does not there touch, he is verily touching, though he does not touch (what is [usually] to be touched); for there is no cessation of the touching of a toucher, because of his imperishability [as a toucher]. It is not, however, a second thing, other than himself and separate, which he may touch.

30. Verily, while he does not there know, he is verily knowing, though he does not know (what is [usually] to be known); for there is no cessation of the knowing of a knower, because of his imperishability [as a knower]. It is not, however, a second thing, other than himself and separate, which he may know.

31. Verily where there seems to be another, there the one might see the other; the one might smell the other; the one might taste the other; the one might speak to the other; the one might hear the other; the one might think of the other; the one might touch the other; the one might know the other.

32. An ocean, a seer alone without duality, becomes he whose world is Brahma, O King!"—thus Yajnavalkya instructed him. "This is a man's highest path. This is his highest achievement. This is his highest world. This is his highest bliss. On a part of just this bliss other creatures have their living.

33. If one is fortunate among men and wealthy, lord over others, best provided with all human enjoyments—that is the highest bliss of men. Now a hundredfold the bliss of men is one bliss of those who have won the fathers' world. Now a hundredfold the bliss of those who have won the fathers' world is one bliss in the Gandharva-world. A hundredfold the bliss in the Gandharva-world is one bliss of the gods who gain their divinity by meritorious works. A hundredfold the bliss of the gods by works is one bliss of the gods by birth and of him who is learned in the Vedas, who is without crookedness, and who is free from desire. A hundredfold the bliss of the gods by birth is one

bliss in the Prajapati-world and of him who is learned in the Vedas, who is without crookedness, and who is free from desire. A hundred-fold the bliss in the Prajapati-world is one bliss in the Brahma-world and of him who is learned in the Vedas, who is without crookedness, and who is free from desire. This truly is the highest world. This is the Brahma-world, O king."–Thus spake Yajnavalkya.

[Janaka said:] "I will give you, noble Sir, a thousand [cows]. Speak further than this, for my release."

Then Yajnavalkya feared, thinking: "This intelligent king has driven me out of every corner."

34. [He said:] "Having had enjoyment in this state of sleep, having traveled around and seen good and bad, he hastens again, according to the entrance and place of origin, back to the state of waking.

35. As a heavily loaded cart goes creaking, just so this bodily self, mounted by the intelligent Self, goes groaning when one is breathing one's last.

36. When he comes to weakness—whether he come to weakness through old age or through disease—this person frees himself from these limbs just as a mango, or a fig, or a berry releases itself from its bond; and he hastens again, according to the entrance and place of origin, back to life.

37. As noblemen, policemen, chariot-drivers, village-heads wait with food, drink, and lodgings for a king who is coming, and cry: 'Here he comes! Here he comes!' so indeed do all things wait for him who has this knowledge and cry: 'Here is Brahma coming! Here is Brahma coming!'

38. As noblemen, policemen, chariot-drivers, village-heads gather around a king who is about to depart, just so do all the breaths gather around the soul at the end, when one is breathing one's last.

4

1. When this self comes to weakness and to confusedness of mind, as it were, then the breaths gather around him. He takes to himself those particles of energy and descends into the heart. When the person in the eye turns away, back [to the sun], then one becomes non-knowing of forms.

2. 'He is becoming one,' they say; 'he does not see.' 'He is becoming one,' they say; 'he does not smell.' 'He is becoming one,' they say; 'he does not taste.' 'He is becoming one,' they say; 'he does not speak.' 'He is becoming one,' they say; 'he does not hear.' 'He is becoming one,' they say; 'he does not think.' 'He is becoming one,' they say; 'he does not touch.' 'He is becoming one,' they say; 'he does not know.' The point of his heart becomes lighted up. By that light the self departs, either by the eye, or by the head, or by other bodily parts. After him, as he goes out, the life goes out. After the life, as it goes out, all the breaths go out. He becomes one with intelligence. What has intelligence departs with him. His knowledge and his works and his former intelligence [i.e., instinct] lay hold of him.

3. Now as a caterpillar, when it has come to the end of a blade of grass, in taking the next step draws itself together towards it, just so this soul in taking the next step strikes down this body, dispels its ignorance and draws itself together [for making the transition].

4. As a goldsmith, taking a piece of gold, reduces it to another newer and more beautiful form, just so this soul, striking down this body and dispelling its ignorance, makes for itself another newer and more beautiful form like that either of the fathers, or of the Gandharvas, or of the gods, or of Prajapati, or of Brahma, or of other beings.

5. Verily, this soul is Brahma, made of knowledge, of mind, of breath, of seeing, of hearing, of earth, of water, of wind, of space, of energy and of non-energy, of desire and of non-desire, of anger and of non-anger, of virtuousness and of non-virtuousness. It is made of everything. This is what is meant by the saying 'made of this, made of that.'

According as one acts, according as one conducts himself, so does he become. The doer of good becomes good. The doer of evil becomes evil. One becomes virtuous by virtuous action, bad by bad action.

But people say: 'A person is made [not of acts, but] of desires only.' [In reply to this I say:] As is his desire, such is his resolve; as is his resolve, such the action he performs; what action he performs, that he procures for himself.

6. On this point there is this verse:
> Where one's mind is attached—the inner self
> Goes thereto with action, being attached to it alone.
> Obtaining the end of his action,
> Whatever he does in this world,

He comes again from that world
To this world of action.

—So the man who desires.

Now the man who does not desire—He who is without desire, who is freed from desire, whose desire is satisfied, whose desire is the Soul—his breaths do not depart. Being very Brahma, he goes to Brahma.

7. On this point there is this verse:
When are liberated all
The desires that lodge in one's heart,
Then a mortal becomes immortal!
Therein he reaches Brahma!

As the slough of a snake lies on an ant-hill, dead, cast off, even so lies this body. But this incorporeal, immortal Life is Brahma indeed, is light indeed."

"I will give you, noble Sir, a thousand [cows]," said Janaka, [king] of Videha.

8. [Yajnavalkya continued:] "On this point there are these verses:
The ancient narrow path that stretches far away
Has been touched by me, has been found by me.
By it the wise, the knowers of Brahma, go up
Hence to the heavenly world, released.

9. On it, they say, is white and blue
And yellow and green and red.
That was the path by Brahma found;

By it goes the knower of Brahma, the doer of right, and every shining one.

10. Into blind darkness enter they
That worship ignorance;
Into darkness greater than that, as it were, they
That delight in knowledge.

11. Joyless are those worlds called,
Covered with blind darkness.
To them after death go those
People that have not knowledge, that are not awakened.

12. If a person knew the Soul,
    With the thought "I am he!"
    With what desire, for love of what
    Would he cling unto the body?

13. He who has found and has awakened to the Soul
    That has entered this conglomerate abode—
    He is the maker of everything, for he is the creator of all;
    The world is his: indeed, he is the world itself.

14. Verily, while we are here we may know this.
    If you have known it not, great is the destruction.
    Those who know this become immortal,
    But others go only to sorrow.

15. If one perceives Him
    As the Soul, as God, clearly,
    As the Lord of what has been and of what is to be—
    One does not shrink away from Him.

16. That before which the year
    Revolves with its days—
    That the gods revere as the light of lights,
    As life immortal.

17. On whom the five peoples
    And space are established—
    Him alone I, the knowing, I, the immortal,
    Believe to be the Soul, the immortal Brahma.

18. They who know the breathing of the breath
    The seeing of the eye, the hearing of the ear,
    (The food of food), the thinking of the mind—
    They have recognized the ancient, primeval Brahma.

19. By the mind alone is It to be perceived
    There is on earth no diversity.
    He gets death after death,
    Who perceives here seeming diversity.

20. As a unity only is It to be looked upon—
    This indemonstrable, enduring Being,
    Spotless, beyond space,
    The unborn Soul, great, enduring.

21. By knowing Him only, a wise
Brahman should get for himself intelligence;
He should not meditate upon many words,
For that is a weariness of speech.

22. Verily, he is the great, unborn Soul, who is this [person] consisting of knowledge among the senses. In the space within the heart lies the ruler of all, the lord of all, the king of all. He does not become greater by good action nor inferior by bad action. He is the lord of all, the overlord of beings, the protector of beings. He is the separating dam for keeping these worlds apart.

Such a one the Brahmans desire to know by repetition of the Vedas, by sacrifices, by offerings, by penance, by fasting. On knowing him, in truth, one becomes an ascetic. Desiring him only as their home, mendicants wander forth.

Verily, because they know this, the ancients desired not offspring, saying: 'What shall we do with offspring, we whose is this Soul, this world?' They, verily, rising above the desire for sons and the desire for wealth and the desire for worlds, lived the life of a mendicant. For the desire for sons is the desire for wealth, and the desire for wealth is the desire for worlds; for both these are desires.

That Soul is not this, it is not that. It is unseizable, for it cannot be seized. It is indestructible, for it cannot be destroyed. It is unattached, for it does not attach itself. It is unbound. It does not tremble. It is not injured.

Him [who knows this] these two do not overcome—neither the thought 'Hence I did wrong,' nor the thought 'Hence I did right.' Verily, he overcomes them both. What he has done and what he has not done do not affect him.

23. This very [doctrine] has been declared in the verse:
This eternal greatness of a Brahman
Is not increased by deeds, nor diminished.
One should be familiar with it. By knowing it,
One is not stained by evil action.

Therefore, having this knowledge, having become calm, subdued, quiet, patiently enduring, and collected, one sees the Soul just in the soul. One sees everything as the Soul. Evil does not overcome him; he overcomes all evil. Evil does not burn him; he burns all evil. Free from evil, free from impurity, free from doubt, he becomes a Brahman.

This is the Brahma-world, O king," said Yajnavalkya.

[Janaka said:] "I will give you; noble Sir, the Videhas and myself also to be your slave."

24. [Yajnavalkya continued:] "This is that great, unborn Soul, who eats the food [which people eat], the giver of good. He finds good who knows this.

25. Verily, that great, unborn Soul, undecaying, undying, immortal, fearless, is Brahma. Verily, Brahma is fearless. He who knows this becomes the fearless Brahma."

5

1. Now then, Yajnavalkya had two wives, Maitreyi and Katyayani. Of the two, Maitreyi was a discourser on sacred knowledge; Katyayani had just a woman's knowledge in that matter.

Now then, Yajnavalkya was about to commence another mode of life.

2. "Maitreyi!" said Yajnavalkya, "lo, verily, I am about to wander forth from this state. Behold! Let me make a final settlement for you and that Katyayani."

3. Then spake Maitreyi: "If now, Sir, this whole earth filled with wealth were mine, would I now thereby be immortal?"

"No, no!" said Yajnavalkya. "As the life of the rich, even so would your life be. Of immortality, however, there is no hope through wealth."

4. Then spake Maitreyi: "What should I do with that through which I may not be immortal? What you know, Sir—that, indeed, explain to me."

5. Then spake Yajnavalkya: "Though, verily, you, my lady, were dear to us, you have increased your dearness. Behold, then, lady, I will explain it to you. But, while I am expounding, do you seek to ponder thereon."

6. Then spake he: "Lo, verily, not for love of the husband is a husband dear, but for love of the Soul a husband is dear.

Lo, verily, not for love of the wife is a wife dear, but for love of the Soul a wife is dear.

Lo, verily, not for love of the sons are sons dear, but for love of the Soul sons are dear.

Lo, verily, not for love of the wealth is wealth dear, but for love of the Soul wealth is dear.

Lo, verily, not for love of the cattle are cattle dear, but for love of the Soul cattle are dear.

Lo, verily, not for love of Brahmanhood is Brahmanhood dear, but for love of the Soul Brahmanhood is dear.

Lo, verily, not for love of Kshatrahood is Kshatrahood dear, but for love of the Soul Kshatrahood is dear.

Lo, verily, not for love of the worlds are the worlds dear, but for love of the Soul the worlds are dear.

Lo, verily, not for love of the gods are the gods dear, but for love of the Soul the gods are dear.

Lo, verily, not for love of the Vedas are the Vedas dear, but for love of the Soul the Vedas are dear.

Lo, verily, not for love of the beings are beings dear, but for love of the Soul beings are dear.

Lo, verily, not for love of all is all dear, but for love of the Soul all is dear.

Lo, verily, it is the Soul that should be seen, that should be hearkened to, that should be thought on, that should be pondered on, O Maitreyi.

Lo, verily, in the Soul's being seen, hearkened to, thought on, understood, this world-all is known.

7. Brahmanhood deserts him who knows Brahmanhood in aught else than the Soul. Kshatrahood deserts him who knows Kshatrahood in aught else than the Soul. The worlds desert him who knows the worlds in aught else than the Soul. The gods desert him who knows the gods in aught else than the Soul. The Vedas desert him who knows the Vedas in aught else than the Soul. Beings desert him who knows beings in aught else than the Soul. Everything deserts him who knows everything in aught else than the Soul. This Brahmanhood, this Kshatrahood, these worlds, these gods, these Vedas, all these beings, everything here is what this Soul is.

8. It is—as, when a drum is being beaten, one would not be able to grasp the external sounds, but by grasping the drum or the beater of the drum the sound is grasped.

9. It is—as, when a conch-shell is being blown, one would not be able to grasp the external sounds, but by grasping the conch-shell or the blower of the conch-shell the sound is grasped.

10. It is—as, when a lute is being played, one would not be able to

grasp the external sounds, but by grasping the lute or the player of the lute the sound is grasped.

11. It is—as, from a fire laid with damp fuel, clouds of smoke separately issue forth, so, lo, verily, from this great Being has been breathed forth that which is Rig-Veda, Yajur-Veda, Sama-Veda, [Hymns] of the Atharvans and Angirases, Legend, Ancient Lore, Sciences, Mystic Doctrines, Verses, Aphorisms, Explanations, Commentaries, sacrifice, oblation, food, drink, this world and the other, and all beings. From it, indeed, have all these been breathed forth.

12. It is—as the uniting-place of all waters is the sea, likewise the uniting-place of all touches is the skin; likewise the uniting-place of all tastes is the tongue; likewise the uniting-place of all odors is the nose; likewise the uniting-place of all forms is the eye; likewise the uniting-place of all sounds is the ear; likewise the uniting-place of all intentions is the mind; likewise the uniting-place of all knowledges is the heart; likewise the uniting-place of all actions is the hands; likewise the uniting-place of all pleasures is the generative organ; likewise the uniting-place of all evacuations is the anus; likewise the uniting-place of all journeys is the feet; likewise the uniting-place of all Vedas is speech.

13. It is—as is a mass of salt, without inside, without outside, entirely a mass of taste, even so, verily, is this Soul, without inside, without outside, entirely a mass of knowledge.

Arising out of these elements, into them also one vanishes away. After death there is no consciousness. Thus, lo, say I." Thus spake Yajnavalkya.

14. Then said Maitreyi: "Herein, indeed, you have caused me, Sir, to arrive at the extreme of bewilderment. Verily, I understand It [i.e., this Atman] not."

Then said he: "Lo, verily, I speak not bewilderment. Imperishable, lo, verily, is this Soul, and of indestructible quality.

15. For where there is a duality, as it were, there one sees another; there one smells another; there one tastes another; there one speaks to another; there one hears another; there one thinks of another; there one touches another; there one understands another. But where everything has become just one's own self, then whereby and whom would one see? then whereby and whom would one smell? then whereby and whom would one taste? then whereby and to whom would one speak? then whereby and whom would one hear? then whereby and of whom would one think? then whereby and whom would one touch?

then whereby and whom would one understand? whereby would one understand him by means of whom one understands this All? That Soul is not this, it is not that. It is unseizable, for it can not be seized; indestructible, for it can not be destroyed; unattached, for it does not attach itself; is unbound, does not tremble, is not injured.

Lo, whereby would one understand the understander?

Thus you have the instruction told to you, Maitreyi. Such, lo, indeed, is immortality."

After speaking thus, Yajnavalkya departed.

6

1. Now the Line of Tradition—
   (We [received this teaching] from Pautimashya),
   Pautimashya from Gaupavana,
   Gaupavana from Pautimashya,
   Pautimashya from Gaupavana,
   Gaupavana from Kausika,
   Kausika from Kaundinya,
   Kaundinya from Sandilya,
   Sandilya from Kausika and Gautama,
   Gautama [2] from Agnivesya,
   Agnivesya from Gargya,
   Gargya from Gargya,
   Gargya from Gautama,
   Gautama from Saitava,
   Saitava from Parasaryayana,
   Parasaryayana from Gargyayana,
   Gargyayana from Uddalakayana,
   Uddalakayana from Jabalayana,
   Jabalayana from Madhyamdinayana,
   Madhyamdinayana from Saukarayana,
   Saukarayana from Kashayana,
   Kashayana from Sayakayana,
   Sayakayana from Kausikayani,
   Kausikayani [3] from Ghritakausika,
   Ghritakausika from Parasaryayana,
   Parasaryayana from Parasarya,

Parasarya from Jatukarnya,
Jatukarnya from Asurayana and Yaska,
Asurayana from Traivani,
Traivani from Aupajandhani,
Aupajandhani from Asuri,
Asuri from Bharadvaja,
Bharadvaja from Atreya,
Atreya from Manti,
Manti from Gautama,
Gautama from Gautama,
Gautama from Vatsya,
Vatsya from Sandilya,
Sandilya from Kaisorya Kapya,
Kaisorya Kapya from Kumaraharita,
Kumaraharita from Galava,
Galava from Vidarbhikaundinya,
Vidarbhikaundinya from Vatsanapat Babhrava,
Vatsanapat Babhrava from Pathin Saubhara,
Pathin Saubhara from Ayasya Angirasa,
Ayasya Angirasa from Abhuti Tvashtra,
Abhuti Tvashtra from Visvarupa Tvashtra,
Visvarupa Tvashtra from the two Asvins,
the two Asvins from Dadhyanc Atharvana,
Dadhyanc Atharvana from Atharvan Daiva,
Atharvan Daiva from Mrityu Pradhvamsana,
Mrityu Pradhvamsana from Pradhvamsana,
Pradhvamsana from Eka Rishi,
Eka Rishi from Vipracitti,
Vipracitti from Vyashti,
Vyashti from Sanaru,
Sanaru from Sanatana,
Sanatana from Sanaga,
Sanaga from Parameshthin,
Parameshthin from Brahma.
Brahma is the Self-existent. Adoration to Brahma!

5

1

Om!

The yon is fulness; fulness, this.
From fulness, fulness doth proceed.
Withdrawing fulness's fulness off,
E'en fulness then itself remains.

Om!

"Brahma is the ether—the ether primeval, the ether that blows."
Thus, verily, was the son of Kauravyayani wont to say.

This is the knowledge the Brahmans know. Thereby I know what is to be known.

2

1. The threefold offspring of Prajapati—gods, men, and devils—dwelt with their father Prajapati as students of sacred knowledge.

Having lived the life of a student of sacred knowledge, the gods said: "Speak to us, Sir." To them then he spoke this syllable, "*Da.*" "Did you understand?" "We did understand," said they. "You said to us, 'Restrain yourselves.'" "Yes!" said he. "You did understand."

2. So then the men said to him: "Speak to us, Sir." To them then he spoke this syllable, "*Da.*" "Did you understand?" "We did understand," said they. "You said to us, 'Give.'" "Yes!" said he. "You did understand."

3. So then the devils said to him: "Speak to us, Sir." To them then he spoke this syllable, "*Da.*" "Did you understand?" "We did understand," said they. "You said to us, 'Be compassionate.'" "Yes!" said he. "You did understand."

This same thing does the divine voice here, thunder, repeat: *Da!*

Da! *Da*! that is, restrain yourselves, give, be compassionate. One should practise this same triad: self-restraint, giving, compassion.

3

The heart is the same as Prajapati (Lord of Creation). It is Brahma. It is all.

It is trisyllabic—*hr-da-yam*.

hr is one syllable. Both his own people and others bring offerings unto him who knows this.

da is one syllable. Both his own people and others give unto him who knows this.

yam is one syllable. To the heavenly world goes he who knows this.

4

This, verily, is That. This, indeed, was That, even the Real. He who knows that wonderful being as the first-born—namely, that Brahma is the Real—conquers these worlds. Would he be conquered who knows thus that great spirit as the first-born—namely, that Brahma is the Real? [No!] for indeed, Brahma is the Real.

5

1. In the beginning this world was just Water. That Water emitted the Real—Brahma [being] the Real—; Brahma, Prajapati; Prajapati, the gods. Those gods reverenced the Real. That is trisyllabic: *sa-ti-yam*—*sa* is one syllable, *ti* is one syllable, *yam* is one syllable. The first and last syllables are truth. In the middle is falsehood. This falsehood is embraced on both sides by truth; it partakes of the nature of truth itself. Falsehood does not injure him who knows this.

2. Yonder sun is the same as that Real. The Person who is there in that orb and the Person who is here in the right eye—these two depend the one upon the other. Through his rays that one depends

upon this one; through his vital breaths this one upon that. When one is about to decease, he sees that orb quite clear [i.e., free from rays]; those rays come to him no more.

3. The head of the person who is there in that orb is *Bhur*—there is one head, this is one syllable. *Bhuvar* is the arms—there are two arms, these are two syllables. *Svar* is the feet—there are two feet, these are two syllables. The mystic name thereof is "Day." He slays evil, he leaves it behind who knows this.

4. The head of the person who is here in the right eye is *Bhur*—there is one head, this is one syllable. *Bhuvar* is the arms—there are two arms, these are two syllables. *Svar* is the feet—there are two feet, these are two syllables. The mystic name thereof is "I." He slays evil, he leaves it behind who knows this.

6

This person here in the heart is made of mind, is of the nature of light, is like a little grain of rice, is a grain of barley. This very one is ruler of everything, is lord of everything, governs this whole universe, whatsoever there is.

7

Brahma is lightning, they say, because of unloosing. Lightning unlooses him from evil who knows this, that Brahma is lightning—for Brahma is indeed lightning.

8

One should reverence Speech as a milch-cow. She has four udders: the *Svaha* (Invocation), the *Vashat* (Presentation), the *Hanta* (Salutation), the *Svadha* (Benediction). The gods subsist upon her two udders, the *Svaha* and the *Vashat*; men, upon the *Hanta*; the fathers upon the *Svadha*. The breath is her bull; the mind, her calf.

9

This is the universal fire which is here within a person, by means of which the food that is eaten is cooked. It is the noise thereof that one hears on covering the ears thus. When one is about to depart, one hears not this sound.

10

Verily, when a person departs from this world he goes to the wind. It opens out there for him like the hole of a chariot-wheel. Through it he mounts higher.

He goes to the sun. It opens out there for him like the hole of a drum. Through it he mounts higher.

He goes to the moon. It opens out for him there like the hole of a kettle-drum. Through it he mounts higher.

He goes to the world that is without heat, without cold. Therein he dwells eternal years.

11

Verily, that is the supreme austerity which a sick man suffers. The supreme world, assuredly, he wins who knows this.

Verily, that is the supreme austerity when they carry a dead man into the wilderness. The supreme world, assuredly, he wins who knows this.

Verily, that is the supreme austerity when they lay a dead man on the fire. The supreme world, assuredly, he wins who knows this.

12

"Brahma is food"—thus some say. This is not so. Verily, food becomes putrid without life.

"Brahma is life"—thus some say. This is not so. Verily, life dries up without food. Rather, only by entering into a unity do these deities reach the highest state.

Now it was in this connection that Pratrida said to his father: "What good, pray, could I do to one who knows this? What evil could I do to him?"

He then said, with [a wave of] his hand: "No, Pratrida. Who reaches the highest state [merely] by entering into a unity with these two?"

And he also spoke to him thus: "*vi*"—verily, *vi* is food, for all beings here enter into food; and "*ram*"—verily, *ram* is life, for all beings here delight in life. Verily, indeed, all beings enter into him, all beings delight in him who knows this.

13

1. The *Uktha*: Verily, the Uktha is life, for it is life that causes everything here to rise up. From him there rises up an Uktha-knowing son, he wins co-union and co-status with the Uktha, who knows this.

2. The *Yajus*: Verily the Yajus is life, for in life are all beings here united. United, indeed, are all beings for his supremacy he wins co-union and co-status with the Yajus, who knows this.

3. The *Saman*: Verily, the Saman is life for in life are all beings here combined. Combined, indeed, are all beings here serving him for his supremacy, he wins co-union and co-status with the Saman, who knows this.

4. The *Kshatra*: Verily, rule is life, for verily rule is life. Life Protects one from hurting. He attains a rule that needs no protection, he wins co-union and co-status with the Kshatra, who knows this.

14

1. *bhu-mir* (earth), *au-ta-ri-ksa* (interspace), *dy-aur* (sky)—eight syllables. Of eight syllables, verily, is one line of the Gayatri. And that [series], indeed, is that [line] of it. As much as there is in the three worlds, so much indeed does he win who knows thus that line of it.

2. *r-cas* (verses), *ya-jum-si* (sacrificial formulas), *sa-ma-ni* (chants)—eight syllables. Of eight syllables, verily, is one line of the Gayatri. And

that [series], indeed, is that [line] of it. As much as is this threefold knowledge, so much indeed does he win who knows thus that line of it.

3. *pra-na* (in-breath), *ap-a-na* (out-breath), *vy-a-na* (diffused breath)— eight syllables. Of eight syllables, verily, is one line of the Gayatri. And that [series], indeed, is that [line] of it. As much breathing as there is here, so much indeed does he win who knows thus that line of it.

That is its fourth, the sightly foot, namely the one above-the-darksome who glows yonder. This fourth is the same as the Turiya. It is called the "sightly foot," because it has come into sight, as it were. And he is called "above-the-darksome," because he glows yonder far above everything darksome. Thus he glows with luster and glory who knows thus that foot of it.

4. This Gayatri is based upon that fourth, sightly foot, the one above-the-darksome. That is based upon truth. Verily, truth is sight, for verily, truth is sight. Therefore if now two should come disputing, saying "I have seen!" "I have heard!" we should trust the one who would say "I have seen."

Verily, that truth is based on strength. Verily, strength is life. It is based on life. Therefore they say, "Strength is more powerful than truth."

Thus is that Gayatri based with regard to the Self. It protects the house-servants. Verily, the house-servants are the vital breaths. So it protects the vital breaths. Because it protects the house-servants, therefore it is called Gayatri. That Savitri stanza which one repeats is just this. For whomever one repeats it, it protects his vital breaths.

5. Some recite this Savitri stanza as Anushtubh meter, saying: "The speech is Anushtubh meter. We recite the speech accordingly." One should not so do. One should recite the Savitri stanza as Gayatri meter. Verily, even if one who knows thus receives very much, that is not at all in comparison with one single line of the Gayatri.

6. If one should receive these three worlds full, he would receive that first line of it [i.e., the Gayatri]. If one should receive as much as is this threefold knowledge, he would receive that second line of it. If one should receive as much as there is breathing here, he would receive that third line of it. But that fourth, sightly foot, the one above-the-darksome, who glows yonder, is not obtainable by any one whatsoever. Whence, pray, would one receive so much!

7. The veneration of it: "O Gayatri, you are one-footed, two-footed, three-footed, four-footed. You are without a foot, because you do not

go afoot. Adoration to your fourth, sightly foot, the one above-the-darksome!—Let not so-and-so obtain such-and-such!"—namely, the one whom one hates. Or, "So-and-so—let not his wish prosper!"—Indeed, that wish is not prospered for him in regard to whom one venerates thus. Or, "Let me obtain such-and-such!"

8. On this point, verily, Janaka, [king] of Videha, spoke as follows to Budila Asvatarasvi: "Ho! Now if you spoke of yourself thus as a knower of the Gayatri, how then have you come to be an elephant and are carrying?"

"Because, great king, I did not know its mouth," said he.

Its mouth is fire. Verily, indeed, even if they lay very much on a fire, it burns it all. Even so one who knows this, although he commits very much evil, consumes it all and becomes clean and pure, ageless and immortal.

15

With a golden vessel
The Real's face is covered o'er.
That do thou, O Pushan, uncover
For one whose law is the Real to see.

O Nourisher, the sole Seer, O Controller, O Sun, offspring of Praja-pati, spread forth thy rays! Gather thy brilliance! What is thy fairest form—that of thee I see. He who is yonder, yonder Person—I myself am he!

[My] breath to the immortal wind! This body then ends in ashes! Om!

O Purpose, remember! The deed remember!
O Purpose, remember! The deed remember!

O Agni, by a goodly path to prosperity lead us,
Thou god who knowest all the ways!
Keep far from us crooked-going sin!
Most ample expression of adoration to thee would we render.

6

1

1. Om! Verily, he who knows the chiefest and best, becomes the chiefest and best of his own [people].

Breath, verily, is chiefest and best. He who knows this becomes the chiefest and best of his own [people] and even of those of whom he wishes so to become.

2. Verily, he who knows the most excellent becomes the most excellent of his own [people].

Speech verily is the most excellent. He who knows this becomes the most excellent of his own [people] and even of those of whom he wishes so to become.

3. Verily, he who knows the firm basis has a firm basis on even ground, has a firm basis on rough ground.

The Eye, verily, is a firm basis, for with the eye both on even ground and on rough ground one has a firm basis. He has a firm basis on even ground, he has a firm basis on rough ground, who knows this.

4. Verily, he who knows attainment—for him, indeed, is attained what wish he wishes.

The Ear, verily, is attainment, for in the ear all these Vedas are attained. The wish that he wishes is attained for him who knows this.

5. Verily, he who knows the abode becomes the abode of his own [people], an abode of folk.

The Mind, verily, is an abode. He becomes an abode of his own [people], an abode of folk, who knows this.

6. Verily, he who knows procreation procreates himself with progeny and cattle.

Semen, verily, is procreation. He procreates himself with progeny and cattle, who knows this.

7. These vital Breaths, disputing among themselves on self-

superiority, went to Brahma. Then they said: "Which of us is the most excellent?"

Then he said: "The one of you after whose going off this body is thought to be worse off, he is the most excellent of you."

8. Speech went off. Having remained away a year, it came back and said: "How have you been able to live without me?"

They said: "As the dumb, not speaking with speech, but breathing with breath, seeing with the eye, hearing with the ear, knowing with the mind, procreating with semen. Thus have we lived." Speech entered in.

9. The Eye went off. Having remained away a year, it came back and said: "How have you been able to live without me?"

They said: "As the blind, not seeing with the eye, but breathing with breath, speaking with speech, hearing with the ear, knowing with the mind, procreating with semen. Thus have we lived." The eye entered in.

10. The Ear went off. Having remained away a year, it came back and said: "How have you been able to live without me?"

They said: "As the deaf, not hearing with the ear, but breathing with breath, speaking with speech, seeing with the eye, knowing with the mind, procreating with semen. Thus have we lived." The ear entered in.

11. The Mind went off. Having remained away a year, it came back and said: "How have you been able to live without me?"

They said: "As the stupid, not knowing with the mind, but breathing with breath, speaking with speech, seeing with the eye, hearing with the ear, procreating with semen. Thus have we lived." The mind entered in.

12. The Semen went off. Having remained away a year, it came back and said: "How have you been able to live without me?"

They said: "As the emasculated, not procreating with semen, but breathing with breath, speaking with speech, seeing with the eye, hearing with the ear, knowing with the mind. Thus have we lived." The semen entered in.

13. Then Breath was about to go off. As a large fine horse of the Indus-land might pull up the pegs of his foot-tethers together, thus indeed did it pull up those vital breaths together. They said: "Sir, go not off! Verily, we shall not be able to live without you!"

"If such I am, make me an offering."

"So be it."

14. Speech said: "Verily, wherein I am the most excellent, therein are you the most excellent."

"Verily, wherein I am a firm basis, therein are you a firm basis," said the eye.

"Verily, wherein I am attainment, therein are you attainment," said the ear.

"Verily, wherein I am an abode, therein are you an abode," said the mind.

"Verily, wherein I am procreation, therein are you procreation," said the semen.

"If such I am, what is my food? what is my dwelling?"

"Whatever there is here, even to dogs, worms, crawling and flying insects—that is your food. Water is your dwelling."

Verily, what is not food is not eaten; what is not food is not taken by him who thus knows that [i.e., water] as the food of breath. Those who know this, who are versed in sacred learning, when they are about to eat, take a sip; after they have eaten, they take a sip. So, indeed, they think they make that breath not naked.

2

1. Verily, Svetaketu Aruneya went up to an assembly of Pancalas. He went up to Pravahana Jaibali while the latter was having himself waited upon. He, looking up, said unto him, "Young man!"

"Sir!" he replied.

"Have you been instructed by your father?"

"Yes," said he.

2. "Know you how people here, on deceasing, separate in different directions?"

"No," said he.

"Know you how they come back again to this world?"

"No," said he.

"Know you why yonder world is not filled up with the many who continually thus go hence?"

"No," said he.

"Know you in which oblation that is offered the water becomes the voice of a person, rises up, and speaks?"

"No," said he.

"Know you the access of the path leading to the gods, or of the one leading to the fathers? by doing what, people go to the path of the gods or of the fathers? for we have heard the word of the seer:

Two paths, I've heard—the one that leads to fathers,
And one that leads to gods—belong to mortals.
By these two, every moving thing here travels,
That is between the Father and the Mother."

"Not a single one of them do I know," said he.

3. Then he addressed him with an invitation to remain. Not respecting the invitation to remain, the boy ran off. He went to his father. He said to him: "Verily, aforetime you have spoken of me, Sir, as having been instructed!"

"How now, wise one?"

"Five questions a fellow of the princely class has asked me. Not a single one of them do I know."

"What are they?"

"These"—and he repeated the topics.

4. He said: "You should know me, my dear, as such, that whatsoever I myself know, I have told all to you. But, come! Let us go there and take up studentship."

"Go yourself, Sir."

So Gautama went forth to where [the place] of Pravahana Jaibali was.

He brought him a seat, and had water brought; so he made him a respectful welcome. Then he said to him: "A boon we offer to the honorable Gautama!"

5. Then he said: "The boon acceptable to me is this:Pray tell me the word which you spoke in the presence of the young man."

6. Then he said: "Verily, Gautama, that is among divine boons. Mention [one] of human boons."

7. Then he said: "It is well known that I have a full share of gold, of cows and horses, of female slaves, of rugs, of apparel. Be not ungenerous toward me, Sir, in regard to that which is the abundant, the infinite, the unlimited."

"Then, verily, O Gautama, you should seek in the usual manner."

"I come to you, Sir, as a pupil!"—with [this] word, verily, indeed, men aforetime came as pupils—So with the acknowledgment of coming as a pupil he remained.

8. Then he said: "As truly as this knowledge has never heretofore

dwelt with any Brahman whatsoever, so truly may not you and your grandfathers injure us. But I will tell it to you, for who is able to refuse you when you speak thus!" He continued:

9. "Yonder world, verily, is a sacrificial fire, O Gautama. The sun, in truth, is its fuel; the light-rays, the smoke; the day, the flame; the quarters of heaven, the coals; the intermediate quarters, the sparks. In this fire the gods offer faith. From this oblation King Soma arises.

10. A rain-cloud, verily, is a sacrificial fire, O Gautama. The year, in truth, is its fuel; the thunder-clouds, the smoke; the lightning, the flame; the thunder-bolts, the coals; the hail-stones, the sparks. In this fire the gods offer King Soma. From this oblation rain arises.

11. This world, verily, is a sacrificial fire, O Gautama. The earth, in truth, is its fuel; fire, the smoke; night, the flame; the moon, the coals; the stars, the sparks. In this fire the gods offer rain. From this oblation food arises.

12. Man, verily, is a sacrificial fire, O Gautama. The open mouth, verily, is its fuel; breath, the smoke; speech, the flame; the eye, the coals; the ear, the sparks. In this fire the gods offer food. From this oblation semen arises.

13. Woman, verily, is a sacrificial fire, O Gautama. The sexual organ, in truth, is its fuel; the hairs, the smoke; the vulva, the flame; when one inserts, the coals; the feelings of pleasure, the sparks. In this oblation the gods offer semen. From this oblation a person arises.

He lives as long as he lives. Then when he dies, [14] then they carry him to the fire. His fire, in truth, becomes the fire; fuel, the fuel; smoke, the smoke; flame, the flame; coals, the coals; sparks, the sparks. In this fire the gods offer a person. From this oblation the man arises, having the color of light.

15. Those who know this, and those too who in the forest truly worship faith, pass into the flame [of the cremation-fire]; from the flame, into the day; from the day, into the half month of the waxing moon; from the half month of the waxing moon, into the six months during which the sun moves northward; from these months, into the world of the gods; from the world of the gods, into the sun; from the sun, into the lightning-fire. A Person consisting of mind goes to those regions of lightning and conducts them to the Brahma-worlds. In those Brahma-worlds they dwell for long extents. Of these there is no return.

16. But they who by sacrificial offering, charity, and austerity con-quer the worlds, pass into the smoke [of the cremation-fire]; from the

smoke, into the night; from the night, into the half month of the waning moon; from the half month of the waning moon, into the six months during which the sun moves southward; from those months, into the world of the fathers; from the world of the fathers, into the moon. Reaching the moon, they become food. There the gods—as they say to King Soma, 'Increase! Decrease!'—even so feed upon them there. When that passes away for them, then they pass forth into this space; from space, into air; from air, into rain; from rain, into the earth. On reaching the earth they become food. Again they are offered in the fire of man. Thence they are born in the fire of woman. Rising up into the world, they cycle round again thus.

But those who know not these two ways, become crawling and flying insects and whatever there is here that bites."

3

1. Whoever may wish, "I would attain something great!"—in the northern course of the sun, on an auspicious day of the half month of the waxing moon, having performed the Upasad ceremony for twelve days, having collected in a dish of the wood of the sacred fig-tree, or in a cup, all sorts of herbs including fruits, having swept around, having smeared around, having built up a fire, having strewn it around, having prepared the melted butter according to rule, having compounded the mixed potion under a male star, he makes an oblation, saying:

"However many gods in thee, All-knower,
Adversely slay desires of a person,
To them participation I here offer!
Let them, pleased, please me with all desires!
    Hail!

Whoever lays herself adverse,
And says, 'I the deposer am!'
To thee, O such appeasing one,
With stream of ghee I sacrifice.
    Hail!"

2. "To the chiefest, hail! To the best, hail!"—he makes an oblation in the fire and pours off the remainder in the mixed potion. A Hail to breath!

"To the most excellent, hail!"—he makes an oblation in the fire and pours off the remainder in the mixed potion. A Hail to speech!

"To the firm basis, hail!"—he makes an oblation in the fire and pours off the remainder in the mixed potion. A Hail to the eye!

"To attainment, hail!"—he makes an oblation in the fire and pours off the remainder in the mixed potion. A Hail to the ear!

"To the abode, hail!"—he makes an oblation in the fire and pours off the remainder in the mixed potion. A Hail to the mind!

"To procreation, hail!"—he makes an oblation in the fire and pours off the remainder in the mixed potion. A Hail to the semen!

Thus he makes an oblation in the fire and pours off the remainder in the mixed potion.

3. "To Agni (fire), hail!"—he makes an oblation in the fire and pours off the remainder in the mixed potion.

"To Soma, hail!"—he makes an oblation in the fire and pours off the remainder in the mixed potion.

"O Earth, hail!"—he makes an oblation in the fire and pours off the remainder in the mixed potion.

"O Atmosphere, hail!"—he makes an oblation in the fire and pours off the remainder in the mixed potion.

"O Sky, hail!"—he makes an oblation in the fire and pours off the remainder in the mixed potion.

"O Earth, Atmosphere and Sky, hail!"—he makes an oblation in the fire and pours off the remainder in the mixed potion.

"To the Brahmanhood, hail!"—he makes an oblation in the fire and pours off the remainder in the mixed potion.

"To the Kshatrahood, hail!"—he makes an oblation in the fire and pours off the remainder in the mixed potion.

"To the past, hail!"—he makes an oblation in the fire and pours off the remainder in the mixed potion.

"To the future, hail!"—he makes an oblation in the fire and pours off the remainder in the mixed potion.

"To everything, hail!"—he makes an oblation in the fire and pours off the remainder in the mixed potion.

"To the All, hail!"—he makes an oblation in the fire and pours off the remainder in the mixed potion.

"To Prajapati, hail!"—he makes an oblation in the fire and pours off the remainder in the mixed potion.

4. Then he touches it, saying: "Thou art the moving. Thou art

the glowing. Thou art the full. Thou art the steadfast. Thou art the sole resort. Thou art the sound *hin* that is made. Thou art the making of the sound *hin*. Thou art the Loud Chant. Thou art the chanting. Thou art that which is proclaimed. Thou art that which is proclaimed in the antiphone. Thou art the flaming in the moist. Thou art the pervading. Thou art surpassing. Thou art food. Thou art light. Thou art destruction. Thou art the despoiler."

5. Then he raises it, saying: "Thou thinkest. Think of thy greatness! He is, indeed, king and ruler and overlord. Let the king and ruler make me overlord."

6. Then he takes a sip, saying:
"On this desired [glory] of Savitri—
'Tis sweetness, winds for pious man—
'Tis sweetness, too, the streams pour forth.
Sweet-filled for us let be the herbs!
    To Earth, hail!

[On this desired] glory of the god let us meditate.
Sweet be the night and morning glows!
Sweet be the atmosphere of earth!
And sweet th' Heaven-father be to us!
    To Atmosphere, hail!

And may he himself inspire our thoughts!
The tree be full of sweet for us!
And let the sun be full of sweet!
Sweet-filled the cows become for us!
    To the Sky, hail!"

He repeats all the Savitri Hymn and all the "Sweet-verses," and says: "May I indeed become this world-all! O Earth and Atmosphere and Sky! Hail!"

Finally, having taken a sip, having washed his hands, he lies down behind the fire, head eastward. In the morning he worships the sun, and says: "Of the quarters of heaven thou art the one lotus-flower! May I of men become the one lotus-flower!"

Then he goes back the same way that he came, and, seated behind the fire, mutters the Line of Tradition.

7. This, indeed, did Uddalaka Aruni tell to his pupil Vajasaneya Yajnavalkya, and say: "Even if one should pour this on a dry stump, branches would be produced and leaves would spring forth."

8. This, indeed, did Vajasaneya Yajnavalkya tell to his pupil Madhuka Paingya, and say: "Even if one should pour this on a dry stump, branches would be produced and leaves would spring forth."

9. This, indeed, did Madhuka Paingya tell to his pupil Cula Bhagavitti, and say: "Even if one should pour this on a dry stump, branches would be produced and leaves would spring forth."

10. This, indeed, did Cula Bhagavitti tell to his pupil Janaki Ayasthuna, and say: "Even if one should pour this on a dry stump, branches would be produced and leaves would spring forth."

11. This, indeed, did Janaki Ayasthuna tell to his pupil Satyakama Jabala, and say: "Even if one should pour this on a dry stump, branches would be produced and leaves would spring forth."

12. This, indeed, did Satyakama Jabala tell to his pupils, and say: "Even if one should pour this on a dry stump, branches would be produced and leaves would spring forth."

One should not tell this to one who is not a son or to one who is not a pupil.

13. Fourfold is the wood of the sacred fig-tree [in the ceremony]: the spoon is of the wood of the sacred fig-tree; the cup is of the wood of the sacred fig-tree; the fuel is of the wood of the sacred fig-tree; the two mixing-sticks are of the wood of the sacred fig-tree. There are ten cultivated grains [used]: rice and barley, sesamum and beans, millet and panic, and wheat, and lentils, and pulse, and vetches. These, when they have been ground, one sprinkles with curdled milk, honey, and ghee; and one makes an oblation of melted butter.

4

1. Verily, of created things here earth is the essence; of earth, water; of water, plants; of plants, flowers; of flowers, fruits; of fruits, man; of man, semen.

2. Prajapati ("Lord of creatures") bethought himself: "Come, let me provide him a firm basis!" So he created woman. When he had created her, he revered her below—Therefore one should revere woman below—He stretched out for himself that stone which projects. With that he impregnated her.

3. Her lap is a sacrificial altar; her hairs, the sacrificial grass; her skin, the soma-press. The two lips of the vulva are the fire in the middle. Verily, indeed, as great as is the world of him who sacrifices with the Vajapeya ("Strength-libation") sacrifice, so great is the world of him who practises sexual intercourse, knowing this; he turns the good deeds of women to himself. But he who practises sexual intercourse without knowing this—women turn his good deeds unto themselves.

4. This, verily, indeed, it was that Uddalaka Aruni knew when he said:

This, verily, indeed, it was that Naka Maudgalya knew when he said:

This, verily, indeed, it was that Kumaraharita knew when he said: "Many mortal men, Brahmans by descent, go forth from this world, impotent and devoid of merit, namely those who practise sexual intercourse without knowing this."

[If] even this much semen is spilled, whether of one asleep or of one awake, [5] then he should touch it, or [without touching] repeat:

"What semen has of mine to earth been spilt now,
Whate'er to herb has flowed, whate'er to water—

This very semen I reclaim!
Again to me let vigor come!
Again, my strength; again, my glow!
Again the altars and the fire
Be found in their accustomed place!"

Having spoken thus, he should take it with ring-finger and thumb, and rub it on between his breasts or his eye-brows.

6. Now, if one should see himself in water, he should recite over it the formula: "In me be vigor, power, beauty, wealth, merit!"

This, verily, indeed, is loveliness among women: when [a woman] has removed the [soiled] clothes of her impurity. Therefore when she has removed the [soiled] clothes of her impurity and is beautiful, one should approach and invite her.

7. If she should not grant him his desire, he should bribe her. If she still does not grant him his desire, he should hit her with a stick or with his hand, and overcome her, saying: "With power, with glory I take away your glory!" Thus she becomes inglorious.

8. If she should yield to him, he says: "With power, with glory I give you glory!" Thus they two become glorious.

9. The woman whom one may desire with the thought, "May she enjoy love with me!"—after coming together with her, joining mouth with mouth, and stroking her lap, he should mutter:

"Thou that from every limb art come,
That from the heart art generate,
Thou art the essence of the limbs!
Distract this woman here in me,
As if by poisoned arrow pierced!"

10. Now, the woman whom one may desire with the thought, "May she not conceive offspring!"—after coming together with her and joining mouth with mouth, he should first inhale, then exhale, and say: "With power, with semen, I reclaim the semen from you!" Thus she comes to be without seed.

11. Now, the woman whom one may desire with the thought, "May she conceive!"—after coming together with her and joining mouth with mouth, he should first exhale, then inhale, and say: "With power, with semen, I deposit semen in you!" Thus she becomes pregnant.

12. Now, if one's wife have a paramour, and he hate him, let him put fire in an unannealed vessel, spread out a row of reed arrows in inverse order, and therein sacrifice in inverse order those reed arrows, their heads smeared with ghee, saying:

"You have made a libation in my fire! I take away your in-breath and out-breath—you, so-and-so!

You have made a libation in my fire! I take away your sons and cattle—you, so-and-so!

You have made a libation in my fire! I take away your sacrifices and meritorious deeds—you, so-and-so!

You have made a libation in my fire! I take away your hope and expectation—you, so-and-so!"

Verily, he whom a Brahman who knows this curses—he departs from this world impotent and devoid of merit. Therefore one should not desire sport with the spouse of a person learned in sacred lore who knows this, for indeed he who knows this becomes superior.

13. Now, when the monthly sickness comes upon any one's wife, for three days she should not drink from a metal cup, nor put on fresh clothes. Neither a low-caste man nor a low-caste woman should touch her. At the end of the three nights she should bathe and should have rice threshed.

14. In case one wishes, "That a white son be born to me! that he may be able to repeat a Veda! that he may attain the full length of life!"—they two should have rice cooked with milk and should eat it prepared with ghee. They two are likely to beget [him].

15. Now, in case one wishes, "That a tawny son with reddish-brown eyes be born to me! that he may be able to recite two Vedas! that he may attain the full length of life!"—they two should have rice cooked with sour milk and should eat it prepared with ghee. They two are likely to beget [him].

16. Now, in case one wishes, "That a swarthy son with red eyes be born to me! that he may be able to repeat three Vedas! that he may attain the full length of life!"—they two should have rice boiled with water and should eat it prepared with ghee. They two are likely to beget [him].

17. Now, in case one wishes, "That a learned daughter be born to me! that she may attain the full length of life!"—they two should have rice boiled with sesame and should eat it prepared with ghee. They two are likely to beget [her].

18. Now, in case one wishes, "That a son, learned, famed, a frequenter of council-assemblies, a speaker of discourse desired to be heard, be born to me! that he be able to repeat all the Vedas! that he attain the full length of life!"—they two should have rice boiled with meat and should eat it prepared with ghee. They two are likely to beget [him], with meat, either veal or beef.

19. Now, toward morning, having prepared melted butter in the manner of the Sthalipaka, he takes of the Sthalipaka and makes a libation, saying: "To Agni, hail! To Anumati, hail! To the god Savitri, whose is true procreation, hail!" Having made the libation, he takes and eats. Having eaten, he offers to the other [i.e., to her]. Having washed his hands, he fills a vessel with water and therewith sprinkles her thrice, saying:

"Arise from hence, Visvavasu!
Some other choicer maiden seek!
This wife together with her lord—"

20. Then he comes to her and says:
"This man am I; that woman, thou!
That woman, thou; this man am I!
I am the Saman; thou, the Rig!
I am the heaven; thou, the earth!

> Come, let us two together clasp!
> Together let us semen mix,
> A male, a son for to procure!"

21. Then he spreads apart her thighs, saying: "Spread yourselves apart, heaven and earth!" Coming together with her and joining mouth with mouth, he strokes her three times as the hair lies, saying:

> "Let Vishnu make the womb prepared!
> Let Tvashtri shape the various forms!
> Prajapati—let him pour in!
> Let Dhatri place the germ for thee!

> O Sinivali, give the germ;
> O give the germ, thou broad-tressed dame!
> Let the Twin Gods implace thy germ—
> The Asvins, crowned with lotus-wreaths!

22. With twain attrition-sticks of gold
> The Asvin Twins twirl forth a flame;
> 'Tis such a germ we beg for thee,
> In the tenth month to be brought forth.

> As earth contains the germ of Fire,
> As heaven is pregnant with the Storm,
> As of the points the Wind is germ,
> E'en so a germ I place in thee,
> 　　So-and-so!"

23. When she is about to bring forth, he sprinkles her with water, saying:

> "Like as the wind doth agitate
> A lotus-pond on every side,
> So also let thy fetus stir.
> Let it come with its chorion.

> This fold of Indra's has been made
> With barricade, enclosed around.
> O Indra, cause him to come forth—
> The after-birth along with babe!"

24. When [the son] is born, he [i.e., the father] builds up a fire, places him on his lap, mingles ghee and coagulated milk in a metal

dish, and makes an oblation, ladling out of the mingled ghee and coagulated milk, and saying:

> "In this son may I be increased,
> And have a thousand in mine house!
> May nothing rob his retinue
> Of offspring or of animals!
> Hail!

The vital powers which are in me, my mind, I offer in you.

> Hail!
> Or What in this rite I overdid,
> Or what I have here scanty made—
> Let Agni, wise, the Prosperer,
> Make fit and good our sacrifice!
> Hail!"

25. Then he draws down to the child's right ear and says "Speech! Speech!" three times. Then he mingles coagulated milk, honey, and ghee and feeds [his son] out of a gold [spoon] which is not placed within [the mouth], saying: "I place in you *Bhur*! I place in you *Bhuvas*! I place in you *Svar*! *Bhur, Bhuvas, Svar*—everything I place in you!"

26. Then he gives him a name, saying "You are Veda." So this becomes his secret name.

27. Then he presents him to the mother and offers the breast, saying:

> "Thy breast which is unfailing and refreshing,
> Wealth-bearer, treasure-finder, rich bestower,
> With which thou nourishest all things esteemed—
> Give it here, O Sarasvati, to suck from."

28. Then he addresses the child's mother:

> "You are Ila, of the lineage of Mitra and Varuna!
> O heroine! She has borne a hero!
> Continue to be such a woman abounding in heroes—
> She who has made us abound in a hero!"

Of such a son, verily, they say: "Ah, you have gone beyond your father! Ah, you have gone beyond your grandfather!"

Ah, he reaches the highest pinnacle of splendor, glory, and sacred knowledge who is born as the son of a Brahman who knows this!

5

1. Now the Line of Tradition—
> The son of Pautimashi [received this teaching] from
>> the son of Katyayani,
> the son of Katyayani from the son of Gautami,
> the son of Gautami from the son of Bharadvaji,
> the son of Bharadvaji from the son of Parasari,
> the son of Parasari from the son of Aupasvasti,
> the son of Aupasvasti from the son of Parasari,
> the son of Parasari from the son of Katyayani,
> the son of Katyayani from the son of Kausiki,
> the son of Kausiki from the son of Alambi
>> and the son of Vaiyaghrapadi,
> the son of Vaiyaghrapadi from the son of Kanvi
>> and the son of Kapi,
> the son of Kapi [2] from the son of Atreyi,
> the son of Atreyi from the son of Gautami,
> the son of Gautami from the son of Bharadvaji,
> the son of Bharadvaji from the son of Parasari,
> the son of Parasari from the son of Vatsi,
> the son of Vatsi from the son of Parasari,
> the son of Parasari from the son of Varkaruni,
> the son of Varkaruni from the son of Varkaruni,
> the son of Varkaruni from the son of Artabhagi,
> the son of Artabhagi from the son of Saungi,
> the son of Saungi from the son of Sankriti,
> the son of Sankriti from the son of Alambayani,
> the son of Alambayani from the son of Alambi,
> the son of Alambi from the son of Jayanti,
> the son of Jayanti from the son of Mandukayani,
> the son of Mandukayani from the son of Manduki,
> the son of Manduki from the son of Sandili,
> the son of Sandili from the son of Rathitari,
> the son of Rathitari from the son of Bhaluki,
> the son of Bhaluki from the two sons of Kraunciki,
> the two sons of Kraunciki from the son of Vaidribhati,
> the son of Vaidribhati from the son of Karsakeyi,
> the son of Karsakeyi from the son of Pracinayogi,

the son of Pracinayogi from the son of Sanjivi,
the son of Sanjivi from the son of Prasni, the Asurivasin,
the son of Prasni from Asurayana,
Asurayana from Asuri,
Asuri [3] from Yajnavalkya,
Yajnavalkya from Uddalaka,
Uddalaka from Aruna,
Aruna from Upavesi,
Upavesi from Kusri,
Kusri from Vajasravas,
Vajasravas from Jihvavant Vadhyoga,
Jihvavant Vadhyoga from Asita Varshagana,
Asita Varshagana from Harita Kasyapa,
Harita Kasyapa from Silpa Kasyapa,
Silpa Kasyapa from Kasyapa Naidhruvi,
Kasyapa Naidhruvi from Vac (Speech),
Vac from Ambhini,
Ambhini from Aditya (the Sun).

These white sacrificial formulas which come from Aditya are declared by Yajnavalkya of the Vajasaneyi school.

4. Up to the son of Sanjivi it is the same.
The son of Sanjivi from Mandukayani,
Mandukayani from Mandavya,
Mandavya from Kautsa,
Kautsa from Mahitthi,
Mahitthi from Vamakakshayana,
Vamakakshayana from Sandilya,
Sandilya from Vatsya,
Vatsya from Kusri,
Kusri from Yajnavacas Rajastambayana,
Yajnavacas Rajastambayana from Tura Kavasheya,
Tura Kavasheya from Prajapati,
Prajapati from Brahma.
Brahma is the Self-existent. Adoration to Brahma!

CHANDOGYA UPANISHAD

1

1

1. *Om*! One should reverence the Udgitha as this syllable, for one sings the loud chant [beginning] with "*Om.*"

The further explanation thereof [is as follows]—

2. The essence of things here is the earth.

The essence of the earth is water.

The essence of water is plants.

The essence of plants is a person.

The essence of a person is speech.

The essence of speech is the Rig.

The essence of the Rig is the Saman.

The essence of the Saman is the Udgitha.

3. This is the quintessence of the essences, the highest, the supreme, the eighth—namely the Udgitha.

4. "Which one is the Rig? Which one is the Saman? Which one is the Udgitha?"—Thus has there been a discussion.

5. The Rig is speech. The Saman is breath. The Udgitha is this syllable "*Om.*"

Verily, this is a pair—namely speech and breath, and also the Rig and the Saman.

6. This pair is joined together in this syllable "*Om.*"

Verily, when a pair come together, verily, the two procure each the other's desire.

7. A procurer of desires, verily, indeed, becomes he who, knowing this thus, reverences the Udgitha as this syllable.

8. Verily, this syllable is assent; for whenever one assents to anything he says simply "*Om.*" This, indeed, is fulfilment—that is, assent is.

A fulfiller of desires, verily, indeed, becomes he who, knowing this thus, reverences the Udgitha as this syllable.

9. This threefold knowledge proceeds with it: saying "*Om,*" one calls forth; saying "*Om,*" one recites; saying "*Om,*" one sings aloud, to the honor of that syllable, with its greatness, with its essence.

10. He who knows this thus and he who knows not, both per-

form with it. Diverse, however, are knowledge and ignorance. What, indeed, one performs with knowledge, with faith, with mystic doctrine—that, indeed, becomes the more effective.

—Such is the further explanation of this syllable.

2

1. Verily, when the gods and the devils, both descendants of Prajapati, contended with each other, the gods took unto themselves the Udgitha, thinking: "With this we shall overcome them!"

2. Then they reverenced the Udgitha as the breath in the nose. The devils afflicted that with evil. Therefore with it one smells both the sweet-smelling and the ill-smelling, for it is afflicted with evil.

3. Then they reverenced the Udgitha as speech. The devils afflicted that with evil. Therefore with it one speaks both the true and the false, for it is afflicted with evil.

4. Then they reverenced the Udgitha as the eye. The devils afflicted that with evil. Therefore with it one sees both the sightly and the unsightly, for it is afflicted with evil.

5. Then they reverenced the Udgitha as the ear. The devils afflicted that with evil. Therefore with it one hears both what should be listened to and what should not be listened to, for it is afflicted with evil.

6. Then they reverenced the Udgitha as the mind. The devils afflicted that with evil. Therefore with it one imagines both what should be imagined and what should not be imagined, for it is afflicted with evil.

7. Then they reverenced the Udgitha as that which is the breath in the mouth. When the devils struck that, they fell to pieces, as one would fall to pieces in striking against a solid stone.

8. As a lump of clay would fall to pieces in striking against a solid stone, so falls to pieces he who wishes evil to one who knows this, and he, too, who injures him. Such a one is a solid stone.

9. With this [breath] one discerns neither the sweet-smelling nor the ill-smelling, for it is free from evil. Whatever one eats with this, whatever one drinks with this, he protects the other vital breaths. And, not finding this [breath in the mouth], one finally deceases; one finally leaves his mouth open.

10. Angiras reverenced this as the Udgitha. People think that it is indeed Angiras, because it is the essence of the limbs—for that reason.

11. Brihaspati reverenced this as the Udgitha. People think that it is indeed Brihaspati, because speech is great and it is the lord thereof—for that reason.

12. Ayasya reverenced this as the Udgitha. People think that it is indeed Ayasya, because it goes from the mouth—for that reason.

13. Baka Dalbhya knew it. He became Udgatri priest of the people of Naimisha. He used to sing to them their desires.

14. An effective singer of desires, verily, indeed, becomes he who, knowing this thus, reverences the syllable as the Udgitha.

—Thus with reference to the self.

3

1. Now with reference to the divinities—

Him who glows yonder [i.e., the sun] one should reverence as an Udgitha. Verily, on rising, he sings aloud for creatures. On rising, he dispels darkness and fear. He, verily, who knows this becomes a dispeller of fear and darkness.

2. This [breath in the mouth] and that [sun] are alike. This is warm. That is warm. People designate this as sound, that as sound and as the reflecting. Therefore, verily, one should reverence this and that as an Udgitha.

3. But one should also reverence the diffused breath as an Udgitha. When one breathes in—that is the in-breath. When one breathes out—that is the out-breath. The junction of the in-breath and the out-breath is the diffused breath. Speech is the diffused breath. Therefore one utters speech without in-breathing, without out-breathing.

4. The Ric is speech. Therefore one utters the Ric without in-breathing, without out-breathing. The Saman is the Ric. Therefore one sings the Saman without in-breathing, without out-breathing. The Udgitha is the Saman. Therefore one chants the Udgitha without in-breathing, without out-breathing.

5. Whatever other actions than these there are that require strength, like the kindling of fire by friction, the running of a race, the bending of a stiff bow—one performs them without in-breathing,

without out-breathing. For this reason one should reverence the diffused breath as an Udgitha.

6. But one should also reverence the syllables of the Udgitha—*ud*, *gi*, *tha*. *ud* is breath, for through breath one arises; *gi* is speech, for people designate speeches as words; *tha* is food, for upon food this whole world is established.

7. *ud* is heaven; *gi* is atmosphere; *tha* is the earth. *ud* is the sun; *gi* is wind; *tha* is fire.

ud is Sama-Veda; *gi* is Yajur-Veda; *tha* is Rig-Veda.

Speech yields milk—that is, the milk of speech itself—for him, he becomes rich in food, an eater of food, who knows and reverences these syllables of the Udgitha thus: *ud*, *gi*, *tha*.

8. Now then, the fulfilment of wishes—

One should reverence the following as places of refuge.

One should take refuge in the Saman with which he may be about to sing a Stotra.

9. One should take refuge in the Ric in which it was contained, in the Rishi who was the poet, in the divinity unto whom he may be about to sing a Stotra.

10. One should take refuge in the meter with which he may be about to sing a Stotra. One should take refuge in the hymn-form with which he may be about to sing a Stotra for himself.

11. One should take refuge in the quarter of heaven toward which he may be about to sing a Stotra.

12. Finally, one should go unto himself and sing a Stotra, meditating carefully upon his desire. Truly the prospect is that the desire will be fulfilled for him, desiring which he may sing a Stotra—yea, desiring which he may sing a Stotra!

4

1. Om! One should reverence the Udgitha as this syllable, for one sings the loud chant [beginning] with "Om."

The further explanation thereof [is as follows]—

2. Verily, the gods, when they were afraid of death, took refuge in the threefold knowledge [i.e., the three Vedas], They covered themselves with meters. Because they covered themselves with these, therefore the meters are called *chandas*.

3. Death saw them there, in the Ric, in the Saman, in the Yajus, just as one might see a fish in water. When they found this out, they arose out of the Ric, out of the Saman, out of the Yajus, and took refuge in sound.

4. Verily, when one finishes an Ric, he sounds out "Om" similarly a Saman; similarly a Yajus. This sound is that syllable. It is immortal, fearless. By taking refuge in it the gods became immortal, fearless.

5. He who pronounces the syllable, knowing it thus, takes refuge in that syllable, in the immortal, fearless sound. Since the gods became immortal by taking refuge in it, therefore he becomes immortal.

5

1. Now then, the Udgitha is Om; Om is the Udgitha. And so, verily, the Udgitha is yonder sun, and it is Om, for it is continually sounding "Om."

2. "I sang praise unto it alone; therefore you are my only [son]," spake Kaushitaki unto his son. "Reflect upon its [various] rays. Verily, you will have many [sons]."

3. Now with reference to the self—
One should reverence the Udgitha as that which is the breath in the mouth, for it is continually sounding "Om."

4. "I sang praise unto it alone; therefore you are my only [son]," spake Kaushitaki unto his son. "Sing praise unto the breaths as a multitude. Verily, you will have many [sons]."

5. Now then, the Udgitha is Om; Om is the Udgitha. With this thought, verily, from the seat of a Hotri priest one puts in order again the Udgitha which has been falsely chanted—yea, puts it in order again.

6

1. The Ric is this [earth]; the Saman is fire. This Saman rests upon that Ric. Therefore the Saman is sung as resting upon the Ric. sa is this [earth]; ama is fire. That makes sama.

2. The Ric is the atmosphere; the Saman is the wind. This Saman

rests upon that Ric. Therefore the Saman is sung as resting upon the Ric. *sa* is the atmosphere; *ama* is the wind. That makes *sama*.

3. The Ric is heaven; the Saman is the sun. This Saman rests upon that Ric. Therefore the Saman is sung as resting upon the Ric. *sa* is heaven; *ama* is the sun. That makes *sama*.

4. The Ric is the lunar mansions; the Saman is the moon. This Saman rests upon that Ric. Therefore the Saman is sung as resting upon the Ric. *sa* is the lunar mansions; *ama* is the moon. That makes *sama*.

5. Now, the Ric is the white shining of the sun; the Saman is the dark, the ultra-black. This Saman rests upon that Ric. Therefore the Saman is sung as resting upon the Ric.

6. Now, *sa* is the white shining of the sun; *ama* is the dark, the ultra-black. That makes *sama*.

Now, that golden Person who is seen within the sun has a golden beard and golden hair. He is exceedingly brilliant, all, even to the finger-nail tips.

7. His eyes are even as a Kapyasa lotus-flower. His name is High. He is raised high above all evils. Verily, he who knows this rises high above all evils.

8. His songs are the Ric and the Saman. Therefore [they are called] the Udgitha. Therefore also the Udgatri priest [is so called], for he is the singer of this [High]. He is lord of the worlds which are beyond yonder sun, and also of the gods' desires.

7

1. Now with reference to the self—

The Ric is speech; the Saman is breath. This Saman rests upon that Ric. Therefore the Saman is sung as resting upon the Ric. *sa* is speech; *ama* is breath. That makes *sama*.

2. The Ric is the eye; the Saman is the soul. This Saman rests upon that Ric. Therefore the Saman is sung as resting upon the Ric. *sa* is the eye; *ama* is the soul. That makes *sama*.

3. The Ric is the ear; the Saman is the mind. This Saman rests upon that Ric. Therefore the Saman is sung as resting upon the Ric. *sa* is the ear; *ama* is the mind. That makes *sama*.

4. Now, the Ric is the bright shining of the eye; the Saman is the

dark, the ultra-black. This Saman rests upon that Ric. Therefore the Saman is sung as resting upon the Ric. *sa* is the bright shining of the eye; *ama* is the dark, the ultra-black. That makes *sama*.

5. Now, this person who is seen within the eye is the hymn, is the chant, is the recitation, is the sacrificial formula, is the prayer.

The form of this one is the same as the form of that [Person seen in the sun]. The songs of the former are the songs of this. The name of the one is the name of the other.

6. He is lord of the worlds which are under this one, and also of men's desires. So those who sing on the lute sing of him. Therefore they are winners of wealth.

7. Now, he who sings the Saman, knowing it thus, sings of both; through the former he wins the worlds which are beyond the former, and also the gods' desires.

8. Through the latter he wins the worlds which are under the latter, and also men's desires. Therefore an Udgatri priest who knows this may say: [9] "What desire may I win for you by singing?" For truly he is lord of the winning of desires by singing, who, knowing this, sings the Saman—yea, sings the Saman!

8

1. There were three men proficient in the Udgitha: Silaka Salavatya, Caikitayana Dalbhya, and Pravahana Jaivali. These said: "We are proficient in the Udgitha. Come! Let us have a discussion on the Udgitha!"

2. "So be it," said they, and sat down together. Then Pravahana Jaivali said: "Do you two, Sirs, speak first. While there are two Brahmans speaking, I will listen to their word."

3. Then Silaka Salavatya said to Caikitayana Dalbhya: "Come! Let me question you."

"Question!" said he.

4. "To what does the Saman go back?"

"To sound," said he.

"To what does sound go back?"

"To breath," said he.

"To what does breath go back?"

"To food," said he.

"To what does food go back?"

"To water," said he.

5. "To what does water go back?"

"To yonder world," said he.

"To what does yonder world go back?"

"One should not lead beyond the heavenly world," said he.

"We establish the Saman upon the heavenly world, for the Saman is praised as heaven."

6. Then Silaka Salavatya said to Caikitayana Dalbhya: "Verily, indeed, your Saman, O Dalbhya, is unsupported. If some one now were to say 'Your head will fall off,' your head would fall off."

7. "Come! Let me learn this from you, Sir."

"Learn," said he.

"To what does yonder world go back?"

"To this world," said he.

"To what does this world go back?"

"One should not lead beyond the world-support," said he. "We establish the Saman upon the world as a support, for the Saman is praised as a support."

8. Then Pravahana Jaivali said to him: "Verily, indeed, your Saman, O Salavatya, comes to an end. If some one now were to say 'Your head will fall off,' your head would fall off."

"Come! Let me learn this from you, Sir."

"Learn," said he.

9

1. "To what does this world go back?"

"To space," said he. "Verily, all things here arise out of space. They disappear back into space, for space alone is greater than these; space is the final goal.

2. This is the most excellent Udgitha. This is endless. The most excellent is his, the most excellent worlds does he win, who, knowing it thus, reverences the most excellent Udgitha.

3. When Atidhanvan Saunaka told this Udgitha to Udara-sandilya, he also said: 'As far as they shall know this Udgitha among your off-spring, so far will they have the most excellent life in this world, [4] and likewise a world in yonder world.' He who knows and reverences

it thus has the most excellent life in this world, and likewise a world in yonder world—yea, a world in yonder world."

10

1. Among the Kurus, when they were struck by hailstorms, there lived in the village of a rich man a very poor man, Ushasti Cakrayana, with his wife Atiki.

2. He begged of the rich man while he was eating beans. The latter said to him: "I have no others than these which are set before me."

3. "Give me some of them," said he.

He gave them to him and said: "Here is drink."

"Verily, that would be for me to drink leavings!" said he.

4. "Are not these [beans] also leavings?" "Verily, I could not live, if I did not eat those," said he. "The drinking of water is at my will."

5. When he had eaten, he took what still remained to his wife. She had already begged enough to eat. She took these and put them away.

6. On the morrow he arose and said: "Oh, if we could get some food, we might get a little money! The king over there is going to have a sacrifice performed for himself. He might choose me to perform all the priestly offices."

7. His wife said to him: "Here, my lord, are the beans." He ate them and went off to that sacrifice, which had already been begun.

8. There he approached the Udgatri priests as they were about to sing the Stotra in the place for the singing. Then he said to the Prastotri priest: [9] "Prastotri priest, if you shall sing the Prastava (Introductory Praise) without knowing the divinity which is connected with the Prastava, your head will fall off."

10. Similarly also he said to the Udgatri priest: "Udgatri priest, if you shall chant the Udgitha (Loud Chant) without knowing the divinity which is connected with the Udgitha, your head will fall off."

11. Similarly also he said to the Pratihartri priest: "Pratihartri priest, if you shall take up the Pratihara (Response) without knowing the divinity which is connected with the Pratihara, your head will fall off."

Then they ceased and quietly seated themselves.

11

1. Then the institutor of the sacrifice said to him: "Verily, I would wish to know you, Sir."

"I am Ushasti Cakrayana," said he.

2. Then he [i.e., the institutor] said: "Verily, I have been searching around for you, Sir, for all these priestly offices. Verily, not finding you, Sir, I have chosen others. [3] But do you, Sir, perform all the priestly offices for me."

"So be it," said he. "But in this matter let these, indeed, being permitted, sing the Stotra; but you should give me as much money as you would give them."

"So be it," said the institutor of the sacrifice.

4. Then the Prastotri priest approached him and said: "You, Sir, said unto me: 'Prastotri priest, if you shall sing the Prastava without knowing the divinity which is connected with the Prastava, your head will fall off.' Which is that divinity?"

5. "Breath," said he. "Verily, indeed, all beings here enter [into life] with breath and depart [from life] with breath. This is the divinity connected with the Prastava. If you had sung the Prastava without knowing it, your head would have fallen off, after you had been told so by me."

6. Then the Udgatri priest approached him and said: "You, Sir, said unto me: 'Udgatri priest, if you shall chant the Udgitha without knowing the divinity which is connected with the Udgitha, your head will fall off.' Which is that divinity?"

7. "The Sun," said he. "Verily, indeed, all beings here sing of the sun when he is up. This is the divinity connected with the Udgitha. If you had chanted the Udgitha without knowing it, your head would have fallen off, after you had been told so by me."

8. Then the Pratihartri priest approached him and said: "You, Sir, said unto me: 'Pratihartri priest, if you shall take up the Pratihara without knowing the divinity which is connected with the Pratihara, your head will fall off.' Which is that divinity?"

9. "Food," said he. "Verily, indeed, all beings here live by taking up to themselves food. This is the divinity connected with the Pratihara. If you had taken up the Pratihara without knowing it, your head would have fallen off, after you had been told so by me."

12

1. Now next, the Udgitha of the Dogs—
So Baka Dalbhya—or Glava Maitreya—went forth for Veda-study.
2. Unto him there appeared a white dog. Around this one other dogs gathered and said: "Do you, Sir, obtain food for us by singing. Verily, we are hungry."
3. Then he said to them: "In the morning you may assemble unto me here at this spot." So Baka Dalbhya—or Glava Maitreya—kept watch.
4. Then, even as [priests] here, when they are about to chant with the Bahishpavamana Stotra, glide hand in hand, so did they glide on. Then they sat down together and performed the preliminary vocalizing.
5. They sang: "Om! Let us eat. Om! Let us drink. Om! May the god Varuna, Prajapati, and Savitri bring food here! O Lord of food, bring food here!—yea, bring it here! Om!"

13

1. Verily, the sound ha-u is the world, [for this interjectional trill occurs in the Rathantara Saman, which is identified with the earth].
The sound ha-i is wind. [for this interjectional trill occurs in the Vamadevya Saman, which has for its subject the origin of wind and water].
The sound atha is the moon, [for on food everything is established, and the moon consists of food].
The sound iha is oneself, [for oneself is here].
The sound i is Agni, [for all Samans sacred to Agni end with the sound i].
2. The sound u is the sun, [for people sing of the sun when it is up].
The sound e is the Invocation, [for people call with "Come!"]
The sound au-ho-i is the Visvadeva gods, [for this interjectional trill occurs in the Saman to the Visvadeva gods].
The sound hin is Prajapati, [for Prajapati is undefined, and the sound hin also is indistinct].

svara (sound) is breath, [for that is the source of sound].

ya is food, [for everything here moves through the help of food].

vac is Viraj, [for this interjectional trill occurs in the Saman to Viraj].

3. The sound *hum*, the variable thirteenth interjectional trill, is the Undefined.

4. Speech yields milk—that is, the milk of speech itself—for him, he becomes rich in food, an eater of food, who knows thus this mystic meaning of the Samans—yea, who knows the mystic meaning!

2

1

1. *Om*! Assuredly, the reverence of the Saman entire is good. Assuredly, anything that is good, people call *saman*; anything that is not good, *a-saman*.

2. So also people say: "He approached him with *saman*"; that is, they say: "He approached him with good manner."—"He approached him with no *saman*"; that is, they say: "He approached him with no good manner."

3. So also, further, people say: "Oh! we have *saman*!" if it is something good; that is, they say: "Oh! good!"—"Oh! we have no *saman*!" if it is not good; that is, they say: "Oh! no good!"

4. He who, knowing this, reverences the Saman as good—truly the prospect is that good qualities will come unto him and attend him.

2

1. In the worlds one should reverence a fivefold Saman.
The earth is a Hinkara.
Fire is a Prastava.
The atmosphere is an Udgitha.
The sun is a Pratihara.
The sky is a Nidhana.

2. Now in their reverse order—
The sky is a Hinkara.
The sun is a Prastava.
The atmosphere is an Udgitha.
Fire is a Pratihara.
The earth is a Nidhana.

3. The worlds, both in their ascending order and in their reverse

order, serve him who, knowing this thus, reverences a fivefold Saman in the worlds.

3

1. In a rain-storm one should reverence a fivefold Saman.
   The preceding wind is a Hinkara.
   A cloud is formed—that is a Prastava.
   It rains—that is an Udgitha.
   It lightens, it thunders—that is a Pratihara.

   2. It lifts—that is a Nidhana.

It rains for him, indeed, he causes it to rain, who, knowing this thus, reverences a fivefold Saman in a rain-storm.

4

1. In all waters one should reverence a fivefold Saman.
   When a cloud gathers—that is a Hinkara.
   When it rains—that is a Prastava.
   Those [waters] which flow to the east—they are an Udgitha.
   Those which flow to the west—they are a Pratihara.
   The ocean is a Nidhana.

   2. He perishes not in water, he becomes rich in water, who, knowing this thus, reverences a fivefold Saman in all waters.

5

1. In the seasons one should reverence a fivefold Saman.
   The spring is a Hinkara.
   The summer is a Prastava.
   The rainy season is an Udgitha.
   The autumn is a Pratihara.
   The winter is a Nidhana.

2. The seasons serve him, he becomes rich in seasons, who, knowing this thus, reverences a fivefold Saman in the seasons.

6

1. In animals one should reverence a fivefold Saman.
   Goats are a Hinkara.
   Sheep are a Prastava.
   Cows are an Udgitha.
   Horses are a Pratihara.
   Man is a Nidhana.

2. Animals come into his possession, he becomes rich in animals, who, knowing this thus, reverences a fivefold Saman in animals.

7

1. In the vital breaths one should reverence the most excellent fivefold Saman.
   Breath is a Hinkara.
   Speech is a Prastava.
   The eye is an Udgitha.
   The ear is a Pratihara.
   The mind is a Nidhana.

Verily, these are the most excellent.
2. The most excellent becomes his, he wins the most excellent worlds, who, knowing this thus, reverences the most excellent fivefold Saman in the vital breaths.

8

1. Now for the sevenfold—
   In speech one should reverence a sevenfold Saman.
   Whatsoever of speech is *hum*—that is a Hinkara.
   Whatsoever is *pra*—that is a Prastava.
   Whatsoever is *a*—that is an Adi.

2. Whatsoever is *ud*—that is an Udgitha.
Whatsoever is *prati*—that is a Pratihara.
Whatsoever is *upa*—that is an Upadrava.
Whatsoever is *ni*—that is a Nidhana.

3. Speech yields milk—that is, the milk of speech itself—for him, he becomes rich in food, an eater of food, who, knowing this thus, reverences a sevenfold Saman in speech.

9

1. Now, verily, one should reverence yonder sun as a sevenfold Saman. It is always the same; therefore it is a Saman. It is the same with everyone, since people think: "It faces me! It faces me!" Therefore it is a Saman.

2. One should know that all beings here are connected with it.

When it is before sunrise—that is a Hinkara. Animals are connected with this [part] of it. Therefore they perform preliminary vocalizing. Truly, they are partakers in the Hinkara of that Saman.

3. Now, when it is just after sunrise—that is a Prastava. Men are connected with this [part] of it. Therefore they are desirous of praise, desirous of laudation. Truly, they are partakers in the Prastava of that Saman.

4. Now, when it is the cowgathering-time—that is an Adi. The birds are connected with this [part] of it. Therefore they support themselves without support in the atmosphere and fly around. Truly, they are partakers in the Adi of that Saman.

5. Now, when it is just at mid-day—that is an Udgitha. The gods are connected with this [part] of it. Therefore they are the best of Prajapati's offspring. Truly, they are partakers in the Udgitha of that Saman.

6. Now, when it is past mid-day and before [the latter part of] the afternoon—that is a Pratihara. Fetuses are connected with this [part] of it. Therefore they are taken [or, held] up and do not drop down. Truly, they are partakers in the Pratihara of that Saman.

7. Now, when it is past afternoon and before sunset—that is an Upadrava. Wild beasts are connected with this [part] of it. Therefore

when they see a man, they approach a hiding-place as their hole. Truly, they are partakers in the Upadrava of that Saman.

8. Now, when it is just after sunset—that is the Nidhana. The fathers are connected with this [part] of it. Therefore people lay aside the fathers. Truly, they are partakers in the Nidhana of that Saman.

10

1. Now then, one should reverence the Saman, measured in itself, as leading beyond death.

hinkara has three syllables. *prastava* has three syllables. That is the same.

2. *adi* has two syllables. *pratihara* has four syllables. One from there, here—that is the same.

3. *udgitha* has three syllables. *upadrava* has four syllables.

Three and three—that is the same, one syllable left over. Having three syllables—that is the same.

4. *nidhana* has three syllables. That is the same, too. These are twenty-two syllables.

5. With the twenty-one one obtains the sun. Verily, the sun is the twenty-first from here. With the twenty-two one wins what is beyond the sun. That is heaven. That is the sorrowless.

6. He obtains the victory of the sun, indeed, a victory higher than the victory of the sun is his, who, knowing this thus, reverences the sevenfold Saman, measured in itself, as leading beyond death—yea, who reverences the Saman!

11

1. The wind is a Hinkara.
Speech is a Prastava.
The eye is an Udgitha.
The ear is a Pratihara.
The breath is a Nidhana.

This is the Gayatri Saman as woven upon the vital breaths.

2. He who knows thus this Gayatri Saman as woven upon the vital breaths becomes possessor of vital breaths, reaches a full length of life, lives long, becomes great in offspring and in cattle, great in fame. One should be great-minded. That is his rule.

12

1. One rubs the fire-sticks together—that is a Hinkara.
Smoke is produced—that is a Prastava.
It blazes—that is an Udgitha.
Coals are formed—that is a Pratihara.
It becomes extinct—that is a Nidhana.
It becomes completely extinct—that is a Nidhana.

This is the Rathantara Saman as woven upon fire.
2. He who knows thus this Rathantara Saman as woven upon fire becomes an eater of food, eminent in sacred knowledge, reaches a full length of life, lives long, becomes great in offspring and in cattle, great in fame. One should not take a sip and spit toward fire. That is his rule.

13

1. One summons—that is a Hinkara.
He makes request—that is a Prastava.
Together with the woman he lies down—that is an Udgitha.
He lies upon the woman—that is a Pratihara.
He comes to the end—that is a Nidhana.
He comes to the finish—that is a Nidhana.

This is the Vamadevya Saman as woven upon copulation.
2. He who knows thus this Vamadevya Saman as woven upon copulation comes to copulation, procreates himself from every copulation, reaches a full length of life, lives long, becomes great in offspring and in cattle, great in fame. One should never abstain from any woman. That is his rule.

14

1. The rising sun is a Hinkara.
   The risen sun is a Prastava.
   Mid-day is an Udgitha.
   Afternoon is a Pratihara.
   When it is set—that is a Nidhana.

This is the Brihad Saman as woven upon the sun.

2. He who knows thus this Brihad Saman as woven upon the sun becomes a brilliant eater of food, reaches a full length of life, lives long, becomes great in offspring and in cattle, great in fame. One should not find fault with it when it is hot. That is his rule.

15

1. Mists come together—that is a Hinkara.
   A cloud is formed—that is a Prastava.
   It rains—that is an Udgitha.
   It lightens and thunders—that is a Pratihara.
   It holds up—that is a Nidhana.

This is the Vairupa Saman as woven upon rain.

2. He who knows thus this Vairupa Saman as woven upon rain acquires cattle both of various form and of beautiful form, reaches a full length of life, lives long, becomes great in children and in cattle, great in fame. One should not find fault with it when it rains. That is his rule.

16

1. Spring is a Hinkara.
   Summer is a Prastava.
   The rainy season is an Udgitha.
   Autumn is a Pratihara.
   Winter is a Nidhana.

This is the Vairaja Saman as woven upon the seasons.

2. He who knows thus this Vairaja Saman as woven upon the seasons shines like a king with offspring, cattle, and eminence in sacred knowledge, reaches a full length of life, lives long, becomes great in offspring and cattle, great in fame. One should not find fault with the seasons. That is his rule.

17

1. The earth is a Hinkara.
   The atmosphere is a Prastava.
   The sky is an Udgitha.
   The regions of the compass are a Pratihara.
   The ocean is a Nidhana.

These are the verses of the Sakvari Saman as woven upon the worlds.

2. He who knows thus these verses of the Sakvari Saman as woven upon the worlds becomes possessor of a world, reaches a full length of life, lives long, becomes great in offspring and in cattle, great in fame. One should not find fault with the worlds. That is his rule.

18

1. Goats are a Hinkara.
   Sheep are a Prastava.
   Cows are an Udgitha.
   Horses are a Pratihara.
   Man is a Nidhana.

These are the verses of the Revati Saman as woven upon animals.

2. He who knows thus these verses of the Revati Saman as woven upon animals becomes possessor of animals, reaches a full length of life, lives long, becomes great in offspring and in cattle, great in fame. One should not find fault with animals. That is his rule.

19

1. Hair is a Hinkara.
   Skin is a Prastava.
   Flesh is an Udgitha.
   Bone is a Pratihara.
   Marrow is a Nidhana.

This is the Yajnayajniya Saman as woven upon the members of the body.

2. He who knows thus this Yajnayajniya Saman as woven upon the members of the body becomes possessor of the members of his body, does not become defective in any member of the body, reaches a full length of life, lives long, becomes great in offspring and in cattle, great in fame. One should not eat of marrow for a year. That is his rule. Rather, one should not eat of marrow at all.

20

1. Agni is a Hinkara.
   Vayu is a Prastava.
   Aditya is an Udgitha.
   The Nakshatras are a Pratihara.
   Candrama is a Nidhana.

This is the Rajana Saman as woven upon the divinities.

2. He who knows thus this Rajana Saman as woven upon the divinities goes to the same world, to equality and to complete union with those very divinities, reaches a full length of life, lives long, becomes great in offspring and in cattle, great in fame. One should not find fault with the Brahmans. That is his rule.

21

1. The triple knowledge is a Hinkara.
   The three worlds here are a Prastava.

Agni, Vayu, and Aditya are an Udgitha.
Stars, birds, and light-rays are a Pratihara.
Serpents, Gandharvas, and the Fathers are a Nidhana.

This is the Saman as woven upon the world-all.

2. He who knows thus this Saman as woven upon the world-all becomes the world-all itself.

3. On this point there is this verse:
Whatever triple things are fivefold—
Than these things there is nothing better, higher.

4. Who knows this fact, he knows the world-all;
All regions of the compass bring him tribute.

One should reverence the thought "I am the world-all!" That is his rule. That is his rule!

22

1. "I choose the roaring, animal-like form of the Saman"—such is the Udgitha belonging to Agni. The indistinct form belongs to Prajapati; the distinct, to Soma; the soft and smooth, to Vayu; the smooth and strong, to Indra; the heron-like, to Brihaspati; the ill-sounding, to Varuna. One may practise all these, but one should avoid that belonging to Varuna.

2. "Let me obtain immortality for the gods by singing"—thus should one obtain with his singing. "Let me obtain oblation for the fathers by singing, hope for men, grass and water for cattle, a heavenly world for the sacrificer, food for myself"—one should sing the Stotra carefully, meditating these things in mind.

3. All vowels are embodiments of Indra. All spirants are embodiments of Prajapati. All [other] consonants are embodiments of Mrityu.

If one should reproach a person on his vowels, let him say to that one: "I have been a suppliant to Indra for protection. He will answer you."

4. So, if one should reproach him on his spirants, let him say to that one: "I have been a suppliant to Prajapati for protection. He will thrash you."

So, if one should reproach him on his [other] consonants, let him say to that one: "I have been a suppliant to Mrityu for protection. He will burn you up."

5. All the vowels should be pronounced strong and sonant, with the thought: "To Indra let me give strength." All the spirants should be pronounced well open, without being slurred over, without being elided, with the thought: "To Prajapati let me entrust myself." All the [other] consonants should be pronounced slowly, without being merged together, with the thought: "From Mrityu let me withdraw myself."

23

1. There are three branches of duty. Sacrifice, study of the Vedas, alms-giving—that is the first. (2) Austerity, indeed, is the second. A student of sacred knowledge dwelling in the house of a teacher, settling himself permanently in the house of a teacher, is the third.

All these become possessors of meritorious worlds. He who stands firm in Brahma attains immortality.

2 (3). Prajapati brooded upon the worlds. From them, when they had been brooded upon, issued forth the threefold knowledge. He brooded upon this. From it, when it had been brooded upon, issued forth these syllables: *bhur, bhuvah, svar*.

3 (4). He brooded upon them. From them, when they had been brooded upon, issued forth the syllable Om. As all leaves are held together by a spike, so all speech is held together by Om. Verily, Om is the world-all. Verily, Om is this world-all.

24

1. The expounders of sacred knowledge say: "Since to the Vasus belongs the morning Soma-libation, to the Rudras the mid-day Soma-libation, to the Adityas and the Visvadevas the third Soma-libation, [2] where, then, is the sacrificer's world?"

If one knows not, how can he perform [the sacrifice with success]? So let him who knows perform.

3. Before the commencement of the morning litany he sits down behind the Garhapatya fire, facing the north, and sings forth the Saman to the Vasus:

4. "Open the door to thy world,
   And let us see thee,
   For the obtaining of
   The sovereignty!"

5. So he offers the oblation and says: "Adoration to Agni, earth-inhabiting, world-inhabiting! Find a world for me, the sacrificer! Verily, that is the sacrificer's world! I will go [6] thither, I, the sacrificer, after life. Hail! Thrust back the bar!" Thus having spoken, he rises. At the same time the Vasus bestow upon him the morning Soma-libation.

7. Before the commencement of the mid-day Soma-libation he sits down behind the Agnidhriya fire, facing the north, and sings forth the Saman to the Rudras:

8. "Open the door to thy world,
   And let us see thee,
   For the obtaining of
   Wide sovereignty!"

9. So he offers the libation and says: "Adoration to Vayu, atmosphere-inhabiting, world-inhabiting! Find a world for me, the sacrificer! Verily, that is the sacrificer's world! I will go [10] thither, I, the sacrificer, after life. Hail! Thrust back the bar!" Thus having spoken, he rises. At the same time the Rudras bestow upon him the mid-day Soma-libation.

11. Before the commencement of the third Soma-libation he sits down behind the Ahavaniya fire, facing the north, and sings forth the Saman to the Adityas and the Visvadevas:

12. "Open the door to thy world,
    And let us see thee,
    For the obtaining of
    Chief sovereignty!"

13. Thus the [Saman] to the Adityas, Now the [Saman] to the Visvadevas:

    "Open the door to thy world,
    And let us see thee,
    For the obtaining of
    Full sovereignty!"

14. So he offers the oblation and says: "Adoration to the Adityas and to the Visvadevas, sky-inhabiting, world-inhabiting! Find a world for me, the sacrificer! [15] Verily, that is the sacrificer's world! I will go thither, I, the sacrificer, after life. Hail! Thrust back the bar!" Thus having spoken, he rises. At the same time the Adityas and the Visvadevas bestow upon him the third Soma-libation.

Verily, he knows the fulness of the sacrifice who knows this—yea, who knows this!

3

1

1. Verily, yonder sun is the honey of the gods. The cross-beam for it is the sky. The honeycomb is the atmosphere. The brood are the particles of light.

2. The eastern rays of that sun are its eastern honey-cells. The bees are the Rig verses. The flower is the Rig-Veda. The drops of nectar fluid [arose as follows].

Verily, these Rig verses [3] brooded upon that Rig-Veda; from it, when it had been brooded upon, there was produced as its essence splendor, brightness, power, vigor, and food.

4. It flowed forth. It repaired to the sun. Verily, that is what that red appearance of the sun is.

2

1. So its southern rays are its southern honey-cells. The bees are the Yajus formulas. The flower is the Yajur-Veda. The drops of nectar fluid [arose as follows].

2. Verily, these Yajus formulas brooded upon that Yajur-Veda; from it, when it had been brooded upon, there was produced as its essence splendor, brightness, power, vigor, and food.

3. It flowed forth. It repaired to the sun. Verily, that is what that white appearance of the sun is.

3

1. So its western rays are its western honey-cells. The bees are the Saman chants. The flower is the Sama-Veda. The drops of nectar fluid [arose as follows].

2. Verily, those Saman chants brooded upon that Sama-Veda. From it, when it had been brooded upon, there was produced as its essence splendor, brightness, power, vigor, and food.

3. It flowed forth. It repaired to the sun. Verily, that is what that dark appearance of the sun is.

4

1. So its northern rays are its northern honey-cells. The bees are the [Hymns] of the Atharvans and Angirases. The flower is Legend and Ancient Lore. The drops of nectar fluid [arose as follows].

2. Verily, those [Hymns] of the Atharvans and Angirases brooded upon that Legend and Ancient Lore. From it, when it had been brooded upon, there was produced as its essence splendor, brightness, power, vigor, and food.

3. It flowed forth. It repaired to the sun. Verily, that is what that exceedingly dark appearance of the sun is.

5

1. So its upward rays are its upper honey-cells. The bees are the Hidden Teachings [i.e., the Upanishads]. The flower is Brahma. The drops of nectar fluid [arose as follows].

2. Verily, those Hidden Teachings brooded upon that Brahma; from it, when it had been brooded upon, there was produced as its essence splendor, brightness, power, vigor, and food.

3. It flowed forth. It repaired to the sun. Verily, that is what seems to tremble in the middle of the sun.

4. Verily, these are the essences of the essences, for the Vedas are essences and these are their essences. Verily, these are the nectars of the nectars, for the Vedas are nectars and these are their nectars.

6

1. The Vasus live upon that which is the first nectar [i.e., the Rig-Veda] through Agni as their mouth. Verily, the gods neither eat nor drink. They are satisfied merely with seeing that nectar.

2. These enter that [red] form of the sun and come forth from that form.

3. He who knows thus that nectar becomes one of the Vasus themselves and through Agni as his mouth is satisfied merely with seeing that nectar. He enters that very form and comes forth from that form.

4. As long as the sun shall rise in the east and set in the west, so long will he compass the overlordship and the chief sovereignty of the Vasus.

7

1. Now, the Rudras live upon what is the second nectar [i.e., the Yajur-Veda] through Indra as their mouth. Verily, the gods neither eat nor drink. They are satisfied merely with seeing that nectar.

2. These enter that [white] form and come forth from that form.

3. He who knows thus that nectar becomes one of the Rudras themselves and through Indra as his mouth is satisfied merely with seeing that nectar. He enters that very form and comes forth from that form.

4. As long as the sun shall rise in the east and set in the west, twice so long will it rise in the south and set in the north, and just that long will he compass the overlordship and the chief sovereignty of the Rudras.

8

1. Now, the Adityas live upon what is the third nectar [i.e., the Sama-Veda] through Varuna as their mouth. Verily, the gods neither eat nor drink. They are satisfied merely with seeing that nectar.

2. These enter that [dark] form and come forth from that form.

3. He who knows thus that nectar becomes one of the Adityas themselves and through Varuna as his mouth is satisfied merely with seeing that nectar. He enters that very form and comes forth from that form.

4. So long as the sun shall rise in the south and set in the north, twice so long will it rise in the west and set in the east, and just that long will he compass the overlordship and the chief sovereignty of the Adityas.

9

1. Now, the Maruts live upon what is the fourth nectar [i.e., the Atharva-Veda] through Soma as their mouth. Verily, the gods neither eat nor drink. They are satisfied merely with seeing that nectar.

2. These enter that [exceedingly dark] form and come forth from that form.

3. He who knows thus that nectar becomes one of the Maruts themselves and through Soma as his mouth is satisfied merely with seeing that nectar. He enters that very form and comes forth from that form.

4. As long as the sun shall rise in the west and set in the east, twice so long will it rise in the north and set in the south, and just that long will he compass the overlordship and the chief sovereignty of the Maruts.

10

1. Now, the Sadhyas live upon what is the fifth nectar [i.e., the Upanishads] through Brahma as their mouth. Verily, the gods neither eat nor drink. They are satisfied merely with seeing that nectar.

2. These enter that form [which seems to tremble in the middle of the sun] and come forth from that form.

3. He who knows thus that nectar becomes one of the Sadhyas themselves and through Brahma as his mouth is satisfied merely with seeing that nectar. He enters that very form and comes forth from that form.

4. As long as the sun shall rise in the north and set in the south, twice so long will it rise in the zenith and set in the nadir, and just that long will he compass the overlordship and the chief sovereignty of the Sadhyas.

11

1. Henceforth, after having risen in the zenith, it will no more rise nor set. It will stand alone in the middle. On this point there is this verse:

2. In yonder sphere it has not set,
   Nor ever has it risen up;
   And by the truth of this, ye gods,
   Of Brahma let me not be robbed.

3. Verily, it neither rises nor sets for him, it is evermore day for him, who knows thus this mystic doctrine of Brahma.

4. Brahma told this to Prajapati; Prajapati, to Manu; Manu, to his descendants. To Uddalaka Aruni, as being the eldest son, his father declared this Brahma.

5. Verily, a father may teach this Brahma to his eldest son or to a worthy pupil, [6] [but] to no one else at all. Even if one should offer him this [earth] that is encompassed by water and filled with treasure, [he should say]: "This, truly, is more than that! This, truly, is more than that!"

12

1. Verily, the Gayatri meter is everything here that has come to be, whatsoever there is here. Verily, the Gayatri is speech. Verily, speech both sings of and protects everything here that has come to be.

2. Verily, what this Gayatri is—that is the same as what this earth is; for on it everything here that has come to be is established. It does not extend beyond it.

3. Verily, what this earth is —that is the same as what the body in man here is; for in it these vital breaths are established. They do not extend beyond it.

4. Verily, what the body in man is—that is the same as what the heart within man here is; for on it these vital breaths are established. They do not extend beyond it.

5. This is the four-quartered sixfold Gayatri. With reference to it a Rig verse states:

6. His greatness is of such extent,
   Yet Purusha is greater still.
   All beings are one fourth of him;
   Three fourths, the immortal in the sky.

7. Verily, what is called Brahma—that is the same as what the space outside of a person is. Verily, what the space outside of a person is—[8] that is the same as what the space within a person is. Verily, what the space within a person is—[9] that is the same as what the space here within the heart is. That is the Full, the Non-active. Full, non-active prosperity he obtains who knows this.

13

1. Verily, indeed, this heart here has five openings for the gods.
   As for its eastern opening—that is the Prana breath, that is the eye, that is the sun. One should reverence that as glow and as food. He becomes glowing and an eater of food who knows this.

2. Now, as for its southern opening—that is the Vyana breath, that is the ear, that is the moon. One should reverence that as prosperity and splendor. He becomes prosperous and splendid who knows this.

3. Now, as for its western opening—that is the Apana breath, that is speech, that is fire. One should reverence that as eminence in sacred knowledge and as food. He becomes eminent in sacred knowledge and an eater of food who knows this.

4. Now, as for its northern opening—that is the Samana breath, that is mind, that is the rain-god. One should reverence that as fame and beauty. He becomes famous and beauteous who knows this.

5. Now as for its upper opening—that is the Udana breath, that is wind, that is space. One should reverence that as vigor and greatness. He becomes vigorous and great who knows this.

6. Verily, these same are five Brahma-men, door-keepers of the heavenly world. Who knows these thus as five Brahma-men, as door-keepers of the heavenly world, in his family a hero is born. He reaches the heavenly world who knows these thus as five Brahma-men, door-keepers of the heavenly world.

7. Now, the light which shines higher than this heaven, on the backs of all, on the backs of everything, in the highest worlds, than

which there are no higher—verily, that is the same as this light which is here within a person.

There is this seeing of it—[8] when one perceives by touch this heat here in the body. There is this hearing of it—when one closes his ears and hears as it were a sound, as it were a noise, as of a fire blazing. One should reverence that light as something that has been seen and heard. He becomes one beautiful to see, one heard of in renown, who knows this—yea, who knows this!

14

1. "Verily, this whole world is Brahma. Tranquil, let one worship It as that from which he came forth, as that into which he will be dissolved, as that in which he breathes.

Now, verily, a person consists of purpose. According to the purpose which a person has in this world, thus does he become on departing hence. So let him form for himself a purpose.

2. He who consists of mind, whose body is life, whose form is light, whose conception is truth, whose soul is space, containing all works, containing all desires, containing all odors, containing all tastes, encompassing this whole world, the unspeaking, the unconcerned—[3] this Soul of mine within the heart is smaller than a grain of rice, or a barley-corn, or a mustard-seed, or a grain of millet, or the kernel of a grain of millet; this Soul of mine within the heart is greater than the earth, greater than the atmosphere, greater than the sky, greater than these worlds.

4. Containing all works, containing all desires, containing all odors, containing all tastes, encompassing this whole world, the unspeaking, the unconcerned—this is the Soul of mine within the heart, this is Brahma. Into him I shall enter on departing hence.

If one would believe this, he would have no more doubt—Thus used Sandilya to say—yea, Sandilya!

15

1. The chest whose space is atmosphere,
   With earth for bottom, ne'er decays.

Its corners are the poles of heaven.
Its upper opening is the sky.
This chest is one containing wealth.
Within it everything here rests.

2. Its eastern quarter is named Sacrificial Ladle. Its southern quarter is named Over-powering. Its western quarter is named Queen. Its northern quarter is named Wealthy. The wind is the child of these quarters of heaven. He who knows this wind thus as the child of the quarters of heaven mourns not for a son.

"I here know this wind thus as the child of the quarters of heaven. Let me not mourn for a son."

3. "I take refuge in the imperishable chest with this one, with this one, with this one."

"I take refuge in breath with this one, with this one, with this one."

"I take refuge in *bhur* with this one, with this one, with this one."

"I take refuge in *bhuvas* with this one, with this one, with this one."

"I take refuge in *svar* with this one, with this one, with this one."

4. When I said, "I take refuge in breath"—breath, verily, is everything here that has come to be, whatsoever there is. So it was in this I took refuge.

5. So when I said, "I take refuge in *bhur*," what I said was: "I take refuge in earth; I take refuge in atmosphere; I take refuge in sky."

6. So when I said, "I take refuge in *bhuvas*," what I said was: "I take refuge in Agni; I take refuge in Vayu; I take refuge in Aditya."

7. So when I said, "I take refuge in *svar*," what I said was: "I take refuge in the Rig-Veda; I take refuge in the Yajur-Veda; I take refuge in the Sama-Veda." That was what I said.

16

1. Verily, a person is a sacrifice. His [first] twenty-four years are the morning Soma-libation, for the Gayatri meter has twenty-four syllables and the morning Soma-libation is offered with a Gayatri hymn. The Vasus are connected with this part of the sacrifice. Verily, the vital breaths are the Vasus, for they cause everything here to continue.

2. If any sickness should overtake him in this period of life, let

him say: "Ye vital breaths, ye Vasus, let this morning libation of mine continue over to the mid-day libation. Let not me, the sacrifice, be broken off in the midst of the vital breaths, of the Vasus." He arises from it; he becomes free from sickness.

3. Now the [next] forty-four years are the mid-day libation, for the Trishtubh meter has forty-four syllables and the mid-day libation is offered with a Trishtubh hymn. The Rudras are connected with this part of the sacrifice. Verily, the vital breaths are the Rudras, for [on departing] they cause everything here to lament.

4. If any sickness should overtake him in this period of life, let him say: "Ye vital breaths, ye Rudras, let this mid-day libation of mine continue over to the third libation. Let not me, the sacrifice, be broken off in the midst of the vital breaths, of the Rudras." He arises from it; he becomes free from sickness.

5. Now, the [next] forty-eight years are the third libation, for the Jagati meter has forty-eight syllables and the third libation is offered with a Jagati hymn. The Adityas are connected with this part of the sacrifice. Verily, the vital breaths are the Adityas, for [on departing] they take everything to themselves.

6. If any sickness should overtake him in this period of life, let him say: "Ye vital breaths, ye Adityas, let this third libation of mine continue to a full length of life. Let not me, the sacrifice, be broken off in the midst of the vital breaths, of the Adityas." He arises from it; he becomes free from sickness.

7. Verily, it was this that Mahidasa Aitareya knew when he used to say: "Here, why do you afflict me with this sickness—me, who am not going to die with it?" He lived a hundred and sixteen years. He lives to a hundred and sixteen years who knows this.

17

1. When one hungers and thirsts and does not enjoy himself—that is a Preparatory Consecration Ceremony.

2. When one eats and drinks and enjoys himself—then he joins in the Upasada ceremonies.

3. When one laughs and eats and practises sexual intercourse— then he joins in the Chant and Recitation.

4. Austerity, alms-giving, uprightness, harmlessness, truthfulness—these are one's gifts for the priests.

5. Therefore they say: "He will procreate! He has procreated!"—that is his rebirth. Death is an ablution after the ceremony.

6. When Ghora Angirasa explained this to Krishna, the son of Devaki, he also explained—for he had become free from desire—"In the final hour one should take refuge in these three thoughts: 'You are the Indestructible; you are the Unshaken; you are the very essence of life.'" On this point there are these two Rig verses:

7. Proceeding from primeval seed,
   [The early morning light they see,
   That gleameth higher than the heaven].
   From out of darkness all around,
   We, gazing on the higher light—
   Yea, gazing on the higher light—
   To Surya, god among the gods,
   We have attained—the highest light!
   —yea, the highest light!

18

1. One should reverence the mind as Brahma—Thus with reference to the self.

Now with reference to the divinities—One should reverence space as Brahma.

—This is the twofold instruction with reference to the self and with reference to the divinities.

2. That Brahma has four quarters. One quarter is speech. One quarter is breath. One quarter is the eye. One quarter is the ear—Thus with reference to the self.

Now with reference to the divinities—One quarter is Agni. One quarter is Vayu. One quarter is Aditya. One quarter is the quarters of heaven.

—This is the twofold instruction with reference to the self and with reference to the divinities.

3. Speech, truly, is a fourth part of Brahma. It shines and glows

with Agni as its light. He shines and glows with fame, with splendor, and with eminence in sacred knowledge who knows this.

4. Breath, truly, is a fourth part of Brahma. It shines and glows with Vayu as its light. He shines and glows with fame, with splendor, and with eminence in sacred knowledge who knows this.

5. The eye, truly, is a fourth part of Brahma. It shines and glows with Aditya as its light. He shines and glows with fame, with splendor, and with eminence in sacred knowledge who knows this.

6. The ear, truly, is a fourth part of Brahma. It shines and glows with the quarters of heaven as its light. He shines and glows with fame, with splendor, and with eminence in sacred knowledge who knows this—yea, who knows this!

19

1. The sun is Brahma—this is the teaching. A further explanation thereof [is as follows].

In the beginning this world was merely non-being. It was existent. It developed. It turned into an egg. It lay for the period of a year. It was split asunder. One of the two eggshell-parts became silver, one gold.

2. That which was of silver is this earth. That which was of gold is the sky. What was the outer membrane is the mountains. What was the inner membrane is cloud and mist. What were the veins are the rivers. What was the fluid within is the ocean.

3. Now, what was born therefrom is yonder sun. When it was born, shouts and hurrahs, all beings and all desires rose up toward it. Therefore at its rising and at its every return shouts and hurrahs, all beings and all desires rise up toward it.

4. He who, knowing it thus, reverences the sun as Brahma—the prospect is that pleasant shouts will come unto him and delight him—yea, delight him!

4

1

1. *Om!* Now there was Janasruti, the great-grandson [of Janasruta], a pious dispenser, a liberal giver, a preparer of much food. He had rest-houses built everywhere with the thought, "Everywhere people will be eating of my food."

2. Now then, one time swans flew past in the night, and one swan spoke to another thus: "Hey! Ho! Short-sight! Short-sight! The light of Janasruti, the great-grandson [of Janasruta], has spread like the sky. Do not touch it, lest it burn you up!"

3. To it the other one then replied: "Come! Who is that man of whom you speak as if he were Raikva, the man with the cart?"

"Pray, how is it with Raikva, the man with the cart?"

4. "As the lower throws of dice all go to the highest throw, to the winner, so whatever good thing creatures do, all goes to him. I say the same thing of whoever knows what he knows."

5. Now Janasruti, the great-grandson [of Janasruta], overheard this. Then when he rose he said to the attendant: "Lo! you speak [of me] as if I were Raikva, the man with the cart!"

"Pray, how is it with Raikva, the man with the cart?"

6. "As the lower throws of dice all go to the highest throw, to the winner, so to this man, whatever good thing creatures do, all goes to him. I say the same thing of whoever knows what he knows."

7. Then the attendant, having sought, came back, saying, "I did not find him."

Then he said to him: "Oh! Where one searches for a Brahman, there seek for him."

8. He approached a man who was scratching the itch underneath a cart, and said to him: "Pray, Sir, are you Raikva, the man with the cart?"

"Oh! I am, indeed," he acknowledged.

Then the attendant went back, and said: "I have found him."

2

1. Then Janasruti, the great-grandson [of Janasruta], took six hundred cows and a gold necklace and a chariot drawn by a she-mule, and went back to him.

He said to him: [2] "Raikva, here are six hundred cows, and here is a gold necklace, and here is a chariot drawn by a she-mule. Now, Sir, teach me that divinity—the divinity which you reverence."

3. And to him then the other replied: "Oh! Necklace and carriage along with the cows be yours, O Sudra!"

And then again Janasruti, the great-grandson [of Janasruta], taking a thousand cows and a gold necklace and a chariot drawn by a she-mule, and his daughter too, went unto him.

4. Then he spoke unto him: "Raikva, here are a thousand cows, and here is a gold necklace, and here is a chariot drawn by a she-mule, and here is a wife, and here is the village in which you dwell. Pray, Sir, do you teach me."

5. Then, lifting up her face toward himself, he [i.e., Raikva] said: "He has brought these [cows] along!—Sudra, merely with this face you would cause me to speak."

—So those are called the Raikvaparna [villages], among the people of the Mahavrishas, where at his offer he lived.

Then he said to him:

3

1. "The Wind, verily, is a snatcher-unto-itself. Verily, when a fire blows out, it just goes to the Wind. When the sun sets, it just goes to the Wind. When the moon sets, it just goes to the Wind.

2. When water dries, goes up, it just goes to the Wind. For the Wind, truly, snatches all here to itself—Thus with reference to the divinities.

3. Now with reference to oneself—

Breath, verily, is a snatcher-unto-itself. When one sleeps, speech just goes to breath; the eye, to breath; the ear, to breath; the mind, to breath; for the breath, truly, snatches all here to itself.

4. Verily, these are two snatchers-unto-themselves: the Wind among the gods, breath among the vital breaths.

5. Now, once upon a time when Saunaka Kapeya and Abhipra-

tarin Kakshaseni were being served with food, a student of sacred knowledge begged of them. They did not give to him.

6. Then he said:
'One God has swallowed up four mighty beings.
Who is that world's protector, O Kapeya?
Him mortal men perceive not, though abiding
In manifolded forms, Abhipratarin.

Verily, this food has not been offered to whom it belongs.'

7. Then Saunaka Kapeya, considering this, replied:
'The Self of gods, of creatures Procreator,
With golden teeth Devourer, truly Wise One—
His mightiness they say is truly mighty;
He eats what is not food, and is not eaten.

Thus, verily, O student of sacred knowledge, do we reverence It— Give ye him alms.'

8. Then they gave to him.

These five and the other five make ten, and that is the highest throw in dice. Therefore in all regions ten, the highest throw, is food. That is Viraj and an eater of food. Through it this whole world came to light. This whole world comes to light for him, he becomes an eater of food, who knows this—yea, who knows this."

4

1. Once upon a time Satyakama Jabala addressed his mother Jabala: "Madam! I desire to live the life of a student of sacred knowledge. Of what family, pray, am I?"

2. Then she said to him: "I do not know this, my dear—of what family you are. In my youth, when I went about a great deal serving as a maid, I got you. So I do not know of what family you are. However, I am Jabala by name; you are Satyakama by name. So you may speak of yourself as Satyakama Jabala."

3. Then he went to Haridrumata Gautama, and said: "I will live the life of a student of sacred knowledge. I will become a pupil of yours, Sir."

4. To him he then said: "Of what family, pray, are you, my dear?"

Then he said: "I do not know this, Sir, of what family I am. I asked my mother. She answered me: 'In my youth, when I went about a great deal serving as a maid, I got you. So I do not know this, of what family you are. However, I am Jabala by name; you are Satyakama by name.' So I am Satyakama Jabala, Sir."

5. To him he then said: "A non-Brahman would not be able to explain thus. Bring the fuel, my dear. I will receive you as a pupil. You have not deviated from the truth."

After having received him as a pupil, he separated out four hundred lean, weak cows and said: "Follow these, my dear."

As he was driving them on, he said: "I may not return without a thousand." So he lived away a number of years. When they came to be a thousand,

5

[1] then the bull spoke to him, saying: "Satyakama!"

"Sir!" he replied.

"We have reached a thousand, my dear. Bring us to the teacher's house. [2] And let me tell you a quarter of Brahma."

"Tell me, Sir."

To him it then said: "One sixteenth is the east. One sixteenth is the west. One sixteenth is the south. One sixteenth is the north. This, verily, my dear, is the quarter of Brahma, consisting of four sixteenths, named the Shining.

3. He who, knowing it thus, reverences a quarter of Brahma, consisting of four sixteenths, as the Shining, becomes shining in this world. Then he wins shining worlds who, knowing it thus, reverences a quarter of Brahma, consisting of four sixteenths, as the Shining.

6

1. Fire will tell you a quarter."

He then, when it was the morrow, drove the cows on. Where they came at evening, there he built a fire, penned in the cows, laid on fuel, and sat down to the west of the fire, facing the east.

2. The fire spoke to him, saying: "Satyakama!"

"Sir!" he replied.

3. "Let me tell you, my dear, a quarter of Brahma."

"Tell me, Sir."

To him it then said: "One sixteenth is the earth. One sixteenth is the atmosphere. One sixteenth is the sky. One sixteenth is the ocean. This, verily, my dear, is the quarter of Brahma, consisting of four sixteenths, named the Endless.

4. He who, knowing it thus, reverences a quarter of Brahma, consisting of four sixteenths, as the Endless, becomes endless in this world. Then he wins endless worlds who, knowing it thus, reverences a quarter of Brahma, consisting of four sixteenths, as the Endless.

7

1. A swan will tell you a quarter."

He then, when it was the morrow, drove the cows on. Where they came at evening, there he built a fire, penned in the cows, laid on fuel, and sat down to the west of the fire, facing the east.

2. A swan flew down to him, and spoke to him, saying: "Satyakama!"

"Sir!" he replied.

3. "Let me tell you, my dear, a quarter of Brahma."

"Tell me, Sir."

To him it then said: "One sixteenth is fire. One sixteenth is the sun. One sixteenth is the moon. One sixteenth is lightning.

This, verily, my dear, is the quarter of Brahma, consisting of four sixteenths, named the Luminous.

4. He who, knowing it thus, reverences a quarter of Brahma, consisting of four sixteenths, as the Luminous, becomes luminous in this world. Then he wins luminous worlds who, knowing it thus, reverences a quarter of Brahma, consisting of four sixteenths, as the Luminous.

8

1. A diver-bird will tell you a quarter."

He then, when it was the morrow, drove the cows on. Where they came at evening, there he built a fire, penned in the cows, laid on fuel, and sat down to the west of the fire, facing the east.

2. A diver-bird flew down to him, and spoke to him, saying: "Satyakama!"

"Sir!" he replied.

3. "Let me tell you, my dear, a quarter of Brahma."

"Tell me, Sir."

To him it then said: "One sixteenth is breath. One sixteenth is the eye. One sixteenth is the ear. One sixteenth is mind. This, verily, my dear, is the quarter of Brahma, consisting of four sixteenths, named Possessing-a-support.

4. He who, knowing it thus, reverences a quarter of Brahma, consisting of four sixteenths, as Possessing-a-support, comes to possess a support in this world. Then he wins worlds possessing a support who, knowing it thus, reverences a quarter of Brahma, consisting of four sixteenths, as Possessing-a-support."

9

1. Then he reached the teacher's house. The teacher spoke to him, saying: "Satyakama!"

"Sir!" he replied.

2. "Verily, my dear, you shine like a Brahma-knower. Who, pray, has instructed you?"

"Others than men," he acknowledged. "But do you yourself please speak to me; [3] for I have heard from those who are like you, Sir, that the knowledge which has been learned from a teacher best helps one to attain his end."

To him he then declared it. In it then nothing whatsoever was omitted—yea, nothing was omitted.

10

1. Now, verily, Upakosala Kamalayana dwelt with Satyakama Jabala as a student of sacred knowledge. For twelve years he tended his fires. Then, although accustomed to allow other pupils to return home, him he did not allow to return.

2. His wife said to him: "The student of sacred knowledge has

performed his penance. He has tended the fires well. Let not the fires anticipate you in teaching him. Teach him yourself."

But he went off on a journey without having told him.

3. Then, on account of sickness, he [i.e., Upakosala] took to not eating.

The teacher's wife said to him: "Student of sacred knowledge, eat. Why, pray, do you not eat?"

Then he said: "Many and various are the desires here in this man. I am filled up with sicknesses. I will not eat."

4. So then the fires said among themselves: "The student of sacred knowledge has performed his penance. He has tended us well. Come! Let us teach him."

Then they said to him: [5] "Brahma is life. Brahma is joy. Brahma is the void."

Then he said: "I understand that Brahma is life. But joy and void I do not understand."

They said: "Joy—verily, that is the same as the Void. The Void—verily, that is the same as Joy." And then they explained to him life and space.

11

1. So then the householder's fire instructed him: "Earth, fire, food, sun [are forms of me. But] the Person who is seen in the sun—I am he; I am he indeed!"

2. [Chorus of the fires:] "He who knows and reverences this fire thus, repels evil-doing from himself, becomes possessor of a world, reaches a full length of life, lives long. His descendants do not become destroyed. Both in this world and in the yonder we serve him who knows and reverences this fire thus."

12

1. So then the southern sacrificial fire instructed him: "Water, the quarters of heaven, the stars, the moon [are forms of me. But] the Person who is seen in the moon—I am he; I am he indeed!"

2. [Chorus of the fires:] "He who knows and reverences this fire

thus, repels evil-doing from himself, becomes possessor of a world, reaches a full length of life, lives long. His descendants do not become destroyed. Both in this world and in the yonder we serve him who knows and reverences this fire thus."

13

1. So then the eastern fire instructed him: "Breath, space, sky, lightning [are forms of me. But] the Person who is seen in the lightning—I am he; I am he indeed!"
2. [Chorus of the fires:] "He who knows and reverences this fire thus, repels evil-doing from himself, becomes possessor of a world, reaches a full length of life, lives long. His descendants do not become destroyed. Both in this world and in the yonder we serve him who knows and reverences this fire thus."

14

1. Then the fires said: "Upakosala dear, you have this knowledge of ourselves and the knowledge of the Soul. But the teacher will tell you the way."

Then the teacher returned. The teacher spoke to him, saying: "Upakosala!"
2. "Sir!" he then replied.

"Your face, my dear, shines like a Brahma-knower's. Who, pray, has instructed you?"

"Who, pray, would instruct me, Sir?"—Here he denied it, as it were—"These! They are of this appearance now, but they were of a different appearance!"—Here he alluded to the fires—

"What, pray, my dear, did they indeed tell you?"
3. "This—" he acknowledged.

"Verily, my dear, they did indeed tell you the worlds. But I will tell you something. As water adheres not to the leaf of a lotus-flower, so evil action adheres not to him who knows this."

"Tell me, Sir."

To him he then said:

15

1. "That Person who is seen in the eye—He is the Self," said he. "That is the immortal, the fearless. That is Brahma. So even if they pour clarified butter or water on that, it goes away to the edges.

2. They call this 'Loveliness-uniter,' for all lovely things come together unto it. All lovely things come together unto him who knows this.

3. And this is also 'Goods-bringer,' for it brings all goods. He brings all goods who knows this.

4. And this one is also 'Light-bringer,' for it shines in all worlds. He shines in all worlds who knows this.

5. Now, whether they perform the cremation obsequies in the case of such a person or not, they [i.e., the dead] pass over into a flame; from a flame, into the day; from the day, into the half-month of the waxing moon; from the half-month of the waxing moon, into the six months during which the sun moves northwards; from the months, into the year; from the year, into the sun; from the sun, into the moon; from the moon, into lightning. There there is a Person who is non-human.

6. He leads them on to Brahma. This is the way to the gods, the way to Brahma. They who proceed by it return not to the human condition here—yea, they return not!"

16

1. Verily, he who purifies here is a sacrifice. Truly, when he moves, he purifies this whole world. Since when he moves he purifies this whole world, therefore indeed he is a sacrifice.

His two paths are mind and speech.

2. Of these the Brahman priest forms one with his mind; the Hotri, the Adhvaryu, and the Udgatri priests, the other with speech.

In case, after the morning litany has commenced, the Brahman priest interrupts before the concluding verse, [3] he forms only one path. The other becomes discontinued.

3. As a one-legged man walking, or a chariot proceeding with one wheel, suffers injury, so his sacrifice suffers injury. The institutor of

the sacrifice suffers injury after the sacrifice which suffers injury. He becomes worse off by having sacrificed.

4. But in case, after the morning litany has commenced, the Brahman priest does not interrupt before the concluding verse, they form both paths; the other does not become discontinued.

5. As a two-legged man walking, or a chariot proceeding with both wheels, is well supported, so his sacrifice is well supported. The institutor of the sacrifice is well supported after the sacrifice which is well supported. He becomes better off by having sacrificed.

17

1. Prajapati brooded upon the worlds. As they were being brooded upon, he extracted their essences: fire from the earth, wind from the atmosphere, the sun from the sky.

2. Upon these three deities he brooded. As they were being brooded upon, he extracted their essences: from the fire, the Rig verses; from the wind, the Yajus formulas; the Saman chants, from the sun.

3. Upon this threefold knowledge he brooded. As it was being brooded upon, he extracted its essences: *bhur* from the Rig verses, *bhuvas* from the Yajus formulas, *svar* from the Saman chants.

4. So if there should come an injury in connection with the Rig verses, one should make an oblation in the householder's fire with the words "*bhur!* Hail!" So by the essence of the Rig verses themselves, by the power of the Rig verses he mends the injury to the Rig verses of the sacrifice.

5. Moreover, if there should come an injury in connection with the Yajus formulas, one should make an oblation in the southern fire with the words "*bhuvas!* Hail!" So by the essence of the Yajus formulas themselves, by the power of the Yajus formulas he mends the injury to he Yajus formulas of the sacrifice.

6. Moreover, if there should come an injury in connection with the Saman chants, one should make an oblation in the eastern fire with the words "*svar!* Hail!" So by the essence of the Saman chants, by the power of the Saman chants he mends the injury to the Saman chants of the sacrifice.

7. So, as one would mend gold with borax-salt, silver with gold, tin with silver, lead with tin, iron with lead, wood with iron or with leather, [8] even so with the power of those worlds, of those divinities, of that triple knowledge one mends the injury to the sacrifice. Verily, that sacrifice is healed in which there is a Brahman priest who knows this.

9. Verily, that sacrifice is inclined to the north in which there is a Brahman priest who knows this. Verily, there is this song on the Brahman priest who knows this:

> Whichever way he turns himself,
> In that same way goes [10] common man.
> The Brahman priest alone protects
> The sacrificers like a dog.

Verily, the Brahman priest who knows this guards the sacrifice, the institutor of the sacrifice, and all the priests. Therefore one should make as his Brahman priest one who knows this, not one who does not know this—yea, not one who does not know this.

5

1

1. Om! Verily, he who knows the chiefest and best, becomes the chiefest and best. Breath, verily, is the chiefest and best.

2. Verily, he who knows the most excellent, becomes the most excellent of his own [people]. Speech, verily, is the most excellent.

3. Verily, he who knows the firm basis, has a firm basis both in this world and in the yonder. The eye, verily, is a firm basis.

4. Verily, he who knows attainment—for him wishes are attained, both human and divine. The ear, verily, is attainment.

5. Verily, he who knows the abode, becomes an abode of his own [people]. The mind, verily, is the abode.

6. Now, the Vital Breaths disputed among themselves on self-superiority, saying [in turn]: "I am superior!" "I am superior!"

7. Those Vital Breaths went to Father Prajapati, and said: "Sir! Which of us is the most superior?"

He said to them: "That one of you after whose going off the body appears as if it were the very worst off—he is the most superior of you."

8. Speech went off. Having remained away a year, it came around again, and said: "How have you been able to live without me?"

"As the dumb, not speaking, but breathing with the breath, seeing with the eye, hearing with the ear, thinking with the mind. Thus."

Speech entered in.

9. The Eye went off. Having remained away a year, it came around again, and said: "How have you been able to live without me?"

"As the blind, not seeing, but breathing with the breath, speaking with speech, hearing with the ear, thinking with the mind. Thus."

The Eye entered in.

10. The Ear went off. Having remained away a year, it came around again, and said: "How have you been able to live without me?"

"As the deaf, not hearing, but breathing with the breath, speaking with speech, seeing with the eye, thinking with the mind. Thus."

The Ear entered in.

11. The Mind went off. Having remained away a year, it came around again, and said: "How have you been able to live without me?"

"As simpletons, mindless, but breathing with the breath, speaking with speech, seeing with the eye, hearing with the ear. Thus."

The Mind entered in.

12. Now when the Breath was about to go off—as a fine horse might tear out the pegs of his foot-tethers all together, thus did it tear out the other Breaths all together. They all came to it, and said: "Sir! Remain. You are the most superior of us. Do not go off."

13. Then Speech said unto that one: "If I am the most excellent, so are you the most excellent."

Then the Eye said unto that one: "If I am a firm basis, so are you a firm basis."

14. Then the Ear said unto that one: "If I am attainment, so are you attainment."

Then the Mind said unto that one: "If I am an abode, so are you an abode."

15. Verily, they do not call them "Speeches," nor "Eyes," nor "Ears," nor "Minds." They call them "Breaths," for the vital breath is all these.

2

1. It said: "What will be my food?"

"Whatever there is here, even to dogs and birds," they said.

So this, verily, is the food of breath. Verily, breath is its evident name. Verily, in the case of one who knows this, there is nothing whatever that is not food.

2. It said: "What will be my garment?"

"Water," they said.

Therefore, verily, when people are about to eat, they enswathe it [i.e., the breath] with water both before and after. It is accustomed to receive a garment; it becomes not naked.

3. When Satyakama Jabala told this to Gosruti Vaiyagrapadya, he also said: "Even if one should tell this to a dried-up stump, branches would be produced on it and leaves would spring forth."

4. Now, if one should wish to come to something great, let him on the night of a new moon perform the Preparatory Consecration Ceremony, and on the night of the full moon mix a mixed potion of all sorts of herbs with sour milk and honey.

"Hail to the chiefest and best!"—with these words he should offer a libation of melted butter in the fire and pour the residue into the potion.

5. "Hail to the most excellent!"—with these words he should offer a libation of melted butter in the fire and pour the residue into the potion.

"Hail to the firm basis!"—with these words he should offer a libation of melted butter in the fire and pour the residue into the potion.

"Hail to the abode!"—with these words he should offer a libation of melted butter in the fire and pour the residue into the potion.

6. Then, creeping back [from the fire], and taking the potion in his hollowed hands, he mutters: "Thou art He by name, for this whole world is at home in thee, for thou art pre-eminent and supreme, king and overlord. Let him bring me to pre-eminence and supremacy, kingship and overlordship! Let me be all this!"

7. Verily then with this Rig verse he takes a sip at each hemistich:
"The food which is god Savitri's,"
"That for ourselves do we prefer,"
"The best, the all-refreshing food";
"The Giver's strength may we attain!"

8. After having cleansed the drinking-vessel or goblet, he lies down to the west of the fire either on a skin or on the bare ground with voice restrained and self-possessed. If he should see a woman, he may know that the rite is successful.

9. As to this there is the following verse:
> If during rites done for a wish
> One sees a woman in his dream,
> Success he there may recognize
> In this appearance of his dream
> —In this appearance of his dream.

3

1. Svetaketu Aruneya attended an assembly of the Pancalas. Then Pravahana Jaibali said to him: "Young man, has your father instructed you?"

"He has indeed, Sir."

2. "Do you know unto what creatures go forth hence?"

"No, Sir."

"Do you know how they return again?"

"No, Sir."

"Do you know the parting of the two ways, one leading to the gods, and one leading to the fathers?"

"No, Sir."

3. "Do you know how [it is that] yonder world is not filled up?"

"No, Sir."

"Do you know how in the fifth oblation water comes to have a human voice?"

"No, indeed, Sir."

4. "Now, pray, how did you say of yourself that you had been instructed? Indeed, how could one who would not know these things speak of himself as having been instructed?"

Distressed, he then went to his father's place. Then he said to him: "Verily, indeed, without having instructed me, you, Sir, said: 'I have instructed you.'

5. Five questions a fellow of the princely class has asked me. I was not able to explain even one of them."

Then he [i.e., the father] said: "As you have told them to me here, I do not know even one of them. If I had known them, how would I not have told them to you?"

6. Then Gautama went to the king's place. To him, when he arrived, he [i.e., the king] had proper attention shown. Then on the morrow he went up to the audience-hall. Then he [i.e., the king] said to him: "Honored Gautama, you may choose for yourself a boon of human wealth."

Then he said: "Human wealth be yours, O king! The word which you said in the presence of the young man, even that do you speak to me."

Then he became troubled.

7. "Wait a while," he commanded him. Then he said: "As to what you have told me, O Gautama, this knowledge has never yet come to Brahmans before you; and therefore in all the worlds has the rule belonged to the Kshatriya only." Then he said to him:

4

1. "Yonder world, verily, O Gautama, is a sacrificial fire. In this case the sun is the fuel; the light-rays, the smoke; the day, the flame; the moon, the coals; the stars, the sparks.

2. In this fire the gods offer faith. From this oblation arises King Soma.

5

1. The rain-cloud, verily, O Gautama, is a sacrificial fire. In this case wind is the fuel; mist, the smoke; lightning, the flame; the thunderbolt, the coals; hailstones, the sparks.

2. In this fire the gods offer King Soma. From this oblation arises rain.

6

1. The earth, verily, O Gautama, is a sacrificial fire. In this case the year is the fuel; space, the smoke; night, the flame; the quarters of heaven, the coals; the intermediate quarters of heaven, the sparks.

2. In this fire the gods offer rain. From this oblation arises food.

7

1. Man, verily, O Gautama, is a sacrificial fire. In this case speech is the fuel; breath, the smoke; the tongue, the flame; the eyes, the coals; the ear, the sparks.

2. In this fire the gods offer food. From this oblation arises semen.

8

1. Woman, verily, O Gautama, is a sacrificial fire. In this case the sexual organ is the fuel; when one invites, the smoke; the vulva, the flame; when one inserts, the coals; the sexual pleasure, the sparks.

2. In this fire the gods offer semen. From this oblation arises the fetus.

9

1. Thus indeed in the fifth oblation water comes to have a human voice.

After he has lain within for ten months, or for however long it is, as a fetus covered with membrane, then he is born.

2. When born, he lives for as long as is his length of life. When deceased, they carry him hence to the appointed place for the fire from whence indeed he came, from whence he arose.

10

1. So those who know this, and those too who worship in a forest with the thought that 'Faith is austerity,' pass into the flame; from the flame, into the day; from the day, into the half-month of the waxing moon; from the half-month of the waxing moon, into the six months during which the sun moves northward; [2] from those months, into the year; from the year, into the sun; from the sun, into the moon; from the moon, into the lightning. There there is a Person who is non-human. He leads them on to Brahma. This is the way leading to the gods.

3. But those who in the village reverence a belief in sacrifice, merit, and almsgiving—they pass into the smoke; from the smoke, into the night; from the night, into the latter half of the month; from the latter half of the month, into the six months during which the sun

moves southward—these do not reach the year; [4] from those months, into the world of the fathers; from the world of the fathers, into space; from space, into the moon. That is King Soma. That is the food of the gods. The gods eat that.

5. After having remained in it as long as there is a residue [of their good works], then by that course by which they came they return again, just as they came, into space; from space, into wind. After having become wind, one becomes smoke. After having become smoke, he becomes mist.

6. After having become mist, he becomes cloud. After having become cloud, he rains down. They are born here as rice and barley, as herbs and trees, as sesame plants and beans. Thence, verily, indeed, it is difficult to emerge; for only if some one or other eats him as food and emits him as semen, does he develop further.

7. Accordingly, those who are of pleasant conduct here—the prospect is, indeed, that they will enter a pleasant womb, either the womb of a Brahman, or the womb of a Kshatriya, or the womb of a Vaisya. But those who are of stinking conduct here—the prospect is, indeed, that they will enter a stinking womb, either the womb of a dog, or the womb of a swine, or the womb of an outcast.

8. But on neither of these ways are the small, continually returning creatures, [those of whom it is said:] 'Be born, and die'—theirs is a third state.

Thereby [it comes about that] yonder world is not filled up.

Therefore one should seek to guard himself. As to this there is the following verse:

9. The plunderer of gold, the liquor-drinker,
The invader of a teacher's bed, the Brahman-killer—
These four sink downward in the scale,
And, fifth, he who consorts with them.

10. But he who knows these five fires thus, is not stained with evil, even though consorting with those people. He becomes pure, clean, possessor of a pure world, who knows this—yea, he who knows this!"

11

1. Pracinasala Aupamanyava, Satyayajna Paulushi, Indradyumna Bhallaveya, Jana Sarkarakshya, and Budila Asvatarasvi—these great

householders, greatly learned in sacred lore, having come together, pondered: "Who is our Atman [Soul]? What is Brahma?"

2. Then they agreed among themselves: "Verily, Sirs, Uddalaka Aruni here studies exactly this Universal Atman. Come, let us go unto him."

Then unto him they went.

3. Then he agreed with himself: "These great householders, greatly learned in sacred lore, will question me. I may not be able to answer them everything. Come! Let me direct them to another."

4. Then he said to them: "Verily, Sirs, Asvapati Kaikeya studies just this Universal Atman. Come! Let us go unto him."

Then unto him they went.

5. Then to them severally, when they arrived, he had proper attentions shown. He was indeed a man who, on rising, could say:

"Within my realm there is no thief,
No miser, nor a drinking man,
None altarless, none ignorant,
No man unchaste, no wife unchaste."

"Verily, Sirs, I am about to have a sacrifice performed. As large a gift as I shall give to each priest, so large a gift will I give to you, Sirs. Remain, my Sirs."

6. Then they said: "With whatever subject a person is concerned, of that indeed he should speak. You know just this Universal Atman. Him indeed do you tell to us."

7. Then he said to them: "On the morrow will I make reply." Then with fuel in their hands in the morning they returned. Then, without having first received them as pupils, he spoke to them as follows:

12

1. "Aupamanyava, whom do you reverence as the Atman?"

"The heaven indeed, Sir, O King," said he.

"The Universal Atman is, verily, that brightly shining one which you reverence as the Atman. Therefore Soma is seen pressed out and continually pressed out in your family.

2. You eat food; you see what is pleasing. He eats food; he sees what is pleasing. There is eminence in sacred knowledge in the family of him who reverences the Universal Atman thus. That, however, is

only the head of the Atman," said he. "Your head would have fallen off, if you had not come unto me."

13

1. Then he said to Satyayajna Paulushi: "Pracinayogya! Whom do you reverence as the Atman?"

"The sun indeed, Sir, O King," said he.

"The Universal Atman is, verily, that manifold one which you reverence as the Atman. Therefore much of all sorts is seen in your family, [2] [e.g.] a chariot drawn by a she-mule rolled up [before your door], a female slave, a gold necklace. You eat food; you see what is pleasing. He eats food; he sees what is pleasing. There is eminence in sacred knowledge in the family of him who reverences that Universal Atman thus. That, however, is only the eye of the Atman," said he. "You would have become blind, if you had not come unto me."

14

1. Then he said to Indradyumna Bhallaveya: "Vaiyaghrapadya! Whom do you reverence as the Atman?"

"The wind indeed, Sir, O King," said he.

"The Universal Atman is, verily, that which possesses various paths, which you reverence as the Atman. Therefore offerings come unto you in various ways; rows of chariots follow you in various ways.

2. You eat food; you see what is pleasing. He eats food; he sees what is pleasing. There is eminence in sacred knowledge in the family of him who reverences that Universal Atman thus.

That, however, is only the breath of the Atman," said he. "Your breath would have departed, if you had not come unto me."

15

1. Then he said to Jana: "Sarkarakshya! Whom do you reverence as the Atman?"

"Space indeed, Sir, O King," said he.

"The Universal Atman is, verily, that expanded one, which you reverence as the Atman. Therefore you are expanded with offspring and wealth.

2. You eat food; you see what is pleasing. He eats food; he sees what is pleasing. There is eminence in sacred knowledge in the family of him who reverences that Universal Atman thus.

That, however, is only the body of the Atman," said he. "Your body would have fallen to pieces, if you had not come unto me."

16

1. Then he said to Budila Asvatarasvi: Vaiyaghrapadya! Whom do you reverence as the Atman?"

"Water indeed, Sir, O King," said he.

"The Universal Atman is, verily, that wealth, which you reverence as the Atman. Therefore you are wealthy and thriving.

2. You eat food; you see what is pleasing. He eats food; he sees what is pleasing. There is eminence in sacred knowledge in the family of him who reverences that Universal Atman thus.

That, however, is only the bladder of the Atman," said he. "Your bladder would have burst, if you had not come unto me."

17

1. Then he said to Uddalaka Aruni: "Gautama! Whom do you reverence as the Atman?"

"The earth indeed, Sir, O King," said he.

"The Universal Atman is, verily, that support, which you reverence as the Atman. Therefore you are supported with offspring and cattle.

2. You eat food; you see what is pleasing. He eats food; he sees what is pleasing. There is eminence in sacred knowledge in the family of him who reverences that Universal Atman thus.

That, however, is only the feet of the Atman," said he.

"Your feet would have withered away, if you had not come unto me."

18

1. Then he said to them: "Verily, indeed, you here eat food, knowing this Universal Atman as if something separate. He, however, who reverences this Universal Atman that is of the measure of the span—thus, [yet] is to be measured by thinking of oneself—he eats food in all worlds, in all beings, in all selves.

2. The brightly shining [heaven] is indeed the head of that Universal Atman. The manifold [sun] is his eye. That which possesses various paths [i.e., the wind] is his breath. The extended [space] is his body. Wealth [i.e., water] is indeed his bladder. The support [i.e., the earth] is indeed his feet. The sacrificial area is indeed his breast. The sacrificial grass is his hair. The Garhapatya fire is his heart. The Anvaharyapacana fire is his mind. The Ahavaniya fire is his mouth.

19

1. Therefore the first food which one may come to, should be offered. The first oblation which he would offer he should offer with 'Hail to the Prana breath!' The Prana breath is satisfied.

2. The Prana breath being satisfied, the eye is satisfied. The eye being satisfied, the sun is satisfied. The sun being satisfied, the heaven is satisfied. The heaven being satisfied, whatever the heaven and the sun rule over is satisfied. Along with the satisfaction thereof, he is satisfied with offspring, with cattle, with food, with the glow of health, and with eminence in sacred knowledge.

20

1. Then the second oblation which he would offer he should offer with 'Hail to the Vyana breath!' The Vyana breath is satisfied.

2. The Vyana breath being satisfied, the ear is satisfied. The ear being satisfied, the moon is satisfied. The moon being satisfied, the quarters of heaven are satisfied. The quarters of heaven being satisfied, whatever the moon and the quarters of heaven rule over is satis-

fied. Along with the satisfaction thereof, he is satisfied with offspring, with cattle, with food, with the glow of health, and with eminence in sacred knowledge.

21

1. Then the third offering which he would offer he should offer with 'Hail to the Apana breath!' The Apana breath is satisfied.

2. The Apana breath being satisfied, speech is satisfied. Speech being satisfied, fire is satisfied. Fire being satisfied, the earth is satisfied. The earth being satisfied, whatever the earth and fire rule over is satisfied. Along with the satisfaction thereof, he is satisfied with offspring, with cattle, with food, with the glow of health, and with eminence in sacred knowledge.

22

1. Then the fourth offering which he would offer he should offer with 'Hail to the Samana breath!' The Samana breath is satisfied.

2. The Samana breath being satisfied, the mind is satisfied. The mind being satisfied, the rain-god is satisfied. The rain-god being satisfied, lightning is satisfied. Lightning being satisfied, whatever the rain-god and lightning rule over is satisfied. Along with the satisfaction thereof, he is satisfied with offspring, with cattle, with food, with the glow of health, and with eminence in sacred knowledge.

23

1. Then the fifth offering which he would offer he should offer with 'Hail to the Udana breath!' The Udana breath is satisfied.

2. The Udana breath being satisfied, wind is satisfied. Wind being satisfied, space is satisfied. Space being satisfied, whatever wind and space rule over is satisfied. Along with the satisfaction thereof, he is satisfied with offspring, with cattle, with food, with the glow of health, and with eminence in sacred knowledge.

24

1. If one offers the Agnihotra sacrifice without knowing this—that would be just as if he were to remove the live coals and pour the offering on ashes.

2. But if one offers the Agnihotra sacrifice knowing it thus, his offering is made in all worlds, in all beings, in all selves.

3. So, as a rush-reed laid on a fire would be burned up, even so are burned up all the evils of him who offers the Agnihotra sacrifice knowing it thus.

4. And therefore, if one who knows this should offer the leavings even to an outcast, it would be offered in his Universal Atman. As to this there is the following verse:

> As hungry children sit around
> About their mother here in life,
> E'en so all beings sit around
> The Agnihotra sacrifice."

6

1

1. *Om!* Now, there was Svetaketu Aruneya. To him his father said: "Live the life of a student of sacred knowledge. Verily, my dear, from our family there is no one unlearned [in the Vedas], a Brahman by connection as it were.

2. He then, having become a pupil at the age of twelve, having studied all the Vedas, returned at the age of twenty-four, conceited, thinking himself learned, proud.

3. Then his father said to him: "Svetaketu, my dear, since now you are conceited, think yourself learned, and are proud, did you also ask for that teaching whereby what has not been heard of becomes heard of, what has not been thought of becomes thought of, what has not been understood becomes understood?"

4. "How, pray, Sir, is that teaching?"

"Just as, my dear, by one piece of clay everything made of clay may be known—the modification is merely a verbal distinction, a name; the reality is just 'clay'—

5. Just as, my dear, by one copper ornament everything made of copper may be known—the modification is merely a verbal distinction, a name; the reality is just 'copper'—

6. Just as, my dear, by one nail-scissors everything made of iron may be known—the modification is merely a verbal distinction, a name; the reality is just 'iron'—so, my dear, is that teaching."

7. "Verily, those honored men did not know this; for, if they had known it, why would they not have told me? But do you, Sir, tell me it."

"So be it, my dear," said he.

2

1. "In the beginning, my dear, this world was just Being, one only, without a second. To be sure, some people say: 'In the beginning this

world was just Non-being, one only, without a second; from that Non-being Being was produced.'

2. But verily, my dear, whence could this be?" said he. "How from Non-being could Being be produced? On the contrary, my dear, in the beginning this world was just Being, one only, without a second.

3. It bethought itself: 'Would that I were many! Let me procreate myself!' It emitted heat. That heat bethought itself: 'Would that I were many! Let me procreate myself.' It emitted water. Therefore whenever a person grieves or perspires from the heat, then there is produced water [i.e., either tears or perspiration].

4. That water bethought itself: 'Would that I were many! Let me procreate myself.' It emitted food. Therefore whenever it rains, then there is abundant food. So food for eating is produced just from water.

3

1. Now, of these beings here there are just three origins: [there are beings] born from an egg, born from a living thing, born from a sprout.

2. That divinity [i.e., Being] bethought itself: 'Come! Let me enter these three divinities [i.e., heat, water, and food] with this living Soul, and separate out name and form.

3. Let me make each one of them threefold.' That divinity entered into these three divinities with this living Soul, and separated out name and form.

4. It made each of them threefold.

Now, verily, my dear, understand from me how each of these three divinities becomes threefold.

4

1. Whatever red form fire has, is the form of heat; whatever white, the form of water; whatever dark, the form of food. The firehood has gone from fire: the modification is merely a verbal distinction, a name. The reality is just 'the three forms.'

2. Whatever red form the sun has, is the form of heat; whatever white, the form of water; whatever dark, the form of food. The sun-hood has gone from the sun: the modification is merely a verbal distinction, a name. The reality is just 'the three forms.'

3. Whatever red form the moon has, is the form of heat; whatever white, the form of water; whatever dark, the form of food. The moon-hood has gone from the moon: the modification is merely a verbal distinction, a name. The reality is just 'the three forms.'

4. Whatever red form the lightning has, is the form of heat; whatever white, the form of water; whatever dark, the form of food. The lightninghood has gone from the lightning: the modification is merely a verbal distinction, a name. The reality is just 'the three forms.'

5. Verily, it was just this that the great householders, greatly learned in sacred lore, knew when they said of old: 'No one now will bring up to us what has not been heard of, what has not been thought of, what has not been understood.' For from these [three forms] they knew [everything].

6. They knew that whatever appeared red was the form of heat. They knew that whatever appeared white was the form of water. They knew that whatever appeared dark was the form of food.

7. They knew that whatever appeared un-understood, is a combination of just these divinities.

Verily, my dear, understand from me how each of these three divinities, upon reaching man, becomes threefold.

5

1. Food, when eaten, becomes divided into three parts. That which is its coarsest constituent, becomes the feces; that which is medium, the flesh; that which is finest, the mind.

2. Water, when drunk, becomes divided into three parts. That which is its coarsest constituent, becomes the urine; that which is medium, the blood; that which is finest, the breath.

3. Heat, when eaten, becomes divided into three parts. That which is its coarsest constituent, becomes bone; that which is medium, the marrow; that which is finest, the voice.

4. For, my dear, the mind consists of food; the breath consists of water; the voice consists of heat."

"Do you, Sir, cause me to understand even more."
"So be it, my dear," said he.

6

1. "Of coagulated milk, my dear, when churned, that which is the finest essence all moves upward; it becomes butter.

2. Even so, verily, my dear, of food, when eaten, that which is the finest essence all moves upward; it becomes the mind.

3. Of water, my dear, when drunk, that which is the finest essence all moves upward; it becomes the breath.

4. Of heat, my dear, when eaten, that which is the finest essence all moves upward; it becomes the voice.

5. For, my dear, the mind consists of food; the breath consists of water; the voice consists of heat."

"Do you, Sir, cause me to understand even more."
"So be it, my dear," said he.

7

1. "A person, my dear, consists of sixteen parts. For fifteen days do not eat; drink water at will. Breath, which consists of water, will not be cut off from one who drinks water."

2. Then for fifteen days he did not eat. So then he approached him, saying, "What shall I say, Sir?"
"The Rig verses, my dear, the Yajus formulas, the Saman chants."
Then he said: "Verily, they do not come to me, Sir."

3. To him he then said: "Just as, my dear, a single coal of the size of a fire-fly may be left over from a great kindled fire, but with it the fire would not thereafter burn much—so, my dear, of your sixteen parts a single sixteenth part may be left over, but with it you do not now apprehend the Vedas. Eat; then you will understand from me."

4. Then he ate. So then he approached him. Then whatsoever he asked him, he answered everything. To him he then said:

5. "Just as, my dear, one may, by covering it with straw, make

a single coal of the size of a fire-fly that has been left over from a great kindled fire blaze up, and with it the fire would thereafter burn much—[6] so, my dear, of your sixteen parts a single sixteenth part has been left over. After having been covered with food, it has blazed up. With it you now apprehend the Vedas; for, my dear, the mind consists of food, the breath consists of water, the voice consists of heat."

Then he understood from him—yea, he understood.

8

1. Then Uddalaka Aruni said to Svetaketu, his son: "Understand from me, my dear, the condition of sleep. When a person here sleeps, as it is called, then, my dear, he has reached Being, he has gone to his own. Therefore they say of him "he sleeps"; for he has gone to his own.

2. As a bird fastened with a string, after flying in this direction and in that without finding an abode elsewhere, rests down just upon its fastening—even so, my dear, the mind, after flying in this direction and in that without finding an abode elsewhere, rests down just upon breath; for the mind, my dear, has breath as its fastening.

3. Understand from me, my dear, hunger and thirst. When a person here is hungry, as it is called, just water is leading off that which has been eaten. So, as they speak of 'a leader-of-cows' 'a leader-of-horses,' 'a leader-of-men,' so they speak of water as 'a leader-of-food.'

On this point, my dear, understand that this [body] is a sprout which has sprung up. It will not be without a root.

4. What else could its root be than food? Even so, my dear, with food for a sprout, look for water as the root. With water, my dear, as a sprout, look for heat as the root. With heat, my dear, as a sprout, look for Being as the root. All creatures here, my dear, have Being as their root, have Being as their home, have Being as their support.

5. Now, when a person here is thirsty, as it is called, just heat is leading off that which has been drunk. So, as they speak of 'a leader-of-cows,' 'a leader-of-horses,' 'a leader-of-men,' so one speaks of heat as 'a leader-of-water.'

On this point, my dear, understand that this [body] is a sprout which has sprung up. It will not be without a root.

6. Where else could its root be than in water? With water, my dear,

as a sprout, look for heat as the root. With heat, my dear, as a sprout, look for Being as the root. All creatures here, my dear, have Being as their root, have Being as their abode, have Being as their support.

But how, verily, my dear, each of these three divinities, upon reaching man, becomes threefold, has previously been said.

When a person here is deceasing, my dear, his voice goes into his mind; his mind, into his breath; his breath, into heat; the heat, into the highest divinity. That which is the finest essence—[7] this whole world has that as its soul. That is Reality. That is Atman. That art thou, Svetaketu."

"Do you, Sir, cause me to understand even more."

"So be it, my dear," said he.

9

1. "As the bees, my dear, prepare honey by collecting the essences of different trees and reducing the essence to a unity, [2] as they are not able to discriminate "I am the essence of this tree," "I am the essence of that tree"—even so, indeed, my dear, all creatures here, though they reach Being, know not "We have reached Being."

3. Whatever they are in this world, whether tiger, or lion, or wolf, or boar, or worm, or fly, or gnat, or mosquito, that they become.

4. That which is the finest essence—this whole world has that as its soul. That is Reality. That is Atman. That art thou, Svetaketu."

"Do you, Sir, cause me to understand even more."

"So be it, my dear," said he.

10

1. "These rivers, my dear, flow, the eastern toward the east, the western toward the west. They go just from the ocean to the ocean. They become the ocean itself. As there they know not 'I am this one,' 'I am that one'—[2] even so, indeed, my dear, all creatures here, though they have come forth from Being, know not 'We have come forth from Being.' Whatever they are in this world, whether tiger, or lion, or wolf, or boar, or worm, or fly, or gnat, or mosquito, that they become.

3. That which is the finest essence—this whole world has that as its soul. That is Reality. That is Atman. That art thou, Svetaketu."

"Do you, Sir, cause me to understand even more."

"So be it, my dear," said he.

11

1. "Of this great tree, my dear, if some one should strike at the root, it would bleed, but still live. If some one should strike at its middle, it would bleed, but still live. If some one should strike at its top, it would bleed, but still live. Being pervaded by Atman, it continues to stand, eagerly drinking in moisture and rejoicing.

2. If the life leaves one branch of it, then it dries up. It leaves a second; then that dries up. It leaves a third; then that dries up. It leaves the whole; the whole dries up. Even so, indeed, my dear, understand," said he.

3. "Verily, indeed, when life has left it, this body dies. The life does not die.

That which is the finest essence—this whole world has that as its soul. That is Reality. That is Atman. That art thou, Svetaketu."

"Do you, Sir, cause me to understand even more."

"So be it, my dear," said he.

12

1. "Bring hither a fig from there."

"Here it is, Sir."

"Divide it."

"It is divided, Sir."

"What do you see there?"

"These rather fine seeds, Sir."

"Of these, please, divide one."

"It is divided, Sir."

"What do you see there?"

"Nothing at all, Sir."

2. Then he said to him: "Verily, my dear, that finest essence which

you do not perceive—verily, my dear, from that finest essence this great Nyagrodha (sacred fig) tree thus arises.

3. Believe me, my dear," said he, "that which is the finest essence—this whole world has that as its soul. That is Reality. That is Atman. That art thou, Svetaketu."

"Do you, Sir, cause me to understand even more."

"So be it, my dear," said he.

13

1. "Place this salt in the water. In the morning come unto me."

Then he did so.

Then he said to him: "That salt you placed in the water last evening—please, bring it hither."

Then he grasped for it, but did not find it, as it was completely dissolved.

2. "Please, take a sip of it from this end," said he. "How is it?"

"Salt."

"Take a sip from the middle," said he. "How is it?"

"Salt."

"Take a sip from that end," said he. "How is it?"

"Salt."

"Set it aside. Then come unto me."

He did so, saying, "It is always the same."

Then he said to him: "Verily, indeed, my dear, you do not perceive Being here. Verily, indeed, it is here.

3. That which is the finest essence—this whole world has that as its soul. That is Reality. That is Atman. That art thou, Svetaketu."

"Do you, Sir, cause me to understand even more."

"So be it, my dear," said he.

14

1. "Just as, my dear, one might lead away from the Gandharas a person with his eyes bandaged, and then abandon him in an uninhabited place; as there he might be blown forth either to the east, to

the north, or to the south, since he had been led off with his eyes bandaged and deserted with his eyes bandaged; [2] as, if one released his bandage and told him, 'In that direction are the Gandharas; go in that direction!' he would, if he were a sensible man, by asking [his way] from village to village, and being informed, arrive home at the Gandharas—even so here on earth one who has a teacher knows: 'I belong here only so long as I shall not be released [from the body]. Then I shall arrive home.'

3. That which is the finest essence—this whole world has that as its soul. That is Reality. That is Atman. That art thou, Svetaketu."

"Do you, Sir, cause me to understand even more."

"So be it, my dear," said he.

15

1. "Also, my dear, around a [deathly] sick person his kinsmen gather, and ask, 'Do you know me?' 'Do you know me?' So long as his voice does not go into his mind, his mind into his breath, his breath into heat, the heat into the highest divinity—so long he knows.

2. Then when his voice goes into his mind, his mind into his breath, his breath into heat, the heat into the highest divinity—then he knows not.

3. That which is the finest essence—this whole world has that as its soul. That is Reality. That is Atman. That art thou, Svetaketu."

"Do you, Sir, cause me to understand even more."

"So be it, my dear," said he.

16

1. "And also, my dear, they lead up a man seized by the hand, and call: "He has stolen! He has committed a theft! Heat the ax for him!" If he is the doer of the deed, thereupon he makes himself untrue. Speaking untruth, he covers himself with untruth. He seizes hold of the heated ax, and is burned. Then he is slain.

2. But if he is not the doer of the deed, thereupon he makes him-

self true. Speaking truth, he covers himself with truth. He seizes hold
of the heated ax, and is not burned. Then he is released.

3. As in this case he would not be burned [because of the truth],
so this whole world has that [truth] as its soul. That is Reality. That is
Atman. That art thou, Svetaketu."

Then he understood it from him—yea, he understood.

7

1

1. *Om!* "Teach me, Sir!"—with these words Narada came to Sanatku-mara.

To him he then said: "Come to me with what you know. Then I will tell you still further."

2. Then he said to him: "Sir, I know the Rig-Veda, the Yajur-Veda, the Sama-Veda, the Atharva-Veda as the fourth, Legend and Ancient Lore as the fifth, the Veda of the Vedas [i.e., Grammar], Rites for the Manes, Mathematics, Augury, Chronology, Logic, Polity, the Science of the Gods, the Science of Sacred Knowledge, Demonology, Military Science, Astrology, the Science of Snake-charming, and the Fine Arts. This, Sir, I know.

3. Such a one am I, Sir, knowing the sacred sayings, but not know-ing the Soul. It has been heard by me from those who are like you, Sir, that he who knows the Soul crosses over sorrow. Such a sorrowing one am I, Sir. Do you, Sir, cause me, who am such a one, to cross over to the other side of sorrow."

To him he then said: "Verily, whatever you have here learned, ver-ily, that is mere name.

4. Verily, a Name are the Rig-Veda, the Yajur-Veda, the Sama-Veda, the Atharva-Veda as the fourth, Legend and Ancient Lore as the fifth, the Veda of the Vedas [i.e., Grammar], Rites for the Manes, Mathemat-ics, Augury, Chronology, Logic, Polity, the Science of the Gods, the Science of Sacred Knowledge, Demonology, Military Science, Astrol-ogy, the Science of Snake-charming, and the Fine Arts. This is mere Name. Reverence Name.

5. He who reverences Name as Brahma—as far as Name goes, so far he has unlimited freedom, he who reverences Name as Brahma."

"Is there, Sir, more than Name?"

"There is, assuredly, more than Name."

"Do you, Sir, tell me it."

2

1. "Speech, assuredly, is more than Name. Speech, verily, makes known the Rig-Veda, the Yajur-Veda, the Sama-Veda, the Atharva-Veda as the fourth, Legend and Ancient Lore as the fifth, the Veda of the Vedas [i.e., Grammar], Rites for the Manes, Mathematics, Augury, Chronology, Logic, Polity, the Science of the Gods, the Science of Sacred Knowledge, Demonology, Military Science, Astrology, the Science of Snake-charming, and the Fine Arts, as well as heaven and earth, wind and space, water and heat, gods and men, beasts and birds, grass and trees, animals together with worms, flies, and ants, right and wrong, true and false, good and bad, pleasant and unpleasant. Verily, if there were no speech, neither right nor wrong would be known, neither true nor false, neither good nor bad, neither pleasant nor unpleasant. Speech, indeed, makes all this known. Reverence Speech.

2. He who reverences Speech as Brahma—as far as Speech goes, so far he has unlimited freedom, he who reverences Speech as Brahma."

"Is there, Sir, more than Speech?"

"There is, assuredly, more than Speech."

"Do you, Sir, tell me it."

3

1. "Mind, assuredly, is more than Speech. Verily, as the closed hand compasses two acorns, or two kola-berries, or two dice-nuts, so Mind compasses both Speech and Name. When through Mind one has in mind 'I wish to learn the sacred sayings,' then he learns them; 'I wish to perform sacred works,' then he performs them; 'I would desire sons and cattle,' then he desires them; 'I would desire this world and the yonder,' then he desires them. Truly the self is Mind. Truly, the world is Mind. Truly, Brahma is Mind.

2. He who reverences Mind as Brahma—as far as Mind goes, so far he has unlimited freedom, he who reverences Mind as Brahma."

"Is there, Sir, more than Mind?"

"There is, assuredly, more than Mind."

"Do you, Sir, tell me it."

4

1. "Conception, assuredly, is more than Mind. Verily, when one forms a Conception, then he has in Mind, then he utters Speech, and he utters it in Name. The sacred sayings are included in Name; and sacred works in the sacred sayings.

2. Verily, these have Conception as their union-point, have Conception as their soul, are established on Conception. Heaven and earth were formed through Conception. Wind and space were formed through Conception. Water and heat were formed through Conception. Through their having been formed, rain becomes formed. Through rain having been formed, food becomes formed. Through food having been formed, living creatures become formed. Through living creatures having been formed, sacred sayings become formed. Through sacred sayings having been formed, sacred works become [per]formed. Through sacred works having been [per]formed, the world becomes formed. Through the world having been formed, everything becomes formed. Such is Conception. Reverence Conception.

3. He who reverences Conception as Brahma—he, verily, attains the Conception-worlds; himself being enduring, the enduring worlds; himself established, the established worlds; himself unwavering, the unwavering worlds. As far as Conception goes, so far he has unlimited freedom, he who reverences Conception as Brahma."

"Is there, Sir, more than Conception?"

"There is, assuredly, more than Conception."

"Do you, Sir, tell me it."

5

1. "Thought, assuredly, is more than Conception. Verily, when one thinks, then he forms a conception, then he has in Mind, then he utters Speech, and he utters it in Name. The sacred sayings are included in Name; and sacred works in the sacred sayings.

2. Verily, these things have Thought as their union-point, have Thought as their soul, are established on Thought. Therefore, even if one who knows much is without Thought, people say of him: 'He is not anybody, whatever he knows! Verily, if he did know, he would

not be so without Thought!' On the other hand, if one who knows
little possesses Thought, people are desirous of listening to him. Truly,
indeed, Thought is the union-point, Thought is the soul, Thought is
the support of these things. Reverence Thought.

3. He who reverences Thought as Brahma—he, verily, attains the
Thought-worlds; himself being enduring, the enduring worlds; himself
being established, the established worlds; himself being unwavering,
the unwavering worlds. As far as Thought goes, so far he has unlimited freedom, he who reverences Thought as Brahma."

"Is there, Sir, more than Thought?"

"There is, assuredly, more than Thought.?"

"Do you, Sir, tell me it."

6

1. "Meditation, assuredly, is more than Thought, The earth meditates, as it were. The atmosphere meditates, as it were. The heaven
meditates, as it were. Water meditates, as it were. Mountains meditate,
as it were. Gods and men meditate, as it were. Therefore whoever
among men here attain greatness—they have, as it were, a part of the
reward of meditation. Now, those who are small are quarrelers, tale-
bearers, slanderers. But those who are superior—they have, as it were,
a part of the reward of Meditation. Reverence Meditation.

2. He who reverences Meditation as Brahma—as far as Meditation
goes, so far he has unlimited freedom, he who reverences Meditation
as Brahma."

"Is there, Sir, more than Meditation?"

"There is, assuredly, more than Meditation."

"Do you, Sir, tell me it."

7

1. "Understanding, assuredly, is more than Meditation. Verily, by
Understanding one understands the Rig-Veda, the Yajur-Veda, the
Sama-Veda, the Atharva-Veda as the fourth, Legend and Ancient

Lore as the fifth, the Veda of the Vedas [i.e., Grammar], Rites for the Manes, Mathematics, Augury, Chronology, Logic, Polity, the Science of the Gods, the Science of Sacred Knowledge, Demonology, Military Science, Astrology, the Science of Snake-charming, and the Fine Arts, as well as heaven and earth, wind and space, water and heat, gods and men, beasts and birds, grass and trees, animals together with worms, flies, and ants, right and wrong, true and false, good and bad, pleasant and unpleasant, food and drink, this world and the yonder—all this one understands just with Understanding. Reverence Understanding.

2. He who reverences Understanding as Brahma—he, verily, attains the worlds of Understanding and of Knowledge. As far as Understanding goes, so far he has unlimited freedom, he who reverences Understanding as Brahma."

"Is there, Sir, more than Understanding?"

"There is, assuredly, more than Understanding."

"Do you, Sir, tell me it."

8

1. "Strength, assuredly, is more than Understanding. Indeed, one man of Strength causes a hundred men of Understanding to tremble. When one is becoming strong, he becomes a rising man. Rising, he becomes an attendant. Attending, he becomes attached as a pupil. Attached as a pupil, he becomes a seer, he becomes a hearer, he becomes a thinker, he becomes a perceiver, he becomes a doer, he becomes an understander. By Strength, verily, the earth stands; by Strength, the atmosphere; by Strength, the sky; by Strength, the mountains; by Strength, gods and men; by Strength, beasts and birds, grass and trees, animals together with worms, flies, and ants. By Strength the world stands. Reverence Strength.

2. He who reverences Strength as Brahma—as far as Strength goes, so far he has unlimited freedom, he who reverences Strength as Brahma."

"Is there, Sir, more than Strength?"

"There is, assuredly, more than Strength."

"Do you, Sir, tell me it."

9

1. "Food, assuredly, is more than Strength. Therefore, if one should not eat for ten days, even though he might live, yet verily he becomes a non-seer, a non-hearer, a non-thinker, a non-perceiver, a non-doer, a non-understander. But on the entrance of food he becomes a seer, he becomes a hearer, he becomes a thinker, he becomes a perceiver, he becomes a doer, he becomes an understander. Reverence Food.

2. He who reverences Food as Brahma—he, verily, attains the worlds of Food and Drink. As far as Food goes, so far he has unlimited freedom, he who reverences Food as Brahma."

"Is there, Sir, more than Food?"

"There is, assuredly, more than Food."

"Do you, Sir, tell me it."

10

1. "Water, verily, is more than Food. Therefore, when there is not a good rain, living creatures sicken with the thought, 'Food will become scarce.' But when there is a good rain, living creatures become happy with the thought, 'Food will become abundant.' It is just Water solidified that is this earth, that is the atmosphere, that is the sky, that is gods and men, beasts and birds, grass and trees, animals together with worms, flies, and ants; all these are just Water solidified. Reverence Water.

2. He who reverences Water as Brahma obtains all his desires and becomes satisfied. As far as Water goes, so far he has unlimited freedom, he who reverences Water as Brahma."

"Is there, Sir, more than Water?"

"There is, assuredly, more than Water."

"Do you, Sir, tell me it."

11

1. "Heat, verily, is more than Water. That, verily, seizes hold of the wind, and heats the ether. Then people say: 'It is hot! It is burning hot! Surely it will rain!' Heat indeed first indicates this, and then lets

out water. So, with lightnings darting up and across the sky, thunders roll. Therefore people say: 'It lightens! It thunders! Surely it will rain!' Heat indeed first indicates this, and then lets out water. Reverence Heat.

2. He who reverences Heat as Brahma—he, verily, being glowing, attains glowing, shining worlds freed from darkness. As far as Heat goes, so far he has unlimited Freedom, he who reverences Heat as Brahma."

"Is there, Sir, more than Heat?"

"There is, assuredly, more than Heat."

"Do you, Sir, tell me it."

12

1. "Space, assuredly, is more than Heat. In Space, verily, are both sun and moon, lightning, stars and fire. Through Space one calls out; through Space one hears; through Space one answers. In Space one enjoys himself; in Space one does not enjoy himself. In Space one is born; unto Space one is born. Reverence Space.

2. He who reverences Space as Brahma—he, verily, attains spacious, gleaming, unconfined, wide-extending worlds. As far as Space goes, so far he has unlimited freedom, he who reverences Space as Brahma."

"Is there, Sir, more than Space?"

"There is, assuredly, more than Space."

"Do you, Sir, tell me it."

13

1. "Memory, verily, is more than Space. Therefore, even if many not possessing Memory should be assembled, indeed they would not hear any one at all, they would not think, they would not understand. But assuredly, if they should remember, then they would hear, then they would think, then they would understand. Through Memory, assuredly, one discerns his children; through Memory, his cattle. Reverence Memory.

2. He who reverences Memory as Brahma—as far as Memory goes, so far he has unlimited freedom, he who reverences Memory as Brahma."

"Is there, Sir, more than Memory?"

"There is, assuredly, more than Memory."

"Do you, Sir, tell me it."

14

1. "Hope, assuredly, is more than Memory. When kindled by Hope, verily, Memory learns the sacred sayings; [kindled by Hope] one performs sacred works, longs for sons and cattle, for this world and the yonder. Reverence Hope.

2. He who reverences Hope as Brahma—through Hope all his desires prosper, his wishes are not unavailing. As far as Hope goes, so far he has unlimited freedom, he who reverences Hope as Brahma."

"Is there, Sir, more than Hope?"

"There is, assuredly, more than Hope."

"Do you, Sir, tell me it."

15

1. "Life (prana, breath), verily, is more than Hope. Just as, verily, the spokes are fastened in the hub, so on this vital breath everything is fastened. Life goes on with vital breath. Vital breath gives life; it gives [life] to a living creature. One's father is vital breath; one's mother, vital breath; one's brother, vital breath; one's sister, vital breath; one's teacher, vital breath; a Brahman is vital breath.

2. If one answers harshly, as it were, a father or mother, or brother, or sister, or teacher, or a Brahman, people say to him: 'Shame on you! Verily, you are a slayer of your father! Verily, you are a slayer of your mother! Verily, you are a slayer of your brother! Verily, you are a slayer of your sister! Verily, you are a slayer of your teacher! Verily, you are a slayer of a Brahman!'

3. But if, when the vital breath has departed from them, one should even shove them with a poker and burn up every bit of them, people would not say to him: 'You are a slayer of your father,' nor 'You are a slayer of your mother,' nor 'You are a slayer of your brother,' nor 'You are a slayer of your sister,' nor 'You are a slayer of your teacher,' nor 'You are a slayer of a Brahman.'

4. For indeed, vital breath is all these things. Verily, he who sees this, thinks this, understands this, becomes a superior speaker. Even if people should say to him 'You are a superior speaker,' he should say 'I am a superior speaker.' He should not deny it.

16

1. But he, verily, speaks superiorly who speaks superiorly with Truth."

"Then I, Sir, would speak superiorly with Truth."

"But one must desire to understand the Truth."

"Sir, I desire to understand the Truth."

17

1. "Verily, when one understands, then he speaks the Truth. One who does not understand, does not speak the Truth. Only he who understands speaks the Truth. But one must desire to understand Understanding."

"Sir, I desire to understand Understanding."

18

1. "Verily, when one thinks, then he understands. Without thinking one does not understand. Only after having thought does one understand. But one must desire to understand Thought."

"Sir, I desire to understand Thought."

19

1. "Verily, when one has Faith, then he thinks. One who has not Faith does not think. Only he who has Faith thinks. But one must desire to understand Faith."

"Sir, I desire to understand Faith."

20

1. "Verily, when one grows forth, then he has Faith. One who does not grow forth does not have faith. Only he who grows forth has faith. But one must desire to understand the Growing Forth."

"Sir, I desire to understand the Growing Forth."

21

1. "Verily, when one is active, then he grows forth. Without being active one does not grow forth. Only by activity does one grow forth. But one must desire to understand Activity."

"Sir, I desire to understand Activity."

22

1. "Verily, when one gets Pleasure for himself, then he is active. Without getting Pleasure one is not active. Only by getting Pleasure is one active. But one must desire to understand Pleasure."

"Sir, I desire to understand Pleasure."

23

1. "Verily, a Plenum is the same as Pleasure. There is no Pleasure in the small. Only a Plenum is Pleasure. But one must desire to understand the Plenum."

"Sir, I desire to understand the Plenum."

24

1. "Where one sees nothing else, hears nothing else, understands nothing else—that is a Plenum. But where one sees something else—that is the small. Verily, the Plenum is the same as the immortal; but the small is the same as the mortal."

"That Plenum, Sir—on what is it established?"

"On its own greatness—unless, indeed, not on greatness at all.

Here on earth people call cows and horses, elephants and gold, slaves and wives, fields and abodes 'greatness.' I do not speak thus; I do not speak thus," said he; "for [in that case] one thing is established upon another.

25

1. That [Plenum], indeed, is below. It is above. It is to the west. It is to the east. It is to the south. It is to the north. It, indeed, is this whole world—

Now next the instruction with regard to the Ego—

"I, indeed, am below. I am above. I am to the west. I am to the east. I am to the south. I am to the north. I, indeed, am this whole world."—

2. Now next the instruction with regard to the soul—

"The Soul, indeed, is below. The Soul is above. The Soul is to the west. The Soul is to the east. The Soul is to the south. The Soul is to the north. The Soul, indeed, is this whole world.

Verily, he who sees this, who thinks this, who understands this, who has pleasure in the Soul, who has delight in the Soul, who has intercourse with the Soul, who has bliss in the Soul—he is autonomous; he has unlimited freedom in all worlds. But they who know otherwise than this, are heteronomous; they have perishable worlds; in all worlds they have no freedom.

26

1. Verily, for him who sees this, who thinks this, who understands this, Vital Breath arises from the Soul; Hope, from the Soul; Memory,

from the Soul; Space, from the Soul; Heat, from the Soul; Water, from the Soul; appearance and disappearance, from the Soul; Food, from the Soul; Strength, from the Soul; Understanding, from the Soul; Meditation, from the Soul; Thought, from the Soul; Conception, from the Soul; Mind, from the Soul; Speech, from the Soul; Name, from the Soul; sacred sayings, from the Soul; sacred works, from the Soul; indeed this whole world, from the Soul."

2. As to this there is the following verse:
The seer sees not death,
Nor sickness, nor any distress.
The seer sees only the All,
Obtains the All entirely.

That [Soul] is onefold, is threefold, fivefold, sevenfold, and also ninefold;
Again, declared elevenfold,
And hundred-and-eleven-fold,
And also twenty-thousand-fold.

In pure nourishment there is a pure nature. In a pure nature the traditional doctrines become firmly fixed. In acquiring the traditional doctrines there is release from all knots [of the heart]. To such a one who has his stains wiped away the blessed Sanatkumara shows the further shore of darkness. People call him Skanda—yea, they call him Skanda.

8

1

1. Om! [The teacher should say:] "Now, what is here in this city of Brahma, is an abode, a small lotus-flower. Within that is a small space. What is within that, should be searched out; that, assuredly, is what one should desire to understand."

2. If they [i.e., the pupils] should say to him: "This abode, the small lotus-flower that is here in this city of Brahma, and the small space within that—what is there there which should be searched out, which assuredly one should desire to understand?" [3] he should say: "As far, verily, as this world-space extends, so far extends the space within the heart. Within it, indeed, are contained both heaven and earth, both fire and wind, both sun and moon, lightning and the stars, both what one possesses here and what one does not possess; everything here is contained within it."

4. If they should say to him: "If within this city of Brahma is contained everything here, all beings as well as all desires, when old age overtakes it or it perishes, what is left over there-from?" [5] he should say: "That does not grow old with one's old age; it is not slain with one's murder. That is the real city of Brahma. In it desires are contained. That is the Soul, free from evil, ageless, deathless, sorrowless, hungerless, thirstless, whose desire is the Real, whose conception is the Real.

For, just as here on earth human beings follow along in subjection to command; of whatever object they are desirous, whether a realm or a part of a field, upon that they live dependent—

6. As here on earth the world which is won by work becomes destroyed, even so there the world which is won by merit becomes destroyed.

Those who go hence without here having found the Soul and those real desires—for them in all the worlds there is no freedom. But those who go hence having found here the Soul and those real desires—for them in all worlds there is freedom.

2

1. If he becomes desirous of the world of fathers, merely out of his conception fathers arise. Possessed of that world of fathers, he is happy.

2. So, if he becomes desirous of the world of mothers, merely out of his conception mothers arise. Possessed of that world of mothers, he is happy.

3. So, if he becomes desirous of the world of brothers, merely out of his conception brothers arise. Possessed of that world of brothers, he is happy.

4. So, if he becomes desirous of the world of sisters, merely out of his conception sisters arise. Possessed of that world of sisters, he is happy.

5. So, if he becomes desirous of the world of friends, merely out of his conception friends arise. Possessed of that world of friends, he is happy.

6. So, if he becomes desirous of the world of perfume and garlands, merely out of his conception perfume and garlands arise. Possessed of that world of perfume and garlands, he is happy.

7. So, if he becomes desirous of the world of food and drink, merely out of his conception food and drink arise. Possessed of that world of food and drink, he is happy.

8. So, if he becomes desirous of the world of song and music, merely out of his conception song and music arise. Possessed of that world of song and music, he is happy.

9. So, if he becomes desirous of the world of women, merely out of his conception women arise. Possessed of that world of women, he is happy.

10. Of whatever object he becomes desirous, whatever desire he desires, merely out of his conception it arises. Possessed of it, he is happy.

3

1. These same are real desires with a covering of what is false. Although they are real, there is a covering that is false.

For truly, whoever of one's [fellows] departs hence, one does not get him [back] to look at here.

2. But those of one's [fellows] who are alive there, and those who have departed, and whatever else one desires but does not get—all this one finds by going in there [i.e., in the Soul]; for there, truly, are those real desires of his which have a covering of what is false.

So, just as those who do not know the spot might go over a hid treasure of gold again and again, but not find it, even so all creatures here go day by day to that Brahma-world [in deep sleep], but do not find it; for truly they are carried astray by what is false.

3. Verily, this Soul is in the heart. The etymological explanation thereof is this: This one is in the heart; therefore it is the heart. Day by day, verily, he who knows this goes to the heavenly world.

4. Now, that serene one who, rising up out of this body, reaches the highest light and appears with his own form—he is the Soul," said he [i.e., the teacher]. "That is the immortal, the fearless. That is Brahma."

Verily, the name of that Brahma is the Real.

5. Verily, these are the three syllables: sat-ti-yam. The sat (Being)—that is the immortal. The ti—that is the mortal. Now the yam—with that one holds the two together. Because with it one holds the two together, therefore it is yam. Day by day, verily, he who knows this goes to the heavenly world.

4

1. Now, the Soul is the bridge [or, dam], the separation for keeping these worlds apart. Over that bridge [or, dam] there cross neither day, nor night, nor old age, nor death, nor sorrow, nor well-doing, nor evil-doing.

2. All evils turn back therefrom, for that Brahma-world is freed from evil. Therefore, verily, upon crossing that bridge, if one is blind, he becomes no longer blind; if he is sick, he becomes no longer sick. Therefore, verily, upon crossing that bridge, the night appears even as the day, for that Brahma-world is ever illumined.

3. But only they who find that Brahma-world through the chaste life of a student of sacred knowledge—only they posses that Brahma-world. In all worlds they possess unlimited freedom.

5

1. Now, what people call "sacrifice" is really the chaste life of a student of sacred knowledge, for only through the chaste life of a student of sacred knowledge does he who is a knower find that [world].

Now, what people call "what has been sacrificed" is really the chaste life of a student of sacred knowledge, for only after having searched with the chaste life of a student of sacred knowledge does one find the Soul.

2. Now, what people call "the protracted sacrifice" is really the chaste life of a student of sacred knowledge, for only through the chaste life of a student of sacred knowledge does one find the protection of the real Soul.

Now, what people call "silent asceticism" is really the chaste life of a student of sacred knowledge, for only in finding the Soul through the chaste life of a student of sacred knowledge does one [really] think.

3. Now, what people call "a course of fasting" is really the chaste life of a student of sacred knowledge, for the Soul which one finds through the chaste life of a student of sacred knowledge perishes not.

Now, what people call "betaking oneself to hermit life in the forest" is really the chaste life of a student of sacred knowledge. Verily, the two seas in the Brahma-world, in the third heaven from here, are Ara and Nya. There is the lake Airammadiya; there, the fig-tree Somasavana; there, Brahma's citadel, Aparajita, the golden hall of the Lord.

4. But only they who find those two seas, Ara and Nya, in the Brahma-world through the chaste life of a student of sacred knowledge—only they possess that Brahma-world. In all the worlds they possess unlimited freedom.

6

1. Now, as for these arteries of the heart—they arise from the finest essence, which is reddish brown, white, blue, yellow, and red: so it is said. Verily, yonder sun is reddish brown; it is white; it is blue; it is yellow; it is red.

2. Now, as a great extending highway goes to two villages, this one and the yonder, even so these rays of the sun go to two worlds, this one and the yonder. They extend from yonder sun, and creep into these arteries. They extend from these arteries, and creep into yonder sun.

3. Now, when one is thus sound asleep, composed, serene, he knows no dream; then he has crept into these arteries; so no evil touches him, for then he has reached the Bright Power.

4. Now, when one thus becomes reduced to weakness, those sitting around say: "Do you know me?" "Do you know me?" As long as he has not departed from this body, he knows them.

5. But when he thus departs from this body, then he ascends upward with these very rays of the sun. With the thought of Om, verily, he passes up. As quickly as one could direct his mind to it, he comes to the sun. That, verily, indeed, is the world-door, an entrance for knowers, a stopping for non-knowers.

6. As to this there is the following verse:

There are a hundred and one arteries of the heart.
One of these passes up to the crown of the head.
Going up by it, one goes to immortality.

The others are for departing in various directions.

7

1. "The Self, which is free from evil, ageless, deathless, sorrowless, hungerless, thirstless, whose desire is the Real, whose conception is the Real—He should be searched out, Him one should desire to understand. He obtains all worlds and all desires who has found out and who understands that Self."—Thus spake Prajapati.

2. Then both the gods and the devils heard it. Then they said: "Come! Let us search out that Self, the Self by searching out whom one obtains all worlds and all desires!"

Then Indra from among the gods went forth unto him, and Virocana from among the devils. Then, without communicating with each other, the two came into the presence of Prajapati, fuel in hand.

3. Then for thirty-two years the two lived the chaste life of a student of sacred knowledge.

Then Prajapati said to the two: "Desiring what have you been living?"

Then the two said: "'The Self, which is free from evil, ageless, deathless, sorrowless, hungerless, thirstless, whose desire is the Real, whose conception is the Real—He should be searched out, Him one should desire to understand. He obtains all worlds and all desires who has found out and who understands that Self.'—Such do people declare to be your words, Sir. We have been living desiring Him."

4. Then Prajapati said to the two: "That Person who is seen in the eye—He is the Self of whom I spoke. That is the immortal, the fearless. That is Brahma."

"But this one, Sir, who is observed in water and in a mirror—which one is he?"

"The same one, indeed, is observed in all these," said he.

8

1. "Look at yourself in a pan of water. Anything that you do not understand of the Self, tell me."

Then the two looked in a pan of water.

Then Prajapati said to the two: "What do you see?"

Then the two said: "We see everything here, Sir, a Self corresponding exactly, even to the hair and finger-nails!"

2. Then Prajapati said to the two: "Make yourselves well-ornamented, well-dressed, adorned, and look in a pan of water."

Then the two made themselves well-ornamented, well-dressed, adorned, and looked in a pan of water.

Then Prajapati said to the two: "What do you see?"

3. Then the two said: "Just as we ourselves are here, Sir, well-ornamented, well-dressed, adorned—so there, Sir, well-ornamented, well-dressed, adorned."

"That is the Self," said he. "That is the immortal, the fearless. That is Brahma."

Then with tranquil heart the two went forth.

4. Then Prajapati glanced after them, and said: "They go without having comprehended, without having found the Self. Whosoever

shall have such a mystic doctrine, be they gods or be they devils, they shall perish."

Then with tranquil heart Virocana came to the devils. To them he then declared this mystic doctrine: "Oneself is to be made happy here on earth. Oneself is to be waited upon. He who makes his own self happy here on earth, who waits upon himself—he obtains both worlds, both this world and the yonder."

5. Therefore even now here on earth they say of one who is not a giver, who is not a believer, who is not a sacrificer, "Oh! devilish!" for such is the doctrine of the devils. They adorn the body of one deceased with what they have begged, with dress, with ornament, as they call it, for they think that thereby they will win yonder world.

9

1. But then Indra, even before reaching the gods, saw this danger: "Just as, indeed, that one [i.e., the bodily self] is well-ornamented when this body is well-ornamented, well-dressed when this is well-dressed, adorned when this is adorned, even so that one is blind when this is blind, lame when this is lame, maimed when this is maimed. It perishes immediately upon the perishing of this body. I see nothing enjoyable in this."

2. Fuel in hand, back again he came. Then Prajapati said to him: "Desiring what, O Maghavan, have you come back again, since you along with Virocana went forth with tranquil heart?"

Then he said: "Just as, indeed, that one [i.e., the bodily self] is well-ornamented when this body is well-ornamented, well-dressed when this is well-dressed, adorned when this is adorned, even so it is blind when this is blind, lame when this is lame, maimed when this is maimed. It perishes immediately upon the perishing of this body. I see nothing enjoyable in this."

3. "He is even so, O Maghavan," said he. "However, I will explain this further to you. Live with me thirty-two years more."

Then he lived with him thirty-two years more.

To him [i.e., to Indra] he [i.e., Prajapati] then said:

10

1. "He who moves about happy in a dream—he is the Self," said he. "That is the immortal, the fearless. That is Brahma."

Then with tranquil heart he [i.e., Indra] went forth.

Then, even before reaching the gods, he saw this danger: "Now, even if this body is blind, that one [i.e., the Self, Atman] is not blind. If this is lame, he is not lame. Indeed, he does not suffer defect through defect of this. [2] He is not slain with one's murder. He is not lame with one's lameness. Nevertheless, as it were, they kill him; as it were, they unclothe him; as it were, he comes to experience what is unpleasant; as it were, he even weeps. I see nothing enjoyable in this."

3. Fuel in hand, back again he came. Then Prajapati said to him: "Desiring what, O Maghavan, have you come back again, since you went forth with tranquil heart?"

Then he said: "Now, Sir, even if this body is blind, that one [i.e., the Self] is not blind. If this is lame, he is not lame. Indeed, he does not suffer defect through defect of this. [4] He is not slain with one's murder. He is not lame with one's lameness. Nevertheless, as it were, they kill him; as it were, they unclothe him; as it were, he comes to experience what is unpleasant; as it were, he even weeps. I see nothing enjoyable in this."

"He is even so, O Maghavan," said he. "However, I will explain this further to you. Live with me thirty-two years more."

Then he lived with him thirty-two years more.

To him [i.e., to Indra] he [i.e., Prajapati] then said:

11

1. "Now, when one is sound asleep, composed, serene, and knows no dream—that is the Self," said he. "That is the immortal, the fearless. That is Brahma."

Then with tranquil heart he went forth.

Then, even before reaching the gods, he saw this danger: "Assuredly, indeed, this one does not exactly know himself with the thought 'I am he,' nor indeed the things here. He becomes one who has gone to destruction. I see nothing enjoyable in this."

2. Fuel in hand, back again he came. Then Prajapati said to him: "Desiring what, O Maghavan, have you come back again, since you went forth with tranquil heart?"

Then he [i.e., Indra] said: "Assuredly, this [self] does not exactly know himself with the thought 'I am he,' nor indeed the things here. He becomes one who has gone to destruction. I see nothing enjoyable in this."

3. "He is even so, O Maghavan," said he. "However, I will explain this further to you, and there is nothing else besides this. Live with me five years more."

Then he lived with him five years more—That makes one hundred and one years. Thus it is that people say, "Verily, for one hundred and one years Maghavan lived the chaste life of a student of sacred knowledge with Prajapati."—

To him [i.e., to Indra] he [i.e., Prajapati] then said:

12

1. "O Maghavan, verily, this body is mortal. It has been appropriated by Death. [But] it is the standing-ground of that deathless, bodiless Self. Verily, he who is incorporate has been appropriated by pleasure and pain. Verily, there is no freedom from pleasure and pain for one while he is incorporate. Verily, while one is bodiless, pleasure and pain do not touch him.

2. The wind is bodiless. Clouds, lightning, thunder—these are bodiless. Now as these, when they arise from yonder space and reach the highest light, appear each with its own form, [3] even so that serene one, when he rises up from this body and reaches the highest light, appears with his own form. Such a one is the supreme person. There such a one goes around laughing, sporting, having enjoyment with women or chariots or friends, not remembering the appendage of this body. As a draft-animal is yoked in a wagon, even so this spirit is yoked in this body.

4. Now, when the eye is directed thus toward space, that is the seeing person; the eye is [the instrument] for seeing. Now, he who knows 'Let me smell this'—that is the Self; the nose is [the instrument] for smelling. Now, he who knows 'Let me utter this'—that is the Self; the

voice is [the instrument] for utterance. Now, he who knows 'Let me hear this'—that is the Self; the ear is [the instrument] for hearing.

5. Now, he who knows 'Let me think this'—that is the Self; the mind is his divine eye. He, verily, with that divine eye the mind, sees desires here, and experiences enjoyment.

6. Verily, those gods who are in the Brahma-world reverence that Self. Therefore all worlds and all desires have been appropriated by them. He obtains all worlds and all desires who has found out and who understands that Self."

Thus spake Prajapati—yea, thus spake Prajapati!

13

1. From the dark I go to the varicolored. From the varicolored I go to the dark. Shaking off evil, as a horse his hairs; shaking off the body, as the moon releases itself from the mouth of Rahu; I, a perfected soul, pass into the uncreated Brahma-world—yea, into it I pass!

14

1. Verily, what is called space is the accomplisher of name and form. That within which they are, is Brahma. That is the immortal. That is the Self.

I go to Prajapati's abode and assembly-hall.

I am the glory of the Brahmans, the glory of the princes, the glory of the people.

I have attained unto glory.

May I, who am the glory of the glories, not go to hoary and toothless, yea to toothless and hoary and driveling [old age]!

Yea, may I not go to driveling [old age]!

15

1. This did Brahma tell to Prajapati; Prajapati, to Manu; Manu, to human beings.

He who according to rule has learned the Veda from the family of a teacher, in time left over from doing work for the teacher; he who, after having come back again, in a home of his own continues Veda-study in a clean place and produces [sons and pupils]; he who has concentrated all his senses upon the Soul; he who is harmless toward all things elsewhere than at holy places—he, indeed, who lives thus throughout his length of life, reaches the Brahma-world and does not return hither again—yea, he does not return hither again!

AMERICAN LITERATURE

Little Women — Louisa May Alcott
The Last of the Mohicans — James Fenimore Cooper
The Red Badge of Courage and *Maggie* — Stephen Crane
Selected Poems — Emily Dickinson
Narrative of the Life and Other Writings — Frederick Douglass
The Scarlet Letter — Nathaniel Hawthorne
The Call of the Wild and *White Fang* — Jack London
Moby-Dick — Herman Melville
Major Tales and Poems — Edgar Allan Poe
The Jungle — Upton Sinclair
Uncle Tom's Cabin — Harriet Beecher Stowe
Walden and *Civil Disobedience* — Henry David Thoreau
Adventures of Huckleberry Finn — Mark Twain
The Complete Adventures of Tom Sawyer — Mark Twain
Ethan Frome and *Summer* — Edith Wharton
Leaves of Grass — Walt Whitman

WORLD LITERATURE

Tales from the 1001 Nights — Sir Richard Burton
Don Quixote — Miguel de Cervantes
The Divine Comedy — Dante Alighieri
Crime and Punishment — Fyodor Dostoevsky
The Count of Monte Cristo — Alexandre Dumas
The Three Musketeers — Alexandre Dumas
Selected Tales of the Brothers Grimm — Jacob and Wilhelm Grimm
The Iliad — Homer
The Odyssey — Homer
The Hunchback of Notre-Dame — Victor Hugo
Les Misérables — Victor Hugo
The Metamorphosis and *The Trial* — Franz Kafka
The Phantom of the Opera — Gaston Leroux
The Prince — Niccolò Machiavelli
The Art of War — Sun Tzu
The Death of Ivan Ilych and Other Stories — Leo Tolstoy
Around the World in Eighty Days — Jules Verne
Candide and *The Maid of Orléans* — Voltaire
The Bhagavad Gita — Vyasa

BRITISH LITERATURE

Beowulf — Anonymous
Emma — Jane Austen
Persuasion — Jane Austen
Pride and Prejudice — Jane Austen
Sense and Sensibility — Jane Austen
Peter Pan — J. M. Barrie
Jane Eyre — Charlotte Brontë
Wuthering Heights — Emily Brontë
Alice in Wonderland — Lewis Carroll
The Canterbury Tales — Geoffrey Chaucer
Heart of Darkness and Other Tales — Joseph Conrad
Robinson Crusoe — Daniel Defoe
A Christmas Carol and Other Holiday Tales — Charles Dickens
Great Expectations — Charles Dickens
Oliver Twist — Charles Dickens
A Tale of Two Cities — Charles Dickens
The Waste Land and Other Writings — T. S. Eliot
A Passage to India — E. M. Forster
The Jungle Books — Rudyard Kipling
Paradise Lost and Paradise Regained — John Milton
The Sonnets and Other Love Poems — William Shakespeare
Three Romantic Tragedies — William Shakespeare
Frankenstein — Mary Shelley
Dr. Jekyll and Mr. Hyde and Other Strange Tales — Robert Louis Stevenson
Kidnapped — Robert Louis Stevenson
Treasure Island — Robert Louis Stevenson
Dracula — Bram Stoker
Gulliver's Travels — Jonathan Swift
The Time Machine and The War of the Worlds — H. G. Wells
The Picture of Dorian Gray — Oscar Wilde

ANTHOLOGIES

Four Centuries of Great Love Poems

The text of this book is set in 11 point Goudy Old Style, designed by
American printer and typographer Frederic W. Goudy (1865–1947).

The archival-quality, natural paper is composed of recyclable products
made from wood grown in sustainable forests; the manufacturing
processes conform to the environmental regulations
of the country of origin.

The finished volume demonstrates the convergence of Old-World
craftsmanship and modern technology that exemplifies
books manufactured by Edwards Brothers, Inc.
Established in 1893, the family-owned business is a well-respected
leader in book manufacturing, recognized the world over
for quality and attention to detail.

In addition, Ann Arbor Media Group's editorial and design services
provide full-service book publication to business partners.